Headquarters of the National Society of the Sons of the American Revolution at 2412 Massachusetts Avenue, N.W., Washington, D. C.

The History of the
National Society
of the
Sons of the American Revolution

By
JOHN ST. PAUL, Jr.
Historian General

Assisted by
STUART O. LANDRY

A FIREBIRD PRESS BOOK

PELICAN PUBLISHING COMPANY
Gretna 1998

© Copyright 1962
By Stuart O. Landry

Library of Congress Catalog Card Number 62-22214

Manufactured in the United States of America
Published by Pelican Publishing Company, Inc.
1000 Burmaster Street, Gretna, Louisiana 70053

The publication of the History of the National Society of the Sons of the American Revolution has been endorsed by the Board of Trustees of the National Society which sanctioned the project at its meeting on May 10th, 1961. The manuscript has been reviewed by a Committee appointed for that purpose composed of Past Presidents General de la Houssaye, Wentworth and Jones.

I would have you day by day fix your eyes upon the greatness of your country, until you are filled with the love of her; and when you are impressed by the spectacle of her glory, reflect that it has been acquired by men who knew their duty and had the courage to do it.

— Pericles.

A people which takes no pride in the achievements of remote ancestors will never achieve anything worthy to be remembered by remote descendants.

— Thomas Babington Macauley

TABLE OF CONTENTS

CHAPTER	PAGE
I — Origin of the Society	1
II — The Movement Spreads East	7
III — The Beginning of the National Society	10
IV — Annual Congresses from 1890 to 1902	16
V — The Record from 1902 to 1947	30
VI — The Recent Past	64
VII — The Fruitful Years	117
VIII — Constitution and Charter of the National Society of the Sons of the American Revolution	126
IX — Headquarters' Buildings	136
X — Finances	145
XI — Awards and Honors	147
XII — Organization of State Societies	154
XIII — Miscellanies	156
XIV — The Society in France	162
XV — Resolutions	168
XVI — Biographies	171
Appendix — Officials and Prominent Members	213
— Stamp That Caused the Revolution	240
— List of Patrons	241

ILLUSTRATIONS

Headquarters of the National Society   Frontispiece

Past Presidents General

Trustees Meeting — 1960

Interior Scences of Headquarters

Minute Men

French Society Ceremonies   Between Pgs. 16-17

Missouri State Flag by Mrs. Oliver

Four Chaplains Legion of Honor

Jno. Alden May

"Burning of the Mortgage"

Groups and scenes from various states: Alabama - Missouri   Between Pgs. 80-81

Groups and scenes from various states: Nebraska - Wyoming

The Flag that flew over Ft. Henry when it was bombarded in 1814, now at Smithsonian Institution

Bennington Battle Flag—considered earliest American Flag

Copy of 1814 Flag made by President General R. C. Ballard Thurston and presented to National Society

Old Headquarters Building

General Washington's Seal Ring   Between Pgs. 144-145

Memorial to Battle of Cowpens

Group Pictures of Early Officials and Congresses

Old Church at Jamestown, Virginia

Fairfax Outhouse where Washington kept his surveying instruments and records.

Cornwallis Headquarters at Yorktown

Moore House at Yorktown where surrender was signed.

ACKNOWLEDGMENT

This history of the National Society of the Sons of the American Revolution is the result of the labor of many individuals and the cooperative efforts of many Compatriots.

Some of the material has been taken from earlier writings, and I have quoted extensively from the reminiscences of Frank Bartlett Steele, who was Secretary General of the Society from 1921 up to and including May, 1950. Before his death, he had made notes about the various Congresses and Presidents General from 1902 up to 1947. His notes were published by his wife, Mrs. Steele, after his death. I have excerpted much from her brochure, and received other help from her prior to her recent death.

Authorities consulted were: Henry Hall, Historian General of the National Society from 1891 to 1897; W. Seward Webb, "Historical Sketch"; "The Early Days of the National Society and the Connecticut Society of the Sons of the American Revolution," by Wilson B. Roberts; an article by Frank Elliott Myers in the "Overland Monthly," issue October 1895; "History of the Constitution, By-Laws and Member of the California Society of the Sons of the American Revolution," issued in 1897; "The California Society Sons of the American Revolution," by W. W. Winn, an article in the California Historical Society Quarterly; "The National Register, Sons of the American Revolution," 1905. I have also used "Recollections of Congresses I attended," by Howard E. Coe, of the Connecticut Society. I am indebted also, to Harold L. Putnam, Executive Secretary, not only for his contribution concerning the activities of the Society since 1950, but for other assistance.

The files of the Magazines of the Society have been read and lists of officials and other information extracted therefrom.

I want to thank the following living Past Presidents General for substantial contributions covering the periods of their incumbencies: Sterling F. Mutz; Allen L. Oliver; John W. Finger; Wallace C. Hall; Arthur A. de la Houssaye; Milton M. Lory; Edgar Williamson, Jr.; Eugene P. Carver, Jr.; George E. Tarbox, Jr.; Walter A. Wentworth; Charles A. Jones; Herschel S. Murphy, M.D.; and Horace Y. Kitchell.

Compatriot Robert S. W. Walker, Librarian General, rendered assistance and in particular helped check the pictures of Past Presidents General.

My thanks are due to Mrs. Virginia Kagy, Executive Assistant at Headquarters, and other members of the staff for their aid in gathering and checking information.

To all others who aided in various ways I extend my appreciation.

Pictures and Photographs

I want to thank especially Compatriot William M. Cain of Washington, D. C. for his invaluable aid in obtaining the pictures of all the deceased Past Presidents General. He photographed the pictures of them in the frames at Headquarters and made excellent reproductions. I am afraid that I would have had to omit these pictures if Compatriot Cain had not volunteered to help. He also furnished me with copies of illustrations from old SAR magazines.

I also desire to thank the following:

Rev. Dr. Earle V. Conover of Omaha, Neb., for picture of Omaha Chapter group; Nelson L. Payne, Corresponding Secretary of Vermont State Society, SAR, for the picture of the Bennington Battle Flag; and Mr. Chester M. Clark of Bronxville, N. Y., for the photograph of his father, A. Howard Clark.

JOHN ST. PAUL, JR.
Historian General of the National Society of the Sons of the American Revolution.

President Dwight D. Eisenhower's Message to the 69th Congress of the National Society of the Sons of the American Revolution:

George Washington once spoke of the responsibility each citizen bears in the "foundation of our national policy." As the Sons of the American Revolution encourage a broad and intelligent concern for the problems which face our nation and world, they strengthen the basic traditions of the Republic.

PLEDGE OF THE SONS OF THE AMERICAN REVOLUTION

We, descendants of the heroes of the Amercian Revolution, who, by their sacrifices, established the United States of America, reaffirm our faith in the principles of freedom and American Democracy, and solemnly pledge ourselves to defend them against every foe.

(Authored by Harold Putnam and Harold Marshall. First adopted in 1939 by the California Society. Later adopted by the Trustees of the National Society at Washington in 1954).

I

THE ORIGIN OF THE SOCIETY

The National Society of the Sons of the American Revolution came into existence after a number of State Societies had already been formed. It grew out of the desire for a more perfect union.

The beginning, or what might be termed the "ancestor" of the Society, was an organization formed in California, known as "The Sons of Revolutionary Sires".

This was the first of the modern State patriotic Societies. It was planned in October 1875 and instituted July 4, 1876, at San Francisco, Cal., three thousand miles away from the scenes of the struggle for American Independence.

The preparations for the celebration of the Centennial of the Signing of the Declaration of Independence at Philadelphia on July 4th, 1776, spread a wave of patriotic fervor throughout the United States. The momentum of this wave was so great that it reached out to the fartherest shores of our country and broke with force over the Rocky Mountains and rushed on to California, where there lived a number of patriotic Americans whose ancestors had taken part in the Revolutionary War. In fact the records show that many of these men were Real Sons of the American Revolution, that is, sons of revolutionary soldiers—others were grandsons.

So it was not all surprising that there met in San Francisco, on the evening of October 22, 1875, a half dozen men, whom James Lafayette Cogswell, D.D.S., had invited to discuss with him plans for taking part in the Fourth of July procession in 1876, at his office at 230 Kearny Street. Besides Dr. Cogswell, these men were, Peter Wilkins Randle, Emory L. Willard, M.D., Joseph Reed, Ira Root, Richard Rush Randle, Maj. E. A. Sherman, and possibly one other, whose name was not recalled later. They discussed the possibility of forming a society to perpetuate the memory of their ancestors who fought to make this country free. They voted to call themselves "The National Society of Sons of Revolutionary Sires." Cogswell was elected president, Randle vice-president for California and Sherman vice-president for Nevada.

This small band of citizens met several times during the fall and winter of 1875 and '76, and then, as San Francisco was to hold a great celebration on July 4th, 1876, a call was issued in the *Alta California*, in its issue of June 29th, 1876 as follows:

> The descendants of the Revolutionary patriots are requested to meet at the headquarters of the Grand Marshall at No. 212 Kearny Street, at 8 o'clock this evening, for the purpose of making arrangements to participate in the celebration.

Pursuant to the call, a meeting was held on June 29, 1876. On motion of James P. Dameron, Gen. A. M. Winn was elected chairman and Dr. Emory L. Willard secretary. General Winn stated the object of the meeting as he understood it, but he said that he did not know the origin of the call. Dameron explained that he himself was one of those who had called the meeting. Thereupon it was resolved to organize as "Sons of Revolutionary Sires"* for participation in the celebration, and the following persons were enrolled as original members:

> A. M. Winn, 66 years old, grandson of William Winn, a Revolutionary soldier from Maryland.

---

*Henry Hall, historian-general of the National Society of the Sons of the American Revolution from 1891 to 1897, in his Year Book of Societies of Descendants of the Men of the Revolution, published in New York in 1890, gives full credit to the California organization as the pioneer unit of The National Society of Sons of the American Revolution, and his account, written before the destruction of the records of the California Society by the San Francisco fire of 1906, is so complete in many respects that it has been an important source for this historical sketch.

Emory L. Willard, 55 years old, grandson of Abraham Willard, Surgeon from Massachusetts.

Caleb T. Fay, 55 years old, grandson of Francis Fay, Revolutionary soldier from Massachusetts.

Charles Siskron, 37 years old, grandson of Harvey Ellis, a Revolutionary soldier from Connecticut.

J. Doolittle, age 20, great-grandson of Colonel Doolittle, of Massachusetts.

John Paul Jones Davison, 87 years old, son of George W. Davison of Connecticut.

Joseph Sharon, 54 years old, grandson of Joseph Eaton, one of Morgan's riflemen.

H. T. Graves, 52 years old, grandson of Recompense Graves of New York.

Augustus B. Graves, 44 years of age, grandson of R. Graves.

Dallas A. Kneass, 60 years of age, grandson of John Hart of New Jersey.

J. B. Worden, 41 years of age, grandson of Isaac Graham of New York, Surgeon.

William H. Mead, 42 years of age, grandson of John Paulding, one of the men who captured Andre.

W. B. Eastin, 37 years of age, grandson of Adjutant William Eastin from Virginia.

Z. K. Hersum, 46 years of age, grandson of David Hersum from Maine.

A. M. Seabury, 48 years of age, great-grandson of David Seabury from Connecticut.

Thomas H. Greenough, 14 years of age, grandson of Jonathan Greenough, from Maine.

J. P. Dameron, 92 years of age (this is an error in the original; Mr. Dameron was 48 years old), great-grandson of Joseph Dameron, North Carolina.

John Turner, 66 years of age, grandson of John Turner, who fell at Bunker Hill.

J. E. Clark, 51 years old, grandson of Ichabod Clark, New Jersey.

R. R. Strain, 72 years old, grandson of John Strain from Philadelphia.

Lawrence V. Hogeboom, 49 years of age, grandson of Jacob H. Hogeboom.

John N. Finch, 47 years of age, grandson of John Finch of New York.

Charles A. Seeley, 26 years old, great-grandson of Captain Isaac Davis, first man killed at Concord, Mass.

James L. Cogswell, grandson of Amos Cogswell from Connecticut.

The roll was then called and corrected, and the chairman and secretary were directed to make the arrangements necessary for a parade.

On Saturday, July first, at the Palace Hotel, the newly formed association held a second meeting. Winn presiding and Willard acting as secretary. An invitation to join in the Fourth of July procession was read and accepted. Upon recommendation of the two officers above named, it was resolved that persons signing the roll and declaring upon honor that they were descendants of the Revolution should be constituted members. Election of permanent officers was deferred until after the Fourth. Dameron was, however, chosen treasurer-pro-tem; and Fay and Eatin were appointed assistant secretaries, to enroll the names of those persons who were entitled to membership. The chairman was directed to procure carriages for the members on the Fourth. Eastin, Dameron and Sharon were appointed to procure thirteen banners, representing the thirteen original states of the Union. Thirty-one additional names were enrolled.

Tuesday, July 4, at 9:30 A.M., the Society met at the Palace Hotel. New names were enrolled, bringing the total membership (including many who had been added during the intervals between the meetings) to over 80. Among this number were ten actual sons of Revolutionary sires.

Lines having been formed after the meeting by William S. Moses, the marshal, the detachment joined in the public procession in honor of the day. They attracted the attention of the whole city. Thirteen members carried shields (instead of banners, as originally planned), emblematic of the thirteen original states. In passing Folsom Street, the Society was presented with bouquets of flowers by Mrs. A. Dunlap, one of its "Ladies Auxiliary."

The parade attracted a great deal of attention, the line of march starting from the Palace Hotel at 9:30 A.M., and passing through the principal streets, everywhere receiving that homage which would naturally fall to the descendants of those whose services destroyed the yoke of tyranny and made the glorious Stars and Stripes the symbol of a land of freedom in perpetuity.

The *Daily Alta* of July the 6th, 1876 said: "It [the Parade] was a marked feature of the procession, and as the marchers passed in their antique uniforms, one almost fancied that the procession was a pageant of the 17th century rather than a celebration of this age of military and civic enlightenment."

The parade over and the marchers dismissed by the grand marshall, the descendants of the War of the Revolution returned to the Palace Hotel, where Marshal Moses called them to order. Treasurer Dameron delivered an address, congratulating the members on the success of their efforts to commemorate the deeds of their ancestors. He was repeatedly applauded, and at the conclusion it was unanimously resolved to continue the association as a "Society of Sons of Revolutionary Sires." Adjournment was taken for one week. Shortly afterwards, eighteen additional names, which are omitted here, were signed on the membership roll; other persons had been elected but their names were not formally affixed.

On July eleventh, a meeting, attended by about fifty persons, was held at Dashaway Hall for an election of officers. General Winn presided and made an address. On motion of Colonel Fay, the general was chosen president by acclamation. The complete list of officers was as follows: Gen. A. M. Winn, president; Col. Caleb T. Fay, vice-president; Samuel Graves, 2d. vice-president; Ira C. Root, 3rd. vice-president; William B. Eatin, recording secretary; William H. Mead, financial secretary; James P. Dameron, treasurer; William S. Moses, marshall. Augustus C. Taylor, James N. Makins, and A. S. Iredale composed the executive committee. The officers were instructed to prepare a constitution and by-laws, and the meeting adjourned, the members reassembling on August Second at the Palace Hotel, when they heard the president read a report and the proposed constitution and by-laws, with a draught of articles of incorporation (the Society was never incorporated) which were adopted by unanimous vote. The officers did not have the rules of the Society of Cincinnati to guide them, so that their plan of organization presents interesting and original features.

With the exception of the Cincinnati, this was the first Society in the country, whose members were exclusively descendants from Revolutionary Sires.

From its very inception the promoters of the California Society planned that the organization should be National in its operations, and among other objects its first constitution provided for the organization of "auxiliaries, co-equal branches and representative bodies." The California organization was perfected July 11th, 1876, or seven years prior to the formation of any similar organization in any State in the Union.

The first circular, published in August, 1876, stated the objects of the new Society to be:

> To unite the descendants of Revolutionary patriots and perpetuate the memory of those who took part in the American Revolution and maintained the independence of the United States of America; to promote social intercourse, mental improvement, and mutual benefit of the members; to organize auxiliaries, co-equal branches, and representative bodies at such time and places as the Directors may determine.

The California Society grew and prospered.*

---

*Quoted from Dr. W. Seward Webb's Historical Sketch.

II

THE MOVEMENT SPREADS EAST

"The Sons of Revolutionary Sires" was composed exclusively of lineal descendants from heroes and statesmen of the American Revolution. Its constitution provided for "auxiliary" branches, coequal societies, and a national representative body. Copies of this constitution were sent out all over the United States, together with circulars and bulletins of the Society's proceedings. This California Society was the pioneer of the modern hereditary, patriotic society, and its influence led to the formation of all of them.

Some of these constitutions, with the circulars and bulletins of the California Society, were sent year by year, to residents of New York City. The California movement excited interest in the East, but California was a long way off, and had never even been heard of at the time of the American Revolution. And there were those who felt the patriotic societies based on revolutionary ancestry should be formed in the East and not as a child of a society formed in California.

In 1883, however, a few men in New York City met and organized an independent Society there, called "Sons of the Revolution". Thus the seed planted by California had sprouted at last in the metropolis. The new society was small in membership, and at first intended to be purely local, but finally it also adopted a constitution providing that societies might be formed in other States, each of which should be an "auxiliary" branch. That expression, "auxiliary branch", adopted from the California Society's Constitution, was an error of judgment, now at last confessed, but long persisted in. It was that word *auxiliary*, and that alone, which led to the creation of two sets of societies. A "Society of Sons of the Revolution" was organized in Philadelphia in 1888, although refusing to be "auxiliary" to New York.

This movement of 1883 awoke fresh interest in the subject of patriotic societies in the East, but the word "auxiliary" prevented gentlemen in New England and others of the original thirteen states from organizing societies of their own. Massachusetts, Connecticut, and other States each supplied far more men for the American Revolution than New York. A natural pride prevented those States from being "auxiliary" to New York. For about five years, therefore, these two Societies in the East and the pioneer Society in California were the only organizations of patriotic societies in existence.

In 1888 a few New Jersey members of the New York Society of the Sons of the Revolution proposed to form a New Jersey Society. The New York Sons told them they would be recognized as an "auxiliary" Society, and not otherwise, and, further, that they had better join either the New York or Philadelphia Society anyhow, and not have one of their own. These patriotic and enterprising Jerseymen then went to work.

Shortly came the 100th anniversary of the inauguration of George Washington as the first President of the United States, this event stirred patriotic emotions anew, and many descendants of Revolutionary stock in New Jersey organized a "Society of the Sons of the Revolution" on March 7th, 1889. This Society passed a resolution which had far reaching results and as this action was importance in the history of the Society, it is quoted here substantially in full:

> *Resolved*, That the President of this Society when elected, and the two delegates to the National Society, are hereby appointed a committee to invite the appointment of a like committee from the New York and Pennsylvania Societies, to cooperate with them and to meet with the descendants of Revolutionary ancestors from the different States and Territories, and assist in organizing Societies whose memberships shall be com-

posed exclusively of descendants of Revolutionary statesmen, soldiers, and sailors.

In the spring of 1889 the Jersey Society organized, by correspondence and personal visits, state societies of "Sons of the Revolution" in New Hampshire, Vermont, Delaware, Maryland, Ohio, Indiana, Illinois, West Virginia, Arkansas, South Carolina, Kentucky and Tennessee. The endeavor of those leading the movement was to organize a "National Society"—mark the name—"of the Sons of the Revolution" in which each state society should be a coequal organization, and none of them "auxiliary" to any other. They never dreamed of forming a new organization. Their whole purpose was to create enough pressure to influence the New York society to repeal the "auxiliary" article in its constitution.

If, when the New Yorkers heard of this movement, they had promptly met and repealed the "auxiliary" article, there never would have been two sets of societies. No one thought of it. But what did the New Yorkers do? They actually met and adopted a new constitution, in which the "auxiliary" article was made more explicit, and more binding, thus ignoring the patriotic sentiment and natural pride of every sister State, and declaring war upon any movement having for its object the equality of the different State Societies. By making all the other States "auxiliary" to New York, the annual election of national officers would have to be held in New York, and would always have been controlled by the local members.

III

THE BEGINNING OF THE NATIONAL SOCIETY

In accordance with the resolution passed at the meeting of the Jersey group on March 7, 1889, the following committee was appointed: William O. McDowell, J. C. Pumpelly, General William S. Stryker.

Thereafter, on April 10th, 1889, a call was issued by the committee mentioned in the above resolution, inviting delegates from every existing society from all states and territories to met at Fraunce's Tavern in New York, at 9 o'clock on April 30, 1889, to organize a National Society every state to be entitled to one delegate-at-large, and additional delegates proportioned upon the number of members of that state.

Then at the appointed place and hour, twenty delegates from a dozen states met at Fraunce's Tavern in the historic "Long Room"—in the same room in which Washington met the officers of his army and bade them farewell on December 3, 1783.

Eighteen out of the twenty societies including the original one in California were represented, and persons from New York and Pennsylvania.

Mr. McDowell, of New Jersey, called the meeting to order. After a permanent organization had been effected by the election of Mr. McDowell as chairman, and Lieutenant James C. Cresap, United States Navy, as secretary, remarks were made by several gentlemen, all in favor of the organization of a National Society. The necessity of such an organization was apparent to those present. The delegates reasoned that various state societies had come into existence for patriotic purposes, but their patriotic efforts could be best furthered and carried out under a national organization. Their ancestors who fought for freedom are now claimed by the nation as a whole. As one delegate pointed out, a Congress, made up from delegates from all the Colonies, had drafted and promulgated the Declaration of Independence; an army composed of patriots from all the colonies had carried out the sentiments of that Declaration and achieved American Independence; a union of all the American Colonies, under a central government, had preserved the rights so secured; it is fitting that we have one patriotic association representing all the states.

A motion was made to proceed with the organization of a National Society, and that a committee be appointed on constitution and by-laws, and to nominate permanent officers to consist of one delegate from each State. While this motion was being debated, the Pennsylvania delegates took the floor and urged that all the societies should become "auxiliary" to New York. This was debated for a long time. Pennsylvania was asked if her society was "auxiliary" to New York. She replied, "No." The convention then refused point blank to agree to the "auxiliary" relation to New York. Not one State in that whole convention would agree to that proposition. The New Yorkers refused, for their part, to recognize the others as "sister" societies, and both Pennsylvania and New York took no further part in the proceedings.

The question, "What shall be done?" then arose. The convention was there, in actual session, acting in behalf of eighteen States, including the original society of California. The delegates felt deeply the injustice of an attempt to impose an un-American style of organization upon a Society which should be pre-eminently American in all its sentiments, objects and framework, and especially to try to control, in this manner, a movement which New York had not even originated. After discussion, before adjournment, the convention organized as a National Society, taking the name of *Sons of the American Revolution*. The national organization thus began its existence with eighteen state societies, while the Sons of the Revolution had only two; and every one in the eighteen soon thereafter adopted the title, "Sons of the American Revolution."

After a two-day session, the *National Society of the Sons of the American Revolution* came into being. A constitution was adopted and the following officers elected:

President, Hon. Lucius P. Deming, New Haven, Conn.

Vice President-at-Large, William O. McDowell, Newark, N. J.

Vice Presidents, A. S. Hubbard, California; Gov. Simon B. Buckner, Kentucky; Maj. J. C. Kinney, Connecticut; C. H. Denison, Maine; P. C. Washington, West Virginia; Gov. D. R. Francis, Missouri; Col. C. Williams, Arkansas; Hon. G. B. West, Alabama; Gov. Wade Hampton, South Carolina; Gov. Robert S. Green, New Jersey; Rev. John G. Morris, D.D., Maryland; Hon. Luther L. Tarbell, Massachusetts; Hon. Rutherford B. Hayes, Ohio; Hon. H. K. Slayton, New Hampshire; Mons. Edmond de Lafayette, Paris, France; Gov. W. P. Dillingham, Vermont; Adm. D. D. Porter, U.S.N., District of Columbia.

Chaplain, Rev. Timothy Dwight, D.D., LL.D., of Yale University.

Secretary, Lt. James C. Cresap, U.S.N., Annapolis, Md.

Assistant Secretaries, Wilson L. Gill, Columbus, Ohio; G. L. Callaway, Greenville, S. C.; Charles J. King, San Francisco, Calif.

Treasurer, Gaius Paddock, St. Louis, Mo.

Registrar, Hon. Thomas M. Green, Maysville, Ky.

In addition to the above named offices there were present at this initial gathering the following:

Frederick Leighton, N.H.; Frank R. Starr, Conn.; G. V. Abbott, Ill.; Clarence S. Ward, Mass.; Franklin H. Hart, Conn.; John J. Hubbell, N. J.; N. C. Upham, Mass.; Charles C. Page, M.D., Ala.; Andrew J. Woodman, Dela.; Maj. George B. Halstead, Calif.; William E. English and Charles W. Merrill of Indiana.

For seven months the above named officers labored to strengthen the existing state societies and to lay the foundation for new societies to be organized. The first President, Mr. Lucius P. Deming,* finding the duties of this

---

*Compatriot Deming was also the first president of the Connecticut Society S.A.R. His Connecticut membership number was 2 and his National number, 202.

office too arduous tendered his resignation and at the urgent request of a committee appointed for the purpose, Doctor W. Seward Webb of Vermont, who was living in New York at the time, consented to act as President General.

A committee was appointed to officially notify Dr. Webb of his election and on December 7th, 1889, this committee, headed by the former President, Mr. Deming, as Chairman, met at Dr. Webb's residence in New York.

Among the distinguished names of the members of this notification committee were: Hon. Chauncey M. Depew, William K. Vanderbilt, William O. McDowell, Edmund C. Stanton, Henry L. Hall, Luther L. Tarbell, William H. Arnoux, Lieut. James C. Cresap, U.S.N.; J. C. Pumpelly, and many others of distinction.

Due to his inability to be present at the first National Congress, Dr. Webb invited to New York, the officers and prominent members of all the State Societies of the Sons of the American Revolution, in order, he stated: "to strengthen the ties of fraternity between the various branches of the order and to enjoy with his guests mutual felicitation over the progress and prosperity of their work." Invitation were sent to every part of the United States to attend a banquet at Delmonico's on the evening of March 1st. The invitation read as follows:

Dr. William Seward Webb
President
of the
National Society of the Sons of the
American Revolution
Requests the pleasure of your company at
dinner at Delmonico's on Saturday evening,
March 1st, at 7 o'clock, to meet representatives and members of the societies of the
Sons of the American Revolution.

R.S.V.P.   New York, January 25th, 1890

Arrangements were made for special private cars from Chicago, St. Louis and Cincinnati to bring guests from the West and South. The banquet scene was described as most elaborate, the walls of the great room and the balcony for musicians were half hidden from sight by American flags and the tables were laden with roses. The banquet was the first national gathering of the Sons of the American Revolution and was a meeting of men from widely separated states for the first time. Friendships, which would endure for life, were formed there.

The menu, which had been prepared by Tiffany & Co., was an elaborate one, and bore on its first page a beautiful representation of the insignia of the Sons of the American Revolution in colors, France was represented by the language in which the menu was printed. The insignia "S.A.R.," worked in colors, was also seen on every table in the hall, and on the large ornaments which had been prepared for the occasion.

Dr. Webb, with three others, sat at the head table; while Judge Deming with three others, was at the foot. Compatriot Deming was the toastmaster of the evening and following an address by President Webb, Judge Deming was introduced by Dr. Webb, who said: "I now take pleasure in introducing to you the first President of the National Society. The Honorable Lucius P. Deming of New Haven, who will speak of 'The Society and its Objects.'" Judge Deming responded by saying in part: "You have done me a great honor by calling upon me and referring to me as the first President of the National Society of the Sons of the American Revolution. I feel proud of that title and of the Society which has grown up since it was organized on April 30, 1889. In 1876, on July 4th, out in California, an inspiration came to the editor of a paper there, the *Alta-California*, and I don't know but that inspiration always come to editors, they seem to know everything, and think of everything - - - out of it came the first society of this name: the California Society of Revolutionary Sires - - - . Today, Mr. President and gentlemen, we have twenty-six societies, in twenty-six different states, all organized for the great work, which started in California."

Among the speakers presented by Judge Deming were: Chauncey M. Depew, who was introduced as "the next President of the United States," Rev. Dr. Edward Everett Hale, and President Benedict of the Vermont Society, who said: "I say long life and health to the National Society, an organization of the Sons of the American Revolution; long life and health to our genial host of tonight, our worthy and efficient President General, whose efforts to make our organization truly national, I am sure we all appreciate and applaud.

"We of the Green Hills have been glad to adopt him as almost a Vermonter, for his summer home is on land granted to his ancestor for patriotic service in the State of Vermont, and we claim him as half a Vermonter."

Dr. Webb was overwhelmed with congratulations upon the success of the banquet which was said to have welded solidly together the Sons of the American Revolution of the United States; it was further stated that: "If Dr. Webb should never perform another act for the good of the Society of the Sons of the American Revolution, it was the unanimous verdict Saturday night, that he had done enough already to entitle him to the lasting gratitude of every Son of the American Revolution in the United States."

There were also many letters and telegrams from friends and officers of the Society who were unable to attend, some of which were Hon. Edwin S. Barrett, Mass.; Jonathan Trumbull, Conn.; Adjt. General W. S. Stryker, N. J.; Admiral David D. Porter, U.S.N.; Governor Dillingham of Vt.; Governor J. P. Richardson, S. C., and many others.

Dr. Webb continued as President General until 1892, and throughout his administration the Society made great strides and many new state societies were organized and the Society grew and prospered under his leadership and the splendid assistance given him by the active officers throughout the country.

IV

ANNUAL CONGRESSES FROM 1890 TO 1901

CONGRESS OF 1890

During the first year of the Society's organization numerous meetings of the board of managers were held, and the work of instituting State Societies was taken up and prosecuted with such vigor that at a meeting of the first congress at Louisville, ten new State Societies had been organized, making a total of twenty-eight, with a membership of twenty-five hundred.

The first National Congress of the Society was held in Louisville, Kentucky, at the Galt House, on April 30th, 1890, at which General Alexander S. Webb, of New York, was called upon to preside in the absence of Dr. William Seward Webb, who was in Europe.

A banquet was given the delegates on the evening of the second day of the Congress at the Galt House, with about ninety present. At 9 o'clock the orchestra began to play "My Old Kentucky Home," which was "The signal to form for the assault on the feast waiting in the banquet hall. The charging column was headed by Governor Buckner and it was not the first time the old hero had done such a thing, though under less agreeable circumstances—who arm in arm with General Webb, another gallant leader, led the column to the banquet hall."

Governor Buckner presided at the banquet and introduced Judge William Lindsay of Kentucky, who spoke on the Constitution, its trials and triumphs, saying: "That wonderful document has survived all stress and now bound people together for all time, into one country, indissoluble."

Judge Deming, responding to a toast, spoke on "Our

ILLUSTRATIONS

All Past Presidents General are pictured down to and including the incumbent President General Anderson.

In addition to the Presidents General an effort was made to find pictures and photographs from every state society. Most of those shown come from National Headquarters or were reproduced from the S.A.R. Magazine. Some state societies send in more photographs to National Headquarters than others, so that those states have a larger representation.

The pictures have been arbitrarily selected and the choice was based upon their availability and adaptability. There has been no disposition to favor any person, group, chapter or state society. It is easy to see that if an effort had been made to get pictures from all the state societies and chapters, it would have been a colossal undertaking, unsatisfactory in many respects. As it is, the book contains many desirable illustrations and many hundreds of compartiots can be recognized in group pictures. It was not the original idea to have a "pictorial" book, but the pictures shown are representative of the Society's membership.

There are also illustrations of the home of the National Society as well as the Society's former Headquarters building. Several historical and patriotic scences are shown.

MEN PROMINENT IN ORGANIZING THE SONS
OF REVOLUTIONARY SIRES
Left to right: James L. Cogswell, J. P. Dameron, A. M. Winn.

1. Lucius P. Deming, 1889
2. Dr. William Seward Webb, 1890
3. General Horace Porter, 1892
4. Edwin Shepard Barrett, 1897
5. Franklin Murphy, 1899
6. General J. C. Breckinridge, 1900
7. Walter Seth Logan, 1901
8. General Edwin Warfield, 1902

9. General Edwin S. Greeley, 1903
10. James D. Hancock, 1904
11. General Francis H. Appleton, 1905
12. Cornelius A. Pugsley, 1906
13. Nelson A. McClary, 1907
14. Henry Stockbridge, 1908
15. Morris B. Beardsley, 1909
16. William A. Marble, 1910

17. Dr. Moses Greeley Parker, 1911
18. James M. Richardson, 1912
19. R. C. Ballard Thruston, 1913
20. Newell B. Woodworth, 1915
21. Elmer M. Wentworth, 1916
22. Louis Annin Ames, 1918
23. Chancellor L. Jenks, 1919
24. James Harry Preston, 1920

25. Wallace McCamant, 1921
26. W. I. L. Adams, 1922
27. Arthur P. Sumner, 1923
28. Harrison L. Lewis, 1924
29. Harvey F. Remington, 1925
30. Wilbert H. Barrett, 1926
31. Ernest E. Rogers, 1927
32. Ganson Depew, 1928

33. Howard C. Rowley, 1929
34. Josiah A. Van Orsdel, 1930
35. Benjamin N. Johnson, 1931
36. Frederick W. Millspaugh, 1932
37. Arthur M. McCrillis, 1933-34
38. Henry F. Baker, 1935
39. Messmore Kendall, 1936-39
40. Loren E. Souers, 1940

47. G. Ridgley Sappington, 1941
49. Smith L. Multer, 1943-45
51. A. Herbert Foreman, 1947

52. Charles B. Shaler, 1948
53. Ben H. Powell, III, 1948
56. Ray O. Edwards, 1952

Photo by Fabian Bachrach (Copyright)
Sterling F. Mutz, 1942

Photo by Harris & Ewing (Copyright)
Allen L. Oliver, 1946

PAST PRESIDENTS GENERAL

(Below) John W. Finger, 1949

(Below) Wallace C. Hall, 1950-1951

Photo by John L. Herrmann

Arthur A. de la Houssaye, 1953   Milton M. Lory, 1954

PAST PRESIDENTS GENERAL

(Below) Edgar Williamson, Jr., 1955   *(Below)* Eugene P. Carver, Jr., 1956
Photo by Handy-Boesser   *Photo by Alfred Brown*

Photo by Lainson Studio
George E. Tarbox, Jr., 1957

Photo by Blackstone Studio
Walter A. Wentworth, 1958

PAST PRESIDENTS GENERAL

(Below) Charles A. Jones, 1959

(Below) Herschel S. Murphy, M.D., 1960

Photo by Lamb's Studio

Horace Y. Kitchell, 1961
Past President General

Charles A. Anderson, M.D., 1962
President General

Trustees of the National Society at a meeting at Headquarters Oct. 10, 1960

Photo by Wm. M. Cain

(At left)—A. Howard Clark, Secretary General, 1893 and 1904 through 1918 (In 1904 the office of Secretary General was combined with that of Registrar General)

Photo by Harris & Ewing

(Below)—Frank B. Steele, Secretary General and Registrar General, 1921 through 1949.

Photo by Harris & Ewing

(Above)—Harold L. Putnam, Executive Secretary since 1950 to date.

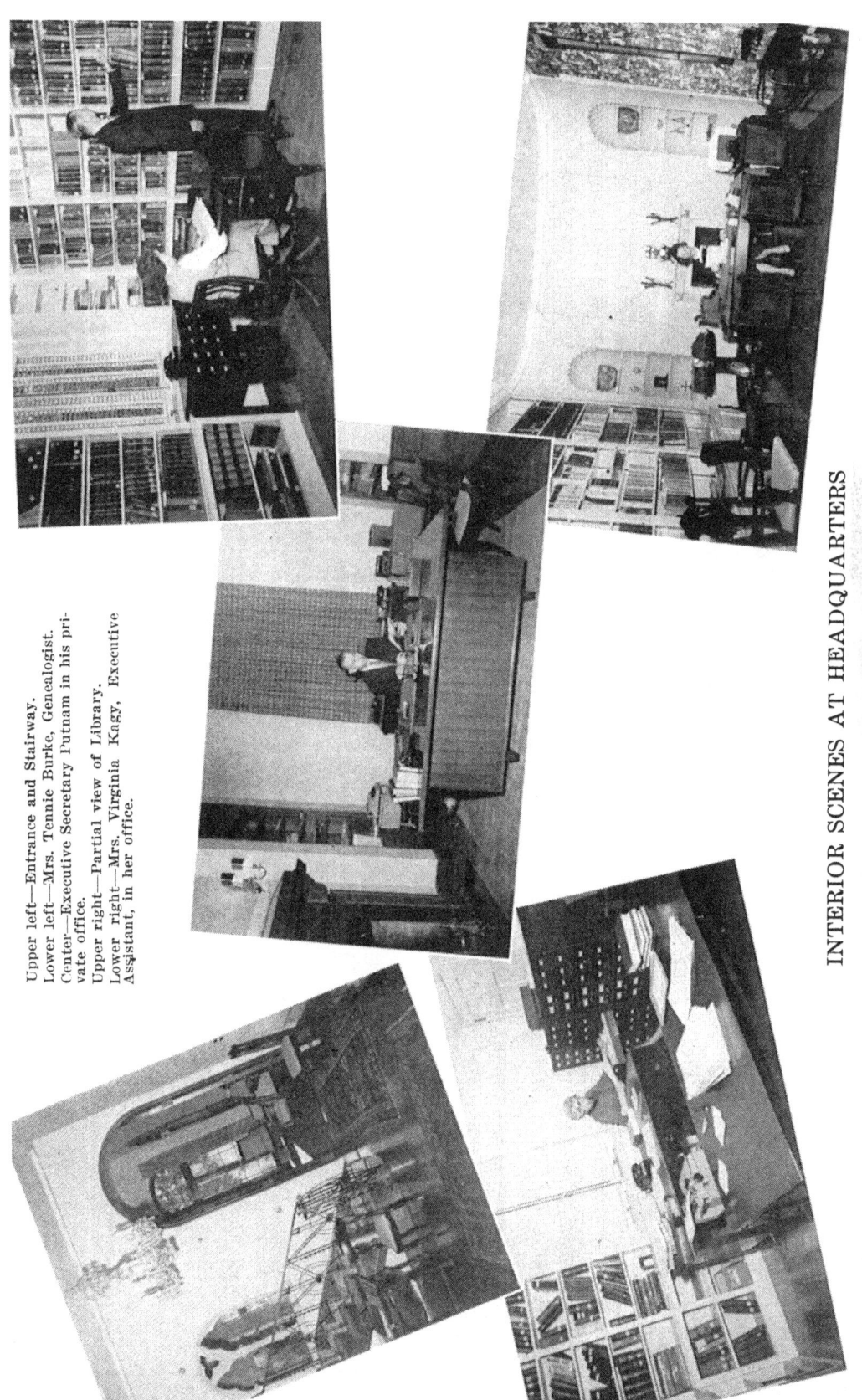

Upper left—Entrance and Stairway.
Lower left—Mrs. Tennie Burke, Genealogist.
Center—Executive Secretary Putnam in his private office.
Upper right—Partial view of Library.
Lower right—Mrs. Virginia Kagy, Executive Assistant, in her office.

INTERIOR SCENES AT HEADQUARTERS

Minute Man Award, May 23, 1955: *(Front row, left to right)* Charles B. Elder, Crawford S. Rogers, Stuart O. Landry, Walter Wentworth, Eugene P. Carver, Jr., Col. William T. Carpenter, Gardner Osborn, Redmond S. Cole and Edwin B. Graham *(Back row)* S.A.R. Officers.

1956 Award: *(Upper left, left to right)* Arthur F. Cole, Brig. Gen'l. Charles D. Y. Ostrom, John E. King and Charles A. Jones.

1958 Award: *(Lower left, left to right)* Dr. William F. Bulkley, John E. Dickinson, Jean A. Hibbard, Col. F. W. Huntington, Judge Augustus M. Roan, Dr. Mott R. Sawyers, and Samuel Hubbard Scott. (President General Tarbox at right of picture.)

1957 Award: *(Upper right, left to right)* Warren M. Taylor, Cyril S. Cain and Judge Stanton T. Lawrence.

1959 Award: *(Lower right, left to right)* Col. Robert P. Waters, Arthur C. Trimble, Dr. T. Earl Pardoe, Stephen C. Luce, Jr., Senator Albert W. Hawkes, Robert P. Gordon, Franklin Blackstone, John G. Ballord. (President General Walter Wentworth presented medals).

MINUTE MEN

1960 Minute Men not shown because group picture unavailable. Receiving the Award were: Reginald Runge, Edward W. Milligan and James C. Cecil.

1961 Award: *(Below, left to right)* John St. Paul, Jr., Dr. Harold I. Meyer and Horace Y. Kitchell. (Calvin Bolles absent).

1962 Award: *(Below, left to right)* Robert S. W. Walker, Augustin G. Rudd, Samuel K. Houston, Chester R. Martin, John F. Lanier, Ross K. Cook and Charles A. Anderson, M.D.

The Society in France of the Sons of the American Revolution observed the 4th of July (1958) at Lafayette's tomb. More than two-hundred leading Franco-American personalities attended.

(At left) AMBASSADOR HERRICK SPEAKING AT THE EXERCISES AT PICPUS CEMETERY, PARIS, JULY 4, 1926.
Left to right: Captain Lhopital, representing Marshal Foch; Hon. Myron T. Herrick, American Ambassador; General Gouraud, Military Governor of Paris; Compatriot Edward H. de Neveu, Secretary of the Society in France and Chairman.

(Below) S. A. R. IN FRANCE HONOR GEORGE WASHINGTON IN 1932
Left to right: Vice-President General Marquis de Rochambeau; Edward de Neveu, Vice-President; Comte de Luppé, Registrar; C. Benoist d'Azy, Secretary.

(Above) At left—Jno. Alden May. *Right*—Frank Forsyth, 85 yrs., of St. Augustine, Fla.

(Above) Original flag of the State of Missouri designed and made by Marie Elizabeth Watkins Oliver, Past President General Allen Oliver's Mother. *At left*—Warren Hearne, Sec. of State of Missouri. *Center*—John M. Dalton, Governor of Missouri. *Right*—Allen L. Oliver.

(At right) The "burning of the mortgage" at the Sixty-Fifth Annual Congress, Chicago, May 23, 1955. *Left to Right*—President General Milton M. Lory, Executive Secretary Harold L. Putnam and Past President General Arthur A. de la Houssaye.

FOUR CHAPLAINS LEGION OF HONOR (Below)

At the 1962 Congress the general officers of the National Society of the Sons of the American Revolution were presented with certificates of membership in the Legion of Honor of the Chapel of Four Chaplains.

Absent President General," giving a history of the Webb family and saying: "Dr. Webb's name is a synonym for generosity, truth and manhood." Compatriot William O. McDowell of New Jersey, received the special honor of a parchment certificate of membership, Number 1 in the National Society, and Number 1 in the New Jersey Society. In honor of the first son of an S.A.R. member since the Society was organized, Compatriot Deming presented to Secretary General Cresap a silver cup for his baby boy.

Regarding the many social events enjoyed at the Congress were the following interesting items: "A great variety of hospitalities were showered on the delegates by the good people of the city. Among them, the dinner of the Blue Grass Club, at which all the speakers were chaffed, will be long remembered."

The first annual National Congress at Louisville was said to have been a great success and it results gave much satisfaction to all delegates. After the Congress had adjourned, the Board of Managers held a meeting for the election of the executive committee. Among those elected to it were, Dr. William S. Webb and Lucius P. Deming.

At this first Congress the Constitution was revised and a new one adopted. After being engrossed, it was signed by all the delegates present.

Other important matters were decided. One was the decision to limit the membership of the Society to males exclusively. Up to this time much pressure had been exerted to include women in the organization, and in one or two states there had actually been a number admitted. The clause in the newly adopted Constitution which defined the status of women reads as follows:

> For the purpose of making more nearly perfect the records of our Revolutionary ancestors and their descendants, any woman of Revolutionary ancestry may *file a record* of her ancestor's services and of her line of descent with any Registrar who shall send a duplicate to the Registrar General.

This clause of the Constitution has of course been long since eliminated.

Another eligibility clause of this early Constitution

might, with pertinence, be quoted here, in view of the erroneous statement sometimes heard to the effect that our Society once admitted on collateral descent:

> Any man is eligible for membership who is of the age of twenty-one, and who is *descended from an ancestor*, who, with unfailing loyalty, rendered material aid to the cause of American Independence, etc., etc.

The word "lineal" was inserted in later years, to make this more emphatic, but one is not "descended" from a *collateral* line.

From the very beginning the National Society of the Sons of the American Revolution has constantly promoted proper use of the American Flag, and has been most influential in securing proper flag legislation in most states where such has been enacted, and was the originator of the observance of June 14th as Flag Day, now nationally recognized.

At this Congress important resolutions were adopted looking toward the correct use of the American Flag and its proper display on all patriotic anniversaries and upon public buildings. So influential had the Society already become with respect to this matter, that Dr. Webb states:

> After the adjournment of the Louisville Convention, and possibly by reason of the resolution there passed and the action there taken, the President of the United States ordered and directed that the National flag shall be constantly displayed over the Executive Mansion, instead of occasionally as heretofore.

In his reminiscences printed by his wife after his death, Frank B. Steele, having known personally nearly all of the early officers, made these comments about the first Congress at Louisville.

> At the Louisville meeting much discussion took place on the question of including women in the membership, and the momentous policy was adopted there not to accept women members! It will surprise many, no doubt, to learn that there already had been filed with the Society a goodly number of applications and lineage papers by women, and these are still filed and bound within the first volume of 200 application papers de-

posited in the Sons of the American Revolution National Headquarters. The final decision made at Louisville, after much debate, was that women might file papers showing their descent from Revolutionary patriots, with our Society, as a place of deposit, and for the preservation of the record. This clause of our early Constitution was long ago eliminated.

Perhaps one reason for this decision on the part of the National Society was that our organization was then largely influenced by military men.

The decision to bar women from the organization caused many regrets and probably still more indignation on the part of the ladies, and very shortly after the Louisville meeting of the S. A. R., and due to the energy and enthusiasm of three splendid women, who got together and worked hard for several months, the organization of the National Society, Daughters of the American Revolution, was inaugurated, with Mrs. Caroline Scott Harrison, wife of the then President of the United States, as the first President General. This accounts for the difference in the dates of origin of the two Societies. Interesting to note, two prominent members of the Sons of the American Revolution, Dr. G. Browne Goode, and A. Howard Clark, assisted the ladies substantially in formulating their constitution and policies. Mrs. Clark was the first Registrar General of the Daughters.

Today the Society of the Sons of the American Revolution is far out-distanced by the Daughters in point of *numbers*, and the writer has frequently observed that it was probably a very good thing for them that the Sons decided to keep to themselves; and further, it has been his observation that *mixed* societies of men and women, as a rule, have not progressed in growth and activities so noticeably. *Witness*: The Society of Mayflower Descendants, Descendants of Huguenots, as examples—very worthy and interesting as to lineage and influence, but not impressive as to *numbers;* whereas, in several societies of Colonial ancestry, such as the War of 1812, Daughters of American Colonists, Colonial Wars, and similar groups where there are separate organizations of men and women, we find the women's groups, especially are more active and numerous.

Another matter of the Louisville Congress of 1890

which deserves special emphasis because of certain allegations which have been made regarding Sons-of-the-American-Revolution eligibility, was a clause in the Constitution there adopted, namely: one who is *"descended from an Ancestor"*; *later*, the word *"lineal"* was inserted to make this descent more emphatic, but it can be seen that the Sons of the American Revolution *never* authorized *collateral* descent.

CONGRESS OF 1891

On the 30th day of April, 1891, the second annual congress of the National Society of the Sons of the American Revolution was held at Hartford, Conn. The attendance was large, and the delegates were full of enthusiasm. Governor Buckley welcomed the delegates at the opening of the congress. Full and interesting reports were received from the State Societies and from the officers of the National Society. The question of unity with the Sons of the Revolution was considered, and such steps taken as led eventually to a conference of committees of both Societies looking to a union. At the close of the congress the Connecticut Society entertained the delegates with an elaborate banquet, at which many eloquent and patriotic addresses were made.

CONGRESS OF 1892

The third annual congress met on April 30, 1892, in the Governor's room in the City Hall in New York City. The use of this room was secured to the Society by special permission of the city authorities; it was decorated appropriately for the occasion. Eighty-nine delegates were present, representing twenty-two States. The report showed thirty State Societies, with a membership aggregatin three thousand five hundred and three. The reports of the officers and of the State Societies showed that the order was in a prosperous condition, and that its influence was not only increasing but that its methods were becoming better understood, and its records and those of its members were being perfected to a degree scarcely to have been expected when it was organized. The usual amount of routine business was transacted, and upon the adjournment of the convention a banquet was served at Delmonico's by the Empire State Society, at which the Honorable Chauncey M. Depew acted as toast-master.

At this Congress General Horace Porter, of New York, was unanimously elected President-General. He held this office until April 30, 1896.

General Porter was deeply interested in the Society and during his administration, although part of the time he was our Minister from the United States to France, many outstanding and lasting accomplishments were inaugurated and successfully completed. In an address made in 1895 at the annual Congress at Boston, General Porter outlined some of these accomplishments (given hereinafter). General Porter, while Minister of France, searched for and found the remains of John Paul Jones, and through his efforts this great naval hero lies in that beautiful sarcophagus at Annapolis.

Congress and Conclave of 1893

Early in 1893 the National Society received an invitation from the Illinois State Society to hold its annual congress and the first Triennial Conclave of the general membership at Chicago, on June 16th and 17th of that year. In order that the constitution should not be violated, the board of managers, on April 30th, held a pro forma session in New York City, at the office of General Horace Porter, President-General, and then adjourned to meet at Chicago on the 16th day of June. At this pro forma session certain constitutional amendments were proposed and referred to the special committee on revision of the constitution, appointed in 1892.

On the 16th day of June, 1893, the adjourned session of the congress met in the Art Institute in the city of Chicago. There were present eighty-five members and a large number of compatriots from Illinois and other State Societies, as well as a number of Daughters of the American Revolution. Twenty-nine State Societies were represented. The reports of the various officers showed that the Society was in a prosperous condition, and that its membership had increased to four thousand one hundred. After the election officers for the ensuing year, the congress adjourned to become the guests of the Illinois Society at a banquet given at the Union League Club at Chicago, at which the Honorable Henry M. Shepard, President of the Illinois Society, presided and welcomed the congress to Chicago. Various toasts were responded to by prominent members of the Society.

On the following day a thousand or more of Sons and Daughters of the American Revolution assembled at the Music Hall on the Exposition Grounds to celebrate the anniversary of the Battle of Bunker Hill. Gen. Horace Porter presided and delivered the opening address, after which addresses were made by Hon. Chauncey M. Depew, of New York, and William Wirt Henry, of Virginia. Adjournment was then had to the Casino for lunch. In the afternoon a spirited meeting was held by the Daughters of the American Revolution in the Women's Building. At this meeting addresses were made by Gen. Porter, Hon. Henry M. Shepard, and also by several of the more prominent Daughters of the American Revolution, after which refreshments were served and the meeting adjourned.

Congress of 1894

The fifth annual congress of the Society convened in the city of Washington on the 30th day of April, 1894. Twenty-seven State Societies were represented. The report of the registrar-general showed that the Societies had been organized in Iowa and Pennsylvania during the year, and that the membership of the Society had increased to four thousand five hundred and ninety-two. During the noon recess the delegates marched in a body to the White House, where they were received by President Cleveland in the East Room, each delegate being presented to the President by General Porter. In the evening the District of Columbia Society tendered a reception to the delegates and their ladies and others, in the parlors of the Arlington Hotel. General J. C. Breckinridge, President of the District of Columbia Society, welcomed the guests, and during the evening addresses were made by General Porter, Judge Whitehead, of New Jersey; Senator Hill, of Connecticut; Judge Good, of Virginia; Mr. Weeks, of Pennsylvania, and others.

Congress of 1895

The sixth annual congress met in the old South Meetinghouse, in the city of Boston, on May 1st, 1895.

Twelve hundred new members had been added to the rolls. A committee on National Legislation was appointed to take charge of all business, both of the National and State Societies, requiring action in the United States Congress. It was also resolved to try to secure through Congressional action the publication in book form of the records of Revolutionary service, which were then being indexed at Washington, at Governmental expenses, and also to request the various State Societies to take steps for the general observation of Flag Day, June 14th, in the several cities and municipalities within their respective jurisdictions.

In the evening the members of the congress were the guests of the Massachusetts Society at the Hotel Vendome. After a reception in the parlors of the hotel, two hundred and fifty Sons of the American Revolution marched to the dining-hall and enjoyed a repast of marked excellence. The day following was devoted to an excursion to the battlefields of Lexington and Concord.

In his address at the annual Congress in Boston, May 1, 1895, President General Horace Porter pointed out some of the accomplishments of the society since its inception:

> —Secured from Congress a law under which the records of Revolution service stored in Executive Departments in Washington were indexed and placed in a fireproof building in the Smithsonian Institution.
> —Secured from Congress a law authorizing officers of the regular army and navy, who are members, to wear the badge of this Society on ceremonial occasions.
> Prevailed upon the New Hampshire Legislature to construct and publicly dedicate the statue of that grand old hero, General John Stark.
> —Originated the beautiful custom of Flag Day, setting aside June 14 as the anniversary of the adoption of the Stars and Stripes as our national ensign for such celebrations.
> —Persuaded the New York Legislature to pass a law forbidding the display of foreign flags upon public

buildings unless the official representatives of a foreign power are guests of a city or the State.

—Took the most prominent part in the celebration of the laying of the cornerstone of the National Capitol, September 18, 1893, when William Wirt Henry, the grandson of the great Patrick Henry, was selected from this Society as the orator of the day.

—Stimulated interest in the American Revolution by participating in more than two hundred public celebrations of anniversaries of important events.

—Initiated the movement, originated by our honored Massachusetts Society, of the plan of marking the graves of the patriots of the American Revolution with bronze and iron markers.

—Advocated the passage of a law by Congress forbidding the desecration of the national flag for advertising purposes.

—Advocated a law passed by the New York Legislature saving from desecration, the old historic building known as City Hall in New York City.

—Erected an expensive monument at Dobbs' Ferry, to commemorate the spot where Washington and Rochambeau planned the Yorktown campaign.

—Brought about the preservation of Washington's Headquarters, (Later the home of President General Messmore Kendall).

—Presented national flags, portraits of Washington and prize medals to large numbers of schools and academies in different parts of the country.

—Secured appropriations from the Legislature of Maryland and private individuals for the erection of a splendid monument in Baltimore to the men of the American Revolution.

Congress of 1896

The seventh annual Congress was held at the city of Richmond, Virginia, on April 30, 1896, President General Horace Porter presiding. The registrar-general's report showed a total membership of seven thousand, seven hundred and eighty-three. Various routine business was transacted, and in the evening a banquet was tendered by the Virginia Society at the Hotel Jefferson, at which William Wirt Henry, President of the Virginia Society, presided.

CONGRESS OF 1897

The eighth annual congress was held October 30, 1897, at Cleveland, Ohio. Edward S. Barrett, Vice-President-General, presided. The reports showed that the number of State Societies had increased to thirty-six, with one Society in Hawaii, and that the total membership of the order had increased to eight thousand nine hundred and ninety-six. In the evening the Western Reserve Society banqueted the delegates at the Hollenden Hotel. At this banquet James M. Richardson, president of the Ohio Society, presided. On the following day the Daughters of the American Revolution tendered the delegates a reception at the Colonial Club.

CONGRESS OF 1898

The ninth annual congress of the Society was held in Lafayette's rooms, adjoining Washington's headquarters, at Morristown, N.J., on the 30th day of April, 1898. The reports showed an average annual increase in the membership of the Society, after deducting losses by death and otherwise, during the nine years of its existence, of one thousand and twenty, and a total membership of nine thousand one hundred and forty-one. At the close of the congress the delegates were entertained at a banquet given by the New Jersey Society.

CONGRESS OF 1899

Detroit, Michigan, was the meeting place of the tenth annual congress. The delegates assembled on May 1 and 2, 1899, in Philharmonic Hall, Vice-President-General Franklin Murphy presiding. A message of congratulation was cabled to compatriot George Dewey.*

---

*One of the most famous compatriots of the Society of The Sons of the American Revolution was Admiral George Dewey.

Dewey, at that time Commodore, was in command of the United States Naval forces in Asiatic waters. In April 1898, while his fleet was at Hong Kong, a cable notified him that the United States and Spain were at war and he was ordered to "capture and destroy the Spanish fleet" which was then in Philippine waters. On the 1st of May he overwhelmingly defeated the Spanish fleet in Manila Bay, when on this occasion he gave the famous command, "You may fire when you are ready, Captain Gridley." The Americans won the victory without losing a man.

The official reports showed that the membership of the order had increased to nine thousand six hundred and ninety. April 30 being Sunday, an evening church service was held, at which Chaplain Rev. Rufus M. Clark preached. On Monday afternoon the Louisa St. Claire Chapter Daughters of the American Revolution tendered the delegates a reception at the Hotel Cadillac. On Tuesday evening a banquet was given at the Russell House, at which Thos. W. Palmer presided, and toasts were responded to by prominent members of the order present.

CONGRESS OF 1900

The eleventh annual congress met at the Waldorf Astoria Hotel, in New York City, April 30 and May 1, 1900. President-General Murphy presided. The reports of the various general officers were read, from which it appeared that the past year had been a generally prosperous one with all of the State Societies. The total active membership was nine thousand six hundred and seventy-one. Several amendments to the constitution were adopted. A banner for the Society was provided for. In the evening a banquet was given in the ball-room of the Waldorf Astoria, at which Hon. Walter Seth Logan acted as toastmaster. Many patriotic and enthusiastic speeches were made by prominent and distinguished members present.

CONGRESS OF 1901

The twelfth annual congress was held at Pittsburgh, Pennsylvania, on April 30 and May 1, 1901. President-General Breckinridge presided. From the reports of the general officers, it appeared that the State Societies had enjoyed great prosperity during the year, and that they had accomplished much good, patriotic work. The registrar-general's report showed that the total active membership of the Society was nine thousand nine hundred and nine, enrolled

---

Congress tendered its thanks to Commodore Dewey and authorized the Secretary of the Navy to present a sword of honor to him. On May the 10th, 1898, Commodore Dewey was promoted to the rank of Rear Admiral. A year later, he was given the rank of Admiral — a title formerly borne only by Farragut and Porter. On the 3rd of October 1899, he arrived in New York City where he received one of the great ovations for which that city is famous.

in thirty-nine State Societies; that during the year Maryland had printed a large quarto volume of muster rolls, and that some lists had been published by South Carolina. The National Flag Committee reported that they had secured the passage in six States of laws preventing the desecration of the national flag by using it for advertising purposes, and that such laws now existed in eighteen States.

The convention also determined to recommend that the Congress of the United States cause to be erected in Washington, D. C., such a memorial to the heroes of the Revolution as would give fitting recognition to the deeds of valor and self-sacrifice exhibited in the struggles of our ancestors to achieve independence and establish our republic.

A resolution was also adopted providing that the board of managers proceed with the publication of the register without any expense to the National Society.

After twelve years the members of the National Society contemplated its progress with pride. It was composed of men of various political opinions; men in army and naval life, men eminent as statesmen, jurists, merchants, bankers, preachers, and in every honorable walk of life; all of the men who take pride in their descent from those Revolutionary sires who, by the sacrifice of energy, wealth, and even life itself, founded this great Republic. Among its distinguished members were our late President, William McKinley; the President of the United States, Theo. Roosevelt; the Commanding General of the Army, Nelson A. Miles; the Admiral of the Navy, George Dewey; Associate Justice of the United States Supreme Court, David J. Brewer; the United States Ambassador to France, Horace Porter; the late United States Ambassador to Spain, Stewart L. Woodford; ex-Vice-President, Levi P. Morton; United States Senators, Chauncey W. Depew, John W. Daniels, Marcus A. Hanna, Henry C. Lodge, Orville H. Platt, and Redfield Proctor. Also Generals Simon B. Buckner, Frederick D. Grant, A. W. Greeley, Chas. King, Thos. M. Anderson, Wm. R. Shafter, J. C. Breckinridge, and Joseph Wheeler.

On May 1, 1901, the organization consisted of thirty-nine different Societies in the United States and France, with the following membership:

Arizona	26	Minnesota	300
Arkansas	24	Missouri	114
California	323	Montana	27
Colorado	110	Nebraska	79
Connecticut	993	New Hampshire	280
Delaware	55	New Jersey	408
Dist. Columbia	427	New York	1205
Florida	35	Ohio	425
France	30	Oregon	116
Hawaii	58	Pennsylvania	314
Illinois	522	Rhode Island	255
Indiana	180	South Dakota	20
Iowa	149	Tennessee	81
Kansas	152	Texas	36
Kentucky	80	Utah	57
Louisiana	44	Vermont	267
Maine	365	Virginia	60
Maryland	180	Washington	119
Massachusetts	1400	Wisconsin	227
		Total	9,909

The early growth and progress of the Society was due to the fact that at the very beginning it was organized upon the broad American principle of one National Society, divided into coequal sister and State Societies, and the latter subdivided, to some extent, into local branches or chapters; and to the further fact that the Society was the only one that admitted no man to membership unless he was a lineal descendant of a patriot of the American Revolution. The wisdom of these provisions has been so apparent that the Sons of the Revolution have, since the events of 1889, repealed the "auxiliary" article in their constitution, and still later have abolished their long-cherished provision for admitting collateral descendants. Because of the strict requirements for membership, and spirit of our members, an exceedingly large number of men of high social position and national reputation have joined our Society in all parts of the country. Our application blank has been adopted by all the different Societies of Sons and Daughters of the Revolution.

During the afternoon of May 1, 1901, the literary exercises were held in Carnegie Music Hall, at which addresses were delivered by prominent members. In the evening the delegates were the guests of the Pennsylvania Society at a banquet given in the ball-room of the Hotel Schenley.

FRANK STEELE'S REMINISCENCES

In the months following his retirement, Frank Bartlett Steele, Secretary-Registrar General from 1921 to May 1950, re-wrote and added to his reminiscences of the Society's activity during his long service to the National Society of the Sons of the American Revolution. Some of these memoirs had already been published in the S.A.R. magazine. He intended to elaborate and print his complete memoirs in the Society's magazine, but death intervened.

At the time of his death, Frank Steele was probably the only living compatriot who knew all the personalities described in his notes, and who had had the privilege of attending many of the annual congresses of the Society over such a long period, both prior to and during his incumbency of the office of Secretary-Registrar General.

Mrs. Steele, after Mr. Steele's death, had his manuscript privately printed. From this brochure, which she sent to the Historian General, with the exception of slight alterations, this chapter is taken from his memoirs. It must be understood that the characterizations of the early presidents and other compatriots are those of Mr. Steele and his comments represent his personal opinion.

We are indeed indebted to Compatriot Steele and his wife for information about the early days that would otherwise have been lost.

—*Editor*

V

THE RECORD FROM 1902 TO 1945, INCLUSIVE

1902
General Edwin Warfield, later Governor of Maryland, was elected President General.

1903
General Edwin S. Greeley, of Connecticut, distinguished Civil War Officer, was elected President General.

1904
Hon. James Denton Hancock, Attorney and distinguished legislator of Pennsylvania, was elected President General.

1905
Following this galaxy of courtly and representative gentlemen, came General Francis H. Appleton of Massachusetts, elected in 1905 at Philadelphia.

1906
General Appleton presided at the Boston Congress of 1906. From the stage of historic Faneuil Hall in Boston the privilege of extending the invitation to the Congress to meet in Buffalo was allotted to Compatriot Steele and he wrote that it was a great distinction and honor.

The dignity and ability of General Appleton were very impressive. He was what we would consider a typical Bostonian, tall, handsome and representative of the acknowledged cultural New England aristocracy. He carried on the meetings most ably. He lived to be past ninety years of age, never ceasing to retain an abiding interest in the affairs of the Society.

The year 1906 should be memorable in the annals of the Society, for it was the year in which the United States

Congress gave the National Society its Charter. This is an impressive document preserved in the safe at National Headquarters, and bears the signatures of Theodore Roosevelt, President of the United States, Charles Warren Fairbanks, Vice President, and President of the United States Senate, and Honorable Joseph Cannon, Speaker of the House of Representatives.

At that time there were only three other national organizations chartered by Congress—the National Society, Daughters of the American Revolution; the National Society, United States Daughters of 1812; and the American Red Cross.

The invitation to come to Buffalo in 1907 was not accepted, and it was decided to go to Denver, Colorado, but Buffalo was given preference for the following year. The Denver Congress was one of the few which the writer [Steele] was unable to attend, but from all accounts it was a delightful meeting and the delegates were given the opportunity to visit Pike's Peak as a special thrill.

1907

The presiding officer at Denver was the Honorable Cornelius C. Pugsley, of Peekskill, New York, whose election at Boston had been unanimous.

Of all the Presidents General who served during this writer's long experience, Mr. Cornelius Pugsley was one of the most devoted and regular in his attendance at our annual Congresses. It is not recalled that he ever missed a meeting from his early membership to the time of his death in 1936. He also served many times on the Executive Committee and was active in all projects of the National Society throughout. He was a very picturesque personality, extremely gallant and attentive to the ladies, a fine orator, and a fine businessman, a longtime banker of Peekskill.

At Denver, the election resulted in choosing Mr. Nelson A. McClary, of Chicago, to guide the Society through the following year. This was the first time the Society had gone so far from the Eastern States in selecting its presiding officer, and it was felt that the rapidly developing Midwest deserved recognition.

Mr. McClary, who presided at the 1908 Congress in

Buffalo, was a charming gentleman, very dignified, who made an excellent presiding officer; a businessman of ability, he brought improved methods into the management of the Society. Contacts with him were most delightful and leave a most agreeable memory.

1908

The Buffalo Congress was considered at that time one of the most delightful and interesting, the memorable feature of which was a special train to carry the delegates to Niagara Falls, and included the famous trip around the Niagara Gorge to Queenstown, Ontario, on the high Canadian side, across the lower river to Lewiston, New York, and upon the historic Gorge Route back to Niagara Falls. This famous scenic trip is no longer possible to the tourist of today, as it was discontinued some years ago; its construction was considered one of the greatest engineering feats accomplished up to that time.

Both delegates and hosts at this Congress were treated to a surprise snowstorm. This being April, it was most untimely, but afforded much fun, especially for the Southern delegates, to a few of whom it was a new experience, and who staged a brief snowball battle with great glee!

In Buffalo the Honorable Henry Stockbridge, of Maryland, was elected President General. He was a very cultured gentleman, a prominent attorney and Judge of Maryland's high court. He presided at the Congress of 1909 held in his home city of Baltimore. During his administration he was instrumental in having compiled for distribution among immigrants in collaboration with the United States Immigration Service a valuable little pamphlet containing much helpful instruction for our incoming and prospective citizens from foreign lands, translated into their several languages.

The Baltimore Compatriots at this Congress arranged a delightful excursion to Annapolis, where a session was held in the historic old Capitol, and the delegates were welcomed and escorted over the Naval Academy grounds and buildings by former President General and Governor of Maryland, Honorable Edwin Warfield, a most courteous and handsome gentleman of the old Southern school.

1909

Following Judge Stockbridge came the Honorable Morris B. Beardsley, of Connecticut, another courtly and able lawyer and gentleman of fine imposing appearance and presence and distinguished ancestry. He gave a most successful administration and was unsparing of his time and abilities in promoting the Society's progress.

1910

At Toledo, Ohio, in 1910, Mr. William A. Marble of New York was elected President General. A successful businessman, and President of the Empire State Society, he devoted himself to the advancement of the work of the organization.

At this Toledo Congress there appeared for the first time a most charming gentleman from Louisville, Kentucky, who, in the opinion of the writer accomplished a most effective work in and for the Society which places him among the country's foremost patriots and historians. This was Mr. Rogers Clark Ballard-Thruston, who came to invite the Congress to meet again in Louisville in 1911 which invitation was accepted.

1911

After Mr. Marble's administration came a loyal and patriotic physician of the Massachusetts Society, Dr. Moses Greeley Parker, President of his State Society. He devoted much time to the organization of chapters throughout the Society, believing this to be the most practical method to increase membership and arouse local interest. He remembered the National Society with a bequest in his will. He was deeply interested in projects for the protection and education of underprivileged boys, and devoted much time to these.

1912

There followed the Honorable James M. Richardson, of Ohio, elected in Boston in 1912. He was greatly handicapped by ill health during his administration, but led the Society very successfully, despite this.

During Mr. Richardson's term geographical districts were allotted to the several Vice Presidents General, holding them responsible for promoting activities and membership growth therein. Also, during this administration, on January 26, 1913, the body of John Paul Jones was reinterred in the beautiful Chapel at the Naval Academy at Annapolis, marking the culmination of the notable achievement of our earlier President General, Admiral Porter. Much credit was given an honored Compatriot of the Society, Rear Admiral George W. Baird, USN Ret., who had been very active and successful in securing the necessary appropriations from Congress for this, thus giving to our Nation one of its most impressive and sacred shrines.

1913 - 1914

Mr. Rogers C. B. Thruston, elected President General at Chicago, was a shining example of a true Southern gentleman, a scion of one of the most influential, aristocratic and wealthy families of Kentucky. He was a direct descendant of George Rogers Clark whose name he bore. By a curious incident he had assumed his mother's name of Thruston as a surname, although born a Ballard, acceding to his mother's wishes, as she hoped thus to perpetuate her own family name. However, this desire was not gratified, as Mr. Thruston never married!

It was during his administration as President General that Mr. Thruston became deeply engrossed in an historical project for which his name is honored, and which places him among the great historians of our American tradition. He discovered to his surprise that there was practically no record of the history, birth places, and burial spots of many of the Signers of the Declaration of Independence, and very little and almost nothing known of their descendants, and upon this discovery he set himself to correct this discrepancy and started the research to which he devoted his life thereafter. He made a systematic and exhaustive search for all available data relating to this history, expended much of his personal fortune, and traveled extensively to examine personally every clue. He compiled his findings into a series of eight manuscript volumes entitled "Signers of the Declaration of Independence." Only three copies of this magnificent and valuable work, are in existence. One was presented to the National Society, Sons of the

American Revolution and is kept under constant guard at National Headquarters; one went to the Library of Congress, and the third is in possession of the Filson Club of Louisville, a Museum and Historical Library founded and endowed by Mr. Thruston.

In addition to this monumental work, the value of which is hard to estimate, Mr. Thruston purchased a valuable collection of eighteen volumes of manuscripts, known as the Leach Manuscripts and entitled "Genealogy, Signers of the Declaration of Independence, Mss. Copies." This is an exhaustive compilation dealing with the Signers and their descendants, collected by a Mr. Leach of Philadelphia, now deceased, and is considered the most complete collection of authentic information on the subject extant. This collection Mr. Thruston also presented to the Sons of the American Revolution.

To commend so emphatically this contribution of Mr. Thruston is not to minimize in any respect the work of other able and fine Presidents or their achievements, but it is conceded that few could undertake such a tremendous job and accomplish it so thoroughly. He had the leisure, as well as the ability and the means, and the results redound to his credit. It would be a boon if this stupendous work could be printed and made available to all historians and researchers. Some attempts have been made to induce Congress to do this, but if not Congress, then private subscription should undertake the task, giving Rogers Clark Ballard Thruston the great credit due him.

Another fine contribution of Mr. Thruston to the work of the National Society was the promotion during his second term of the historical tour called "Washington's Journey," which duplicated the route of General Washington from his home at Mt. Vernon to Boston to take command of the Army of the Revolutionary patriots.

This was a picturesque and enthusiastic celebration of the anniversary of the original journey, the participants wearing Colonial uniforms and the old coach and four of General Washington conveying his representative; as many as possible in the cavalcade being descendants of those who accompanied our first President, and the cities where he stayed overnight, turning out crowds of welcome with floral tributes as on the first occasion, the Sons of the American Revolution societies along the route arranging the necessary ceremonies and welcome in each place.

It was a great success, and the Society has a small brochure giving the details and the historical account which is very interesting.

Mr. Thurston also made an exhaustive study of the history of the development of our American Flag. He lectured with slides and authentic copies of the many flags used by the Colonies up to the final original design for our National Flag as officially adopted. His printed brochure on this subject was endorsed and published by the Congress of the United States as the correct history.

1914

Probably the most eligible bachelor of Syracuse, New York, was Newell B. Woodworth who stood for all things civic and patriotic in his community. He took a great interest in the Syracuse Chapter Sons of the American Revolution, became its President, later served on the Board of the Empire State Society, and finally became a leading candidate for President General following Mr. Thruston's regime. He was the leading spirit in arranging for the Congress held at Syracuse in 1914.

At a meeting of the Empire State Society at Rochester, the Rochester Chapter held a delightful reception and dance, and here our bachelor friend, Mr. Woodworth, became very attentive to a charming young lady, and it was evident the attraction was mutual. A few months later invitations to their wedding were received. Mr. Woodworth was extremely handsome and a delightful person in every way with irresistible charm of manner.

At the Syracuse Congress, also, there was authorized the creation of a junior group to be known as the Washington Guard, to be composed of boys aged sixteen to eighteen years who would be eligible to full membership at the proper time. This was a project of the New Jersey Society and fostered under its auspices. It later became somewhat dormant.

This year at Syracuse marked the completion of the Society's first twenty-five years.

What of the Society's accomplishments during these first twenty-five years?

This is best set forth in a report of Dr. A. Howard Clark, who was first Registrar General, and then Secretary-Registrar General and held this office for some fifteen years of these twenty-five. Dr. Clark was one of the most beloved officers of the Society and did much to forward its objects. Quoting in part from the above report made at the 25th Annual Congress held at Syracuse in 1914, it will be seen what remarkable things were undertaken and completed during this first quarter century of existence.

It has erected or led to the erection of hundreds of monuments and tablets to commemorate events and men of the Revolution and to mark the battlefields and other historic sites of the Revolutionary period. It has secured the preservation of some of the most important battlefields and historical buildings of the Revolution as National Memorials.

It has marked the graves of thousands of those who fought for American Independence. It rescued from oblivion the graves of several of the Signers of the Declaration of Independence and has marked them with appropriate memorials. It has saved from destruction and brought to light valuable records of the Revolution and secured the enactment of laws for gathering together in the War and Navy Departments the valuable muster-rolls and pay-rolls of soldiers and sailors in that war.

It has promoted the patriotic education of the youth of our country by awarding hundreds of medals and other prizes for essays on historic topics and for proficiency in historical studies. It has presented busts and portraits of eminent Americans and facsimiles of the Declaration of Independence to hundreds of schools and colleges. It has encouraged and taken part in the celebration of hundreds of patriotic anniversaries.

Flag Day, June 14, was first publicly observed throughout the country upon the recommendation of a member of the Connecticut Society, and Charles Dudley Warner, of Hartford, published an editorial on this subject as far back as 1861. The Society has helped to secure the enactment in most of the States of laws prohibiting the desecration of the Flag.

Under the enthusiastic direction of Colonel Ralph E. Prime of New York, a tremendous and lasting movement was started to prevent the desecration of the Flag, and we now have a general statute, and state laws in nearly every state.

It has assisted in better citizenship by the wide distribution of leaflets to the aliens, and in the larger cities by illustrated lectures on our country given in their own language.

This was one of the most effective activities of the Society and through the splendid leadership of many of our Compatriots these pamphlets were printed in some thirteen languages, and thousands of copies of the Constitution were widely distributed in places most needed.

It has secured the publication of the rolls of more than 40,000 soldiers and sailors of France who participated in the American Revolution. It is securing the indexing of the valuable genealogical and historical data in the papers of 70,000 pensioners of the Revolution for present reference and future publication.

An interesting and prophetic paragraph is interpolated here and quoted from the report of General Thomas M. Anderson, Chairman of the Committee on Education at the time, and this committee was largely concerned with the aliens. General Anderson says: "We think that the people should take care of the Government, and not that the Government should take care of the people. *Whenever Governments take care of the people, the people become slaves of the governments.*" This was written thirty-five years ago! [now 48]

To continue from Mr. Clark's report:

We are justly proud too, of the personnel of our membership, proving as it does that the spirit of true American citizenship is still safeguarded. On our rolls are two Presidents of the United States, three Justices of the Supreme Court of the United States, many Ambassadors to foreign nations, scores of Senators and

Representatives in Congress, Governors of States, Generals of the Army, Admirals in the Navy, men eminent on the legal bench, in literature, in mercantile life, in the pulpit, in medicine, in all honorable professions—some of the wealthiest men in the land and some of the poorest. Neither riches nor poverty bar from membership. All men of good character are eligible, provided they can prove lineal descent from a soldier or sailor or active patriotic participant in the war of the American Revolution

The Journey in 1914 from Philadelphia to Boston, following the route taken by General Washington in 1775 when he went to take command of the Continental Army was a memorable event, and one of the most ambitious undertakings in our history, and was under the leadership of President General R. C. Ballard Thurston. It had great and far-reaching effects not only on the Society itself but upon the places visited along the historic way, and instilled a wave of patriotism over the entire route. The Society published a brochure compiled by Secretary General A. Howard Clark descriptive of this Journey. Thus was our 25th anniversary appropriately celebrated.

That the first twenty-five years of this Society of the Sons of the American Revolution left a lasting impression on this country cannot be denied and those who accomplished its firm establishment did their work unselfishly and with a fine spirit of patriotism. To them and to their memory every tribute should be given in this our Golden Anniversary year. (From "Retrospect—50 years" by Frank Steele.)

1915

The year 1915 found the Congress meeting at Portland, Oregon, where Mr. Woodworth attended with his bride. This was the second Congress which the writer [Steele] was unable to attend, but Oregon shared honors that year with San Francisco, where a short final session was held, and the delegates were given an opportunity to see a bit of the Pacific coast and California's hospitality which proved to be all that had been alleged. It was here that Mr. Woodworth was elected President General, and he proved as efficient and capable as his predecessors; because of his admiration and devotion to his friend, Mr. Thruston, he continued to carry on the good work inaugurated by the former. Among the projects which Mr. Woodworth promoted was the selection of a design and adoption of an Official Grave Marker for marking the graves of Revolutionary patriots for which there had been a great demand.

1916 - 1917

Returning to the East in 1916 for its annual meeting, the Congress was held at Newark, New Jersey, and there Mr. Elmer Wentworth, of Iowa, was elected President General. Mr. Wentworth served two years. This being the period of the first World War, it was deemed wise not to hold a Congress in 1917; therefore, he held over. Mr. Wentworth was a railroad executive and did much traveling in the interests of the Society during his administration, and in spite of world turmoil succeeded in keeping up the Society's good work in all its projects and objectives. He encouraged the formation of local chapters; he had been Iowa State President, and as a Trustee of the National Society and member of the Executive Committee, gave some twenty-two years of service to the Society. During his service as State President he secured passage of a law in Iowa for the State's observance of Constitution Day, September 17th, and later, as President General, encouraged its observance by the National Society.

1918

In 1918 the Congress met in Rochester, New York, and here Colonel Louis Annin Ames was elected. Colonel Ames had devoted himself to the interests of the Society for years, but, except for service on the Executive Committee and as chairman of various national committees, he had not held national office.

Another outstanding and very interesting contribution of Colonel Ames to Sons of the American Revolutuion history was the inauguration, during his term, of a custom by our French Compatriots in Paris, to keep an American Flag flying continually at the grave of the Marquis de Lafayette in Picpus Cemetery, Paris.* This custom was

---

*See article on the French Society of the Sons of the American Revolution in Chapter XI.

cordially adopted by the French Society, and they have continued this practice ever since. Each year, on July 4th, a fresh Flag is placed, with simple ceremony, and the old one from the preceding year removed. Remarkably, we have been told, this grave and its marker have never been disturbed in spite of the two wars which have devastated France! Also, this practice of keeping the American Flag flying over the grave has had the full sanction of French authorities.

An interesting aftermath of this patriotic gesture has been the sending of the old, worn, and very soiled Flag back to our National Headquarters in Washington each year, and these have often been presented to some patriotic organization which accepted the same with appreciation and patriotic sentiment. The latest recipient has been the Lafayette College Library at Easton, Pennsylvania, where the American Friends of Lafayette, of which our Past President General, Messmore Kendall, is the President, maintains an interesting collection of Lafayette Memorabilia.

During Colonel Ames' term, one of the sad events that occurred which brought sorrow to a great majority of the members was the death of Mr. A. Howard Clark, the beloved Secretary General of the Society who had served and assisted in its upbuilding from very early days. His passing was a very great loss to the Society, and his memory was held very dearly in the hearts of all his contemporaries.

One of the great achievements of the Society was its formal recognition of Constitution Day and its observance throughout the country. As is well known, full credit is due the late David L. Pierson, of New Jersey, for first suggesting this be made a *national* observance, although we noted above that the State of Iowa held the first ceremonies under Mr. Elmer Wentworth's regime as State President, and also that the final adoption of this Observance by the National Society, Sons of the American Revolution was during his term as President General. But Mr. Pierson advocated the idea of national observance, and persistently promoted it until it was adopted formally by the National Society. All praise is due him, and his work, therefore, has been publicly acknowledged and was recognized in the New Jersey Legislature by formal Resolution. To the dismay of the S. A. R., and other patriotic societies, a Resolution was passed by Congress in February, 1952, which merged the recogntion of CONSTITUTION DAY *with* I AM AN AMERICAN DAY, and efforts are currently being taken to restore the first name for September 17th. Equally, in sympathy with both observances, the Society is opposed to demoting recognition of Constitution Day to second place in importance to any other observance.

Mr. Pierson began his campaign in 1917, and it took only a short time for the movement to become national in scope. Mr. Pierson died in 1940.

Lest we forget, the Society also takes credit for inauguration and promotion of the observance of Flag Day, June 14th, and more recently the commemoration of Bill of Rights Day, December 15th, and has brought about "I Am An American Day" as a national observance of the coming into full citizenship of both naturalized and our own young Americans.

1919

The Congress of 1919 met at Detroit and here the new President General elected was Mr. Chancellor L. Jenks, of Chicago. Mr. Jenks, an attorney of fine reputation but with leisure for travel, concentrated his efforts in visiting many State Societies and chapters by the then somewhat unusual method of driving by automobile from place to place. Mrs. Jenks accompanied him and the personal contacts made in this way were a healthy and promising thing for the organization and helped promote growth in membership and the formation of new chapters, and brought about a much greater cooperation of effort.

1920

Going further east again in 1920 the Congress met at Hartford where, after quite a lively election contest, Mr. J. Harry Preston, of Baltimore, was elected. Mr. Preston was the former Mayor of Baltimore, a highly regarded citizen of that city, a lawyer, and man of fine presence and genial personality. He was several times a member of the Maryland Legislature and was Speaker of the House of Delegates in 1894. He served for two years as President of the Maryland Society, Sons of the American Revolution. He was Baltimore's Mayor when the 100th Anniversary of the Star Spangled Banner Celebration was held in that city.

1921

In 1921 the Congress was again entertained in Buffalo, and here they elected the Honorable Wallace McCamant, of Portland, Oregon, as President General. It will be recalled that he was the man who brought about the election of a President of the United States, incidentally, also a Compatriot of our National Society, n a m e l y, Calvin Coolidge.

While the story is quite well known, it bears repeating. At the National Republican Convention which nominated Warren G. Harding (also a Compatriot) for President of the United States, the political leaders had practically decided on the nomination of Senator Lenroot, of Wisconsin, for Vice President, but this selection was not acceptable to the delegates from the Wset Coast, of which Judge McCamant was a prominent leader, and, impulsively, without waiting to go to the platform, Judge McCamant jumped on a chair from his place on the floor, and in a ringing voice—he was a very fine orator—secured recognition, and in a three-minute speech of great eloquence, concluded with, "I nominate Calvin Coolidge, of Massachusetts, for Vice President, a great American!"

This was not long after Coolidge had made himself famous throughout the country by quelling the Boston Policemen's strike, declaring that no official body had the right to strike against the Government, State or National. Thus, Mr. McCamant's ringing statement caught the great crowd at the Convention, and Compatriot Calvin Coolidge was nominated as Vice President of the United States, almost unanimously, and we all know what happened later.

Judge McCamant had interested himself greatly in the matter of school textbooks, and prior to his election as President General, had conducted an exhaustive search and published a severe criticism of subversive books being used as history textbooks, and especially of a very popular history of the United States by David Z. Muzzey. His brochure on this subject was responsible for extensive revision of this particular book, and for its ban in many schools. He was for several years Chairman of the Society's Committee for the survey of school texts. Mr. McCamant gave liberally of his talents and ability in the interests of the Society, made many trips East to attend Executive Committee meetings and later Congresses, visited many State Societies and chapters, and left a lasting impression for constructive work.

Unquestionably, Judge McCamant's fight on subversive history textbooks was a great stimulus to the Society's committees on Patriotic Education and Americanism, and both these committees took on new life and vigor under his example and guidance. Mr. Harry F. Brewer, of the New Jersey Society, was very active in this work and gave practical constructive service, conducting classes in citizenship and personally contacting our foreign born.

It was during Judge McCamant's term, as directed by the Buffalo Congress of 1921, that the publication of the Society's Year Book, which had been issued from the beginning, was discontinued, and the *Bulletin*, which originated in 1906, was expanded to become the official organ of the Sons of the American Revolution, going to every member, and to contain all the official information formerly included in the Year Book, and also the news of activities and doings of both the National and State Societies. Proceedings of the annual Congresses, and of the meetings of the Executive Committee were to be reported, suitably condensed, for the information of the local groups and of the individual members. As the Year Book had had a limited printing, and went only to officers of the National and State Societies, the quarterly was now to contain all important information and announcements, and go to every Compatriot. This change was very acceptable to everyone, and what eventually became our present Sons of the American Revolution Magazine was issued, under successive titles, as the *Quarterly Bulletin*, *The Minute Man*, and finally as the *Sons of the American Revolution Magazine* of today.

It was also at this Buffalo Congress that the writer [Steele] was elected to serve as Secretary General of the Society which office he held continuously until May, 1950.

The death of Mr. A. Howard Clark had made it necessary to select a successor. Mr. William S. Parks served a year, and for two years Mr. Philip Larner, of Washington, D. C., served (1919 and 1920). The new Secretary General succeeded in 1921 and was designated to edit the revised quarterly *Magazine* as part of his official duty.

From this time on until the change of editorship in 1949, the *Magazine* was conducted under the conditions imposed when the Year Book was discontinued, with all formal action of the authoritative directives recorded, and all other information published; whenever space and budget permitted, historical articles and addresses were published, but increasing printing costs and shortages in the treasury made it more and more difficult to include any but the most necessary activities as the years followed.

1922

The Congress of 1922 was held in Springfield, Massachusetts, and the President General elected there was Major Washington Irving Lincoln Adams, of New Jersey. Major Adams was an imposing personality, handsome, and courtly and genial in manner. He traveled extensively during his term and did much to build the society numerically. He presided the following year at Nashville, Tennessee, for which meeting a special train trip was arranged to accommodate the majority of delegates, with special cars starting from Washington and meeting members from other points from the West and North. Nashville was the point farthest South at which the Congress had, up to then, convened, and there was much of interest here, such as the famous Heritage, home of Andrew Jackson, Vanderbilt University, etc., not to mention the traditional Southern hospitality which was most apparent.

1923

This Congress of 1923 elected the Honorable Arthur Preston Sumner, of Providence, Rhode Island, to lead the Society through the year, and in 1924 the organization was royally entertained at beautiful Salt Lake City, Utah.

1924

For this Utah Congress, too, special cars and arrangements were provided to take delegates from the East, all who could do so meeting at Chicago for this exciting and momentous trip. Following the sessions of the Congress, a special excursion was arranged from Salt Lake City through Yellowstone Park which was conducted under the personal guidance of Compatriot Daniel Spencer, an official of the Union Pacific Railroad. It was a wonderful experience, full of scenic and historic interest, and a number of members availed themselves of the opportunity of extending their Western trip by continuing on to California and journeying up and down the California and Northwestern coasts and returning East either via the Southern or the Canadian route.

Before making the National Park excursion, delegates were given an opportunity of visiting one of the important copper mines and, also a gay excursion and picnic luncheon at Great Salt Lake itself, including a swim! This was sponsored by the local organization of the Daughters of the Revolution, and was a most delightful experience.

President General Sumner had accepted the office reluctantly, and found it quite a tax on his time and energies, as he had arduous duties on the Supreme Court of Rhode Island which provided some handicap and prevented his undertaking any extensive traveling and visiting, although his administrative work was effective and his term prosperous.

The Salt Lake Congress elected Marvin Harrison Lewis, of Kentucky.

The National Society, by now, like most growing and expanding organizations, had become more or less imbued with a measure of politics, and some leaders in the Society had influenced the election to some extent. This fact was resented by some who felt that a free choice of officers was difficult, and many sections desiring recognition, overlooked. Mr. Lewis succeeded in breaking up this habit. There were other fine and able men in many State Societies whom their colleagues wished to see in the office of President General which was growing in prestige and importance.

From now on, the candidates for President General were usually quite independent of any special clique or small group.

Mr. Lewis was successful, too, in insisting on the active functioning of the several standing and special committees appointed to conduct the work of the Society. Heretofore, these had been more or less honorary, but President General Lewis insisted on the chairmen actually directing and supervising each committee's work and called for frequent reports which appeared in the *Magazine*, and the new life thus instilled has not abated to this day. Needless to say, the work of the Society became much more effective and expanded its patriotic influence.

1925

In 1925, and upon the invitation of the Massachusetts Society, the Congress met at the lovely ocean resort of Swampscott in the delightful New Ocean House. It was just prior to the seasonal opening of the hotel for summer patronage, and it was thrown open to the exclusive use of our Congress which gave a most delightful character to the sessions uninterrupted by other guests.

At this meeting the so-called "upstate" delegates from the New York-Empire State Society, and comprising the compatriots from the central and western chapters of New York, had insisted on presenting their candidate for President General, in opposition to the "New Yorkers" proper— another instance of the independence action referred to above. This candidate was Judge Harvey Foote Remington, of Rochester, former Chapter and State President, a gentleman of great legal ability and very high principles, religiously inclined and well known throughout the State. Judge Remington was the first President General from an Eastern State to make an extensive trip across the country to the West Coast, and this he did very soon after his election, going to Washington State and combining his contacts with the Sons of the American Revolution groups with his attendance at a meeting of the National Baptist organization of which he was a prominent and devoted member.

Another notable trip was carried out in Judge Remington's administration, a journey undertaken by some twenty or more members of the National Executive Committee and other National officers. This started from Washington in October with a special Pullman furnished through the kind offices of Compatriot Frederick Millspaugh, an officer of the Pullman Company, President of the Tennessee Society, and later President General. The first stop was at Fredericksburg, Virginia, where the company was received and entertained at Kenmore, the home of General Washington's sister, Betty Lewis, thence to Richmond for a meeting with Virginia Compatriots; next to Chattanooga and Lookout Mountain, and then Nashville. From there to Louisville, thence to St. Louis where a meeting of the Executive Committee was held, and returning via Chicago, Indianapolis, and back to Washington. In every place the group was royally entertained by local compatriots of chapter or State, and not only was this journey very fruitful by way of personal contacts and good feelings engendered by this evidence of interest in the local problems and situations, but by the fostering of intimacy among the members of the group itself and the knowledge and information acquired was invaluable.

1926

Following the Congress at Swampscott, Philadelphia was chosen as the next meeting place in 1926 because of the 150th celebration of the Signing of the Declaration of Independence. A memorable session was held in Independence Hall, making the gathering a thrill to remember.

A very lively contest for the office of President General took place here, and resulted in the election of Mr. Wilbert H. Barrett, of Adrian, Michigan, a very outstanding businessman of the finest type and ability.

During Mr. Barrett's administration he came to Buffalo, home city of the writer, and spent several days with the Secretary General in working on a revision of the Sons of the American Revolution Constitution and By-Laws which had been authorized by the Congress at Philadelphia. The old Constitution had become more or less outmoded and did not now fulfill the needs of the ever-growing Society. The proposed revision was adopted at the next Congress, and there were compartively few changes until very recently.

The outstanding accomplishment of Mr. Barrett's administration was the revival of two State societies, namely,

North Carolina and West Virginia, both of which were very nearly defunct. Mr. Barrett visited both States several times and secured able assistants in promoting new interest in each and succeeded in placing both in a firm footing so they are now among our most active and progressive State Societies.

Through his wide business experience, Mr. Barrett was successful in improving some of the routine business processes of the National Society which made errors in records of payment and orders almost fool-proof, and helped greatly to eliminate confusion.

1927

In 1927 the Congress met in Richmond, Virginia, and here the election resulted in the choice of Mr. Ernest E. Rogers, of New London, Connecticut. Mr. Rogers had taken much interest in the Society for several years and was very active in Sons of the American Revolution work in his home State. He was later Lieutenant Governor of Connecticut. His name carried much prestige, and his business ability was unquestioned.

This 1927 Congress and the year following were indeed memorable, for its was in Richmond in 1927 that the Society voted to purchase the former National Headquarters at 1227 Sixteenth Street, Northwest, Washington, D. C. For some years the idea of a National Headquarters had been proposed, and a committee had been appointed to explore the possibilities. Ocassionally a piece of property had been offered, but until now none had met with consideration. Now, however, the agent staged a successful campaign to sell his proposition, showing photographs of the house and floor plans with a more or less attractive price, and at a most surprising session, the resolution for purchase of this property went through unanimously! The proposal included fine furnishings and was altogether an attractive one.

The establishment of our National Headquarters radically changed many matters in the Society. In the first place it made the establishment of a central office for the business of the Society imperative, and under Mr. Rogers' very able direction this was immediately brought about, the first move being to bring the office of the Secretary General to Washington. The Registrar General's office was already located in the Capital City, and the Treasurer General's office in Baltimore, conveniently near. The writer, as Secretary General, was invited to visit Mr. Rogers' home in New London to discuss the possibility of his removing to Washington. This invitation was accepted, and after a very frank and satisfactory discussion, the Secretary General and Mrs. Steele moved to Washington October 1st, 1927, remaining at the Headquarters as Executive Officer and Custodian of Property until retirement in 1950.

In the meantime, the task of raising the purchase price of the building and its contents—$145,000—became the major problem of Mr. Rogers and his "cabinet," for, amazing as it may seem, the Society really had no funds for this, only a meager "Permanent Fund" which it was not feasible to disturb. A campaign was planned, but before this could get under way, it was necessary to raise at least $25,000 to secure the deed. Through the loyalty of five Compatriots this was accomplished by their personal loans, and in August, 1927, the papers were signed and the property transferred to the National Society, Sons of the American Revolution.

Next, the campaign to raise the full amount was organized, and again through the generosity of many Compatriots, and especially through the personal efforts of Mr. Rogers and his immediate successor, Mr. Ganson Depew, Colonel Ames and others, a great deal was accomplished. Mr. Rogers appointed Mr. Henry F. Baker, of Maryland, later President General, as Chairman of the fund-raising committee, and he was very successful in bringing in surprisingly substantial subscriptions, although the full amount of $300,000, which was the goal, was never quite achieved. However, the purchase price was covered, but the Endowment Fund had to be deferred. The accumulation of these funds ran over a period of several years, but the centralization of our administrative functions was a great forward step and resulted in immediate growth and activity. The District of Columbia Society, one of the most active groups in the organization, took up office space in the building, making an annual contribution for the privilege.

Another very worthwhile result of this establishment was the ever-increasing friendly contacts with the National Society, Daughters of the American Revolution, thus made possible. Access to their fine genealogical library and the many other courtesies exchanged, made a very helpful contribution to our progress.

During his term, Mr. Rogers also made a trip to the Pacific Coast, and on his visits and contacts with Sons of the American Revolution groups en route, he preferred to meet our members around the conference table to discuss local problems rather than formal entertainment. He was very successful in securing cooperation and providing stimulus and impetus to our growth and activity.

1928

In 1928 the Congress met in Washington, giving Compatriots the opportunity of seeing the new National Headquarters and visualizing their investment. Here Mr. Ganson Depew, then President of the Empire State Society, was elected, and he contributed largely of his time and business ability, and very generously of his own financial resources to carry on the work so successfully inaugurated by Mr. Rogers.

The rise of Ganson Depew to the Presidency was the result of a definite interest in the Society which began in a sort of family tradition. His uncle, the Honorable Chauncey M. Depew, was one of the Charter Members of the Society, and he had become the President of the Empire State Society and fascinated all by his wonderful oratory. Ganson in his early manhood, took an interest in the Buffalo Chapter in his home city, then succeeded to service on the State Society Board, and then to the Presidency of the Empire State Society, so his nomination to the National Executive Committee, and then to be President General, was a natural evolution. He was very genial and much beloved. He was still serving on the Executive Committee at the time of his death in 1934.

Mr. Depew also did considerable traveling and concentrated especially on visiting the Southern States and particularly North Carolina where he toured with the Secretary General and others, visiting several chapters and soliciting funds for the building. He presided in 1929 at Springfield, Illinois, where the home and traditions of Lincoln were brought close to the delegates and contributed much to the interest of the meeting. Here a day was spent at Salem, Illinois, the scene of Lincoln's early manhood. A visit to the grave of Ann Rutledge, said to be his early love, was not forgotten. The Congress at this meeting continued to secure additional subscriptions to the building fund.

1929

The election of Mr. Howard Rowley, of California, at Springfield brought the desired representation for our far western compatriots and an excellent business administration to the Society. Mr. Rowley was an enthusiastic and hard working officer and gave practical and worthwhile devotion to the interests of the Society. He, too, represented the element determined to prevent concentrated control by certain sections and personalities. His heart and soul centered in the Sons of the American Revolution, and no more loyal and patriotic Compatriot ever worked for its upbuilding.

Mr. Rowley made the expensive and tiresome trip to and from California and Washington for the several meetings of the Executive Committee and other occasions during his term, and was insistent on members of the Committee giving more time on these occasions. He endeavored to secure more advertising for the Magazine, being a practical publisher of an important trade journal, and it was during his term that it became necessary to change the name of the Magazine from *The Minute Man* because of copyright restrictions, and from then on it became the *Sons of the American Revolution Magazine.*

Mr. Rowley presided in 1930 at Asbury Park where the Congress was held on invitation of the New Jersey Society which promoted an interesting, historical tour around New Jersey battlefields of the American Revolution, including a meeting held in the historic halls of Princeton University.

1930

At Asbury Park the delegates elected a most beloved Compatriot as President General in the person of the late Josiah A. Van Orsdel, Judge of the District of Columbia Court of Appeals, though a Westerner by birth. Judge Van Orsdel was a commanding figure, a charming personality, a most profound jurist and orator. His addresses and opinions were of the very highest and finest. He chose for a slogan, "Burn the Mortgage," and set this goal for his objective. Much was accomplished in reducing the Society's debt, and a year or two later, the fine judicial mind of Judge Van Orsdel was to save the Society from near disaster through his counsels. His arduous duties on the bench made his year quite a burden to him, but he devoted much time and attention to the Society, nevertheless, and was always available for meetings and constructive addresses whenever he was able to spare the time.

1931

There had recently been coming to our Congresses for a few years past a very delightful gentleman from New England who had shown great interest in the Society and had been a generous contributor to the funds for the Headqquarters Building. This was Mr. Benjamin Newhall Johnson, of Boston and Lynn, Massachusetts, a very distinguished attorney of his State who headed one of the most important and outstanding law firms of Boston. At Charlotte, North Carolina, where Justice Van Orsdel had presided in 1931, Mr. Johnson was elected President General to carry on through the important historical anniversary year of the Sesquicentennial of Yorktown and the close of the Revolutionary War.

The Charlotte meeting was memorable in many ways, chiefly for the wonderful trip to Kings Mountain where a delightful out-door picnic meeting was held on its summit sponsored by the North Carolina Compatriots, and impressive ceremonies commemorating this vital episode in our history took place. The Secretary General was honored with an invitation to make one of the addresses. Other visits of interest here were to some of the large textile mills with which this section abounds.

Mr. Johnson, a former President of the Massachusetts Society, had recently retired from his law practice and was in a position to devote much time to the interests of the Society, and this he did with deep interest in all its phases and especially the Headquarters building itself which he loved and was eager to see cleared of indebtedness. He not only gave very liberally to this purpose himself, but through his influence secured some very generous contributions.

As plans began to be formulated for a suitable celebration of the Yorktown Sesquicentennial in 1931, in the Fall of his administration, he plunged into these with great enthusiasm, the culmination of which was the wonderful trip to Yorktown made available to Compatriots on a privately chartered ship, the cost of which Mr. Johnson underwrote personally. The individual accommodations for our Compatriots were fully subscribed to cover this expense, and some 300 members were able to take this in and will never forget that delightful and historical occasion of the celebration of our great Revolutionary War victory over the forces of General Lord Cornwallis. Mr. Johnson also saw that the Society was appropriately represented in the historical commemorations of the Sesqui by having a Gateway into the battlegrounds erected as a Sons of American Revolution contribution, and booths and headquarters provided where the Society's literature could be displayed and questions answered. Many prospective members registered who later joined the Society, as well as visiting Compatriots.

This whole affair was one of the most outstanding contributions ever made by our Society and would not have been possible except for Mr. Johnson—his generosity and enthusiasm. He underwrote all the expenses of these projects, so eager was he to have the Society properly represented.

Tragedy, however, fell a few months later, for Mr. Johnson had developed a serious heart condition, and in our great February anniversary week, after a too strenuous Western trip, he succumbed and was buried February 22nd, 1932. His loss seemed irreparable, and those most closely associated with him were not only deeply grieved but almost inconsolable. Without any doubt, had he lived to complete his term, it was almost certain he would have seen that the Society was entirely relieved of its indebtedness. A feeling of modesty had prevented his making this possible while in office, but his intentions were well known.

Mr. Johnson also took a great interest in the *Magazine* and supervised a change in its format and general appearance, all of which made it much more attractive and prevailed until very recently.

Due to Mr. Johnson's death it was necessary to provide for someone to carry on his duties, and upon vote of the Executive Committee, Judge Josiah Van Orsdel was requested to resume his former duties and carry on for the short interval before the next election, to which he consented, and presided over the next Congress held in Washington in 1932.

1932

At Washington Frederick W. Millspaugh, of Nashville, Tennessee, was elected, and he had the hard job of trying to keep the Society on an even financial keel, as this was the period of great financial depression and reverses throughout the country. Our Society suffered, too, and was the victim of a substantial loss of working funds in one of the bank closings where funds were deposited. Mr. Millspaugh was indefatigable in his efforts and was as efficient as it was possible for anyone to be. He had the advantage of transportation benefits as an executive of the Pullman Company, and he was thus able to make his personal contacts with our Society groups helpful both to himself and the Society.

However, by the time the next Congress convened at Cincinnati in 1933, the financial situation in the Society was such that drastic cuts in salaries and running expenses were made. A Ways and Means Committee was named with Judge Van Orsdel as chairman, together with other past presidents general and legal-minded compatriots. Their recommendations were accepted which comprised a plan of retrenchment which, it was felt, would keep the Society within its means and which were cheerfully acquiesced in by all concerned. Here the writer

[Steele] was requested not only to accept a salary cut but to take over the duties of the Registrar General without compensation, thus saving the salary of one officer. It had even been suggested that our lovely Headquarters might have to be disposed of, but fortunately this did not become necessary.

From this time the writer, [Steele] carried both the title and the duties of the Registrar General in addition to those of the Secretary General.

1933-1934

The Cincinnati Congress elected Mr. Arthur M. McCrillis, of Providence, Rhode Island, who proved to be the right man in the right place for this period of rigid economy. Mr. McCrillis was experienced in real estate matters and other business and financial affairs, and his abilities and careful supervision of all expenditures were the means of bringing the Society through without a deficit, though with a very tiny margin. His administration carried over two years, for he was reelected at Baltimore in 1934, and during this time he made a journey to the Pacific Coast where he made friends with Western Compatriots to the advantage of all, and also went to Europe and contacted our French Compatriots and cemented the interest of these fine members in the patriotic work of the Society.

Also, during Mr. McCrillis' administration it became necessary to refinance the Society's indebtedness, and this was accomplished under his very able management and knowledge of finances, to the great advantage of the Society, and enabled the still existing financial burden to be wholly liquidated in a comparatively short time. To do this it was necessary to call a special meeting or interim Congress and Trustees' meeting, to obtain the needed authority to establish a system of Certificates of Indebtedness which were sold to the members and which covered the remaining debt and were paid off to the purchasers at regular intervals. This was a very practical and successful plan. The special Congress was held at National Headquarters, Washington, D. C., on December 8th, 1934, with excellent representation.

It was also during Mr. McCrillis' term that the greatest boon for the Society took place, namely, the exemption of our Headquarters property from taxation. This had been the great goal from the time the property was acquired, and it had taken many years, from 1927 to 1934, to get this legislation passed by Congress. Each succeeding President General had done all in his personal power to try to get the Bill through, and much shoe leather had been worn down by the Secretary General and other Compatriots in patrolling the halls of Congress in the effort. Several times the Bill had come close to being passed, but had been "buried," or adjournment had come before it could come to the floor, and joy was unbounded when it finally came about. Great credit is due to the late Senator Royal S. Copeland, of New York, an honored Compatriot of the Society, whose personal interest and skill finally secured the recommendation of the committee in charge for its passage in the Senate.

It was at the Baltimore Congress of 1934 that action was taken to have our membership applications bound. This was a task long neglected which should have been undertaken from the first. It was essential for the physical preservation of our lineage records, as well as for more convenient handling. Along with this the task of correcting the master card index of the Society was undertaken which slowed down the binding process to an extent. The existing card file was in deplorable shape, and it seemed that the two tasks should be combined. The whole task was arduous but has progressed gradually, if slowly, with 200 applications included in each volume. This work was undertaken by Mrs. Steele, and in June, 1950, one hundred and sixty-seven volumes were completed, comprising 33,399 applications.

Now, even though it has been decided to have the records microfilmed, the binding was continued.

1935

In 1935 the Congress met again at Louisville where old acquaintances were renewed and especially with our beloved Past President General, Mr. Thruston. The first session was held on famous "Derby Day," but, inasmuch as the skies elected to empty themselves with a drenching all-day downpour, no one was tempted to play hooky, and the serious business of the Society was given strict attention. Here our good and beloved Compatriot, Henry F. Baker, of Baltimore, was elected. He, it will be recalled, had served as Chairman of the first fund-raising committee for Headquarters, and his devotion and interest in the Society had continuued unabated. Mr. Baker was, without doubt, one of our most deeply beloved of all our presiding officers—a gentle, charming gentleman of wide business experience and accomplishments. He was "Constitution-minded" and adopted for his patriotic slogan, "Make the Society Constitution Minded," and he bent all his energies to this end, accomplishing much in bringing the State Societies and Chapters to organize their potentials of influence and leadership to make the observance of Constitution Day outstanding in their several communities and of State-wide and national importance. Publicity campaigns were promoted in almost every locality, and splendid results were obtained and prevail today. Mr. and Mrs. Baker spent considerable time at the Headquarters during his service, and they made an important trip through our Southern States, meeting and counseling with the local groups in efforts to build the Society in these weaker organizations, all to the great benefit of the Society as a whole.

Mr. Baker presided at the "down East" Congress held in Portland, Maine, in 1936, the first time it had ever met so far East. This was an enjoyable gathering with many places of historical interest to attract the delegates such as Longfellow's home, the House of the Seven Gables, etc. A trip to the State Capital, Augusta, was a feature of the entertainment provided.

1936-1939

At Portland, the Honorable Messmore Kendall of New York, was elected and served for four consecutive years, having been re-elected at Buffalo in 1937, at Dallas in 1938, and at New London, 1939, the first in many years to serve over such a long period.

All of these meetings were memorable. At Buffalo the Congress was taken to historic Old Fort Niagara, at the confluence of the beautiful Niagara River with Lake Ontario, one of the country's most sacred shrines, now restored through combined efforts of the citizens of the Niagara Frontier and the Government. Here, Mr. Kendall dedicated one of the rooms in the old "Castle," for which he had financed the restoration. This old "Castle" was the original building erected by the French during their occupancy, later it was held by the English and then by the Americans since the War of 1812—truly one of the most historic spots in America—the only fort where the three flags of France, England, and the United States are flown continuously side by side.

A notable group of nationally prominent Compatriots served on Mr. Kendall's Executive Committee. They included, beside Colonel Louis Annin Ames, Past President General, his life-long friend; Past President General Henry F. Baker, his immediate predecessor; United States Senator Tom T. Connally, of Texas; Honorable Wilbur L. Cross, then Governor of Connecticut; former Governor of Pennsylvania and President of the Sons of the American Revolution of that State, John S. Fisher; Honorable Herbert Hoover, former United States President, and United States Senator Honorable Arthur H. Vandenberg, of Michigan.

Early in his administration Mr. Kendall interested himself actively in the nation-wide campaign to defeat the so-called "Court Packing Bill" which was so gloriously "snowed under" through the efforts of right thinking Americans. Through his initiative every State Society and Chapter of the Society waged a definitely effective campaign in protest of this legislation, and many other groups and organizations as well.

At Dallas in 1938 the re-election of Mr. Kendall was desired because of the forthcoming World's Fair in New York in which he took a prominent interest and was Chairman of Patriotic Activities. In this capacity he planned and financed the erection of a building as a center for the patriotic ceremonies and observances to be held throughout the summer. This was the Sons of the American Revolution Building, christened "Washington Hall." Members of the Society attended to the daily raising and lowering of the Sons of the American Revolution Flag, and two Past Presidents General of the Daughters of the American Revolution served regularly as hostesses—Mrs. Becker and Mrs. Pouch—and here every patriotic Society held special programs during the Summer, arranged for by Mr. Kendall who also planned their participation in the main Fair programs at the Peace Court as the "special day" contribution to the patriotic events.

As Chairman of Patriotic Activities for the Fair, Mr. Kendall arranged a remarkable opening ceremony which publicized both the Fair and the Sons of the American Revolution. This was another Journey of Washington from Mount Vernon to New York for his Inauguration as our first President, enacted with as much historical correctness as possible, from the leave-taking of Martha and George at Mount Vernon, stopping at the several cities en route, and boarding a barge at Elizabeth, New Jersey, for the grand entry into New York. The whole cavalcade consumed eight days. As far as available, descendants of the principals portrayed the characters enacting the scenes. Mr. Kendall himself was General Knox, and the author portrayed the Count de Moustier, the French Ambassador to America of the time. The inaugural ceremonies were staged before a reproduction of Federal Hall and were authentically reproduced.

The Sons of the American Revolution Building, Washington Hall, housed a Museum collection of Washingtoniana belonging to Mr. Kendall and loaned for the period of the Fair, with other exhibits. The house was situated on the shore of the little lake skirting the Fair grounds, which made a lovely setting for many of the evening displays of fireworks, and became a favored resting place for our members and their friends. The opportunity to register the names of visitors and providing literature about the Society for eligibles was not neglected.

A very progressive project which developed during Mr. Kendall's administration, was the observance of "Young Citizens' Day," now known as "I Am An American Day." Originated in California by Compatriot A. Watson Brown, it was immediately advocated by our chapters throughout the Society—at first intended to bring new American voters to a realization of their privileges and responsibilities, it later came to include our newly naturalized citizens of foreign birth, and is now a recognized national patriotic observance. The development of this important annual event was greatly furthered by one of the outstanding days at the New York Fair at which Mr. Kendall was Master of Ceremonies and addressed one of the largest crowds of the season, honoring all new voters proud to acknowledge themselves as "I Am An American!"

As the New York Fair continued through a second Summer, Mr. Kendall's re-election at New London was of practical advantage to the Society in every way because of his personal prestige and his generous contribution to the Fair and to the credit of the Sons of the American Revolution, and ceremonies conducted at Washington Hall had brought the name and objectives of the Society into favorable prominence. His own collection of Washington relics and others which were exhibited made it of great historic interest, and thousands of visitors were registered. The Hall itself was a partial replica of a section of his own home at Dobbs Ferry, the site of one of the memorable conferences between Washington and Rochambeau in planning for the Yorktown campaign. A large tablet on the high walls surrounding Mr. Kendall's home tells the story of this famous meeting.

To revert to the Dallas meeting (1938) this was the excuse for a most interesting adventure immediately following the Congress. This was a trip into Mexico arranged especially for those who wished to go, and in a special car a party of about thirty or more left Dallas for San Antonio, where a day of sight seeing was spent, visiting an old Spanish Mission, the great army base of Fort Sam Houston, and other interesting points. Then aboard the Mexican Central Railway for Mexico City. Only a five-day trip but full of delightful experiences and surprises. This is not the place for detailed description of the crowded events of this most interesting adventure. The climax occurred on the return when our train was derailed by the revolutionists then carrying on one of their periodic upheavals so prevalent in Latin America. No harm was done to crew or passengers, only a half-day's delay, but excitement was rife and furnished a wonderful conversation topic for weeks!

Mr. Kendall continued to be a dominant figure in the councils of our Society, serving for several consecutive years on the Executive Committee, and ever ready with wise counsel and assistance on important matters. His provision for one of the interesting annual awards for service to the Society as a Memorial to his beloved mother, Mrs. Florence Kendall, has been of substantial benefit to the Society.

1940

Loren Souers—See next chapter.

1941

Mr. G. Ridgely Sappington, of Baltimore, followed in 1941. He was a leading banker of that city and attorney. Mr. Sappington had had a very hectic experience of legal service and adjustment when the closing of his own bank, along with others, in 1932 gave him a nerve-racking period of many months. He was of much assistance to the Society in its financial affairs during this time, for, as previously mentioned, we suffered from the freezing of our working capital at that time, and his advice and counsel were most helpful.

(Compatriot Sappington was elected President General at the Congress held at Columbus, Ohio, May 21, 1941.—Editor).

1942

Sterling F. Mutz—See next chapter.

1943-1945

In 1943 the Congress met in New York, as did the Daughters of the American Revolution and other groups normally holding their Congresses in Washington, the war conditions making the Capital City impossible, and here Mr. Smith Lewis Multer, of New Jersey, was elected, who served us with great ability and prestige for three years, the meetings being held at Harrisburg, Pennsylvania, in 1944, and at Trenton, New Jersey, in 1946; no meeting was held in 1945 because of war conditions.

The 1943 Congress had been scheduled for a city in up-State New York, either Rochester or Syracuse, but the war conditions made it difficult to carry out plans financially, or with proper personnel, so the Congress was carried to New York City through the generous and constructive offices of Past President General Messmore Kendall, who guaranteed the necessary expense and the cooperation of the Empire State Society Compatriots.

Mr. Multer's great ability as an orator must be mentioned. His addresses were of the greatest value in content and delivery—no flamboyancy—a simple straight-forward discussion, given strictly without notes and impressive with its sound patriotic Americanism. We have had many fine speakers and eloquent orators in our day, but none to exceed in ability Smith L. Multer. His sound judgment and wisdom guided the Society through these hectic war years and kept it not only financially sound, but without loss of membership—in fact with an encouraging *gain!* Mr. Multer was a retired corporation lawyer and had the time to devote to the duties of the President General, and he did this with great loyalty and attention to all phases of the Society's work; he made a number of trips to visit our groups and for addresses, where his sound advice and impressive speeches won him high regard.

This is as good a place as any to state, what probably is known, that not only Mr. Multer, but every one of the distinguished Presidents who preceded him and served so well, conducted all their business with the Society and all travel without remuneration, and all expenses were borne by them personally, so that it can be well understood that whatever honor and prestige accrued to them as individuals was justly due their personal sacrifice and loyalty.

VI

THE RECENT PAST

This chapter is the result of interviews and correspondence with Past Presidents General I have known. Since the beginning of the compilation of the history, Past Presidents General Ben H. Powell and Loren P. Souers have died.

The observations and comments on the activities of these Past Presidents General bring the history right up to the date of publication.—Editor

THE ADMINISTRATION OF LOREN E. SOUERS, 1940-41

At the 51st Congress held in Washington, D. C., on May 20, 21, and 22nd, 1940 at the Wardman Park Hotel, Compatriot Loren Edmunds Souers was elected President General without opposition.

In his inaugural address, Mr. Souers urged that the advice of George Washington be followed; that we think first of the duty of preserving upon this continent the freedom *** established here by our ancestors ***. He emphasized the S.A.R.'s insistence on adequate defense. His sage advice was wasted.

President General Souers also urged that "we need to make more secure our Nation's spiritual defense. We need to stir in the hearts and minds of our people a new realization of the importance of ideals, of character, of a means of moral responsibility, of a recognition of the sovereignty of Almighty God, and of the need we have of His power to help and sustain us in all our affairs."(*)

---

*Instead, we join the United Nations from which Stalin, Alger Hiss and Khrushchev have barred God Almighty. We proceed to build a "Tower of Babel," and we wonder why Castro and Congo came into being. — Editor's Note.

During President General Souers' administration, the W.P.A. located, at Cleveland, Ohio, marked in that vicinity the neglected graves of one-hundred and eight (108) Veterans of the Revolutionary War and also identified many thousand graves of veterans of other Wars.

The President General's message in the October, 1940 issue of the SA.R. Magazine advised that when decisions regarding the Country's defenses are made that all patriots must cooperate in carrying out the determined measures.

However, he warned against the adoption of measures which taken as short cuts to desired results would gravely impair the security of our democratic institutions. He stated that there could be no virtue in any plan for defending America which could itself destroy American constitutional democracy. He further said that a government without constitutional limitations for the protection of the liberties of individuuals would not be worth saving.

President General Souers presided at the Congress in Columbus in May 1941.

THE ADMINISTRATION OF STERLING F. MUTZ,

1942 - 1943

With Pearl Harbor fresh in the minds and hearts of the delegates gathered in Williamsburg, Virginia, in the Spring of 1942, the responsibility of the Sons of the American Resolution loomed large in the plans and thinking of the compatriots who met there to answer the question, "What can we do to aid in the defense of our country in this time of tragedy and uncertainty?" Most were not able to bear the burden of combat, but each could do something to defend this land of ours and contribute to its security and the safety of its people.

At the Williamsburg Congress Sterling F. Mutz was elected President General.

Following the patriotic experience in Wiliamsburg, and before the delegates had returned to their homes, President General Mutz arranged a conference with the F.B.I. in Washington, at which the Society tendered its assistance in combatting the influence of subversive elements, which had filtered into not only the agencies of government, federal, state, and municipal, but were weaving a network of subversion in some of the large corporations, with the design of ultimately overthrowing our government and substituting some form of Communism.

As a result of this conference a plan was evolved and approved by the F.B.I. that the Sons of the American Revolution appoint a corps of "Minute Men" whose loyalty was above question, composed of the President and Secretary of each state society and a select corps of the most loyal and trusted men in each chapter of our Society. Their names were certified to the F.B.I. as persons who could be called upon to supply information from the immediate community as to the loyalty of those being considered for important and sensitive governmental positions.

The officers and members of the S.A.R. responded quickly and enthusiastically to the plan of setting up this "Corps of Minute Men", and at the end of thirty days chapters from more than 33 states had appointed 1100 members of the S.A.R. who were certified to the F.B.I. for this service. And thus began a confidential relationship with the staff of the F.B.I., resulting in eliminating from government and industry, and preventing further infiltration, of many disloyal elements so dangerous at this particular time of our history. Even now, twenty years later, the F.B.I. occasionally calls upon members of the S.A.R. for information as to the loyalty of applicants being considered for appointment to sensitive positions in Government.

No one could foretell whether this plan would work. But it did. One report will suffice to illustrate the help given in one large industrial area. There the president of the local S.A.R. chapter went with the manager of a public utility to the several cities in which the utility operated, and through the help of the members of the S.A.R. discovered and discharged over 100 subversives, some of whom were later discovered in other critical areas of government activity and afterwards dismissed. Our work was so outstanding in this instance that a very complimentary letter from J. Edgar Hoover was addressed to the officers of the National Society of the S.A.R., in which he expressed the need for the reliable men who were selected in this important capacity.

The events of World War II increased the activities of the Society during this period, and the time was ripe to conduct a drive for new members. The establishment of the "Minute Men" had a good effect upon the work of the Membership Committee, and the officers began to search for a man who could head the drive for new members. The unanimous choice was compatriot Wallace Hall of Detroit to act as chairman and conduct the campaign. The outline of a plan for new members was quickly adopted and put in force. The campaign soon began to show results, and produced the largest number of new and reinstated members in a year's time in the history of the Society. (Between 1800 and 1900 added.)

A brief account of how this was done may help future committees. First, Mr. Hall recognized that the reservoir of prospects was in the membership of the Daughters of the American Revolution, whose mothers and sisters could furnish the necessary data for qualification as members. He arranged to exchange advertisements in the official publications of the two Societies, including a coupon that could be clipped and forwarded to the Committee with the names of prospective members. This exchange of advertisements placed in the hands of some 150,000 members of the D.A.R., a potential that far exceeded the one placed in the S.A.R. magazine with only about 15,000 members. This was indeed a profitable deal for the S.A.R. A mail campaign to prospects was conducted. It might be added that every time the Wallace Hall plan has been used later the membership of the S.A.R. has grown. And as a token of appreciation of the members, Compatriot Hall was later elected President General.

Other committees did yeoman duty in their various departments which could be mentioned with proper credit to their personnel, but one particularly, was the Committee on Publicity headed by Compatriot Allen L. Oliver, of Cape Girardeau, Missouri, who later became President General.

The year of S.A.R. activities was brought to a close with the Annual Congress at the Plaza Hotel in the city of New York. On this occasion Senator Robert A. Taft was the principal speaker on a national radio hook-up. His address stimulated the large crowd in attendance to greater activity for the S.A.R. in the years to come.

Smith Lewis Multer, of New York, was elected President General. He was re-elected twice in 1944 and 1945.

(See Chapter VI for Steele's account of his administrations).

THE ADMINISTRATION OF ALLEN L. OLIVER,
1946 - 1947

In 1946 the Congress was held at Trenton, New Jersey. For some years there had been a healthy rivalry between the Empire (New York) and the Pennsylvania State Societies. They were the outstandingly large State Societies at that time. A like rivalry existed between Ohio, West Virginia and Indiana. They were all strong, active, functioning Societies.

As is usual at the annual congress, the election of the president-general was an important issue. Two candidates were put forward—one, Judge Bonniwell from Philadelphia, Pennsylvania, and the other, Allen L. Oliver, a lawyer from a small city in Missouri—Cape Girardeau. Oliver was elected.

President-General Oliver, in accepting the office, said, "It is my hope and wish that we work together as a real team. The potentialities of this patriotic organiaztion are great. We can do things—we should do things worthwhile. I say to you, that in my humble opinion, the time is right in America for such organizations as this, not only to raise its voice but to instill in our respective neighborhoods (that is where public opinion begins) a sense of patriotism which we so badly need today.

"Some of the fundamentals upon which our nation was founded are being daily challenged. Shall we meet that challenge? May we work together. May we push aside bickerings. May we deal in principles and not in personalities. I ask you gentlemen for your help. We will need it. We want it . . . Let's do the best we can. I pledge you that I shall. I ask you to do so, too.

"I wish to make this personal note: The official Missouri flag which was present when I was installed a moment ago was made and designed by my sainted mother.

"The colors will be retired . . . The Congress is adjourned."

Two incidents marked the election. The internationally known bridge-authority, Goren, who did not know Oliver from Adam, flew to Trenton (flying was not commonplace then), registered as a delegate, voted for Oliver, and flew back to New York.

When the result of the election was announced two large state delegations instantly left enmasse before the brief acceptance address and the closing ceremonies. These delegations, however, did not fail to continue to co-operate with the National Society, and their anger was short lived.

When President General Oliver was inaugurated, the movement of troops resulting from World War II was still in progress. Transportation was difficult. After the Congress adjourned, Mr. and Mrs. Oliver packed their suitcases and went to the railroad station to go to Washington. There "was no room at the inn"—literally, no available seat on the long train. So the newly elected and installed president-general and his wife rode in the baggage car as far as Philadelphia. It was an unusual experience, and they thought it was fun. Had there been any tendency toward inflation in the top story as a result of the election, this incident certainly would have provided the necessary deflation. It so happened, however, that both Mr. and Mrs. Oliver knew the president of one of the country's large railroads and knew that he sometimes rode in his private car and sometimes in the baggage car and knew also how very efficient he was.

President-General Oliver spent three days in Washington going into every available detail of the operation of the Society and making a careful inspection of the Society's headquarters.

He thereupon made a full, written report to members of the executive committee and recommended action on matters which he found existing at headquarters and also with reference to personnel. The recommendations were unanimously approved and some unsatisfactory situations clarified.

The president-general in his first official message to the membership wrote:

> I bespeak on the part of each of you a rededication to the fundamental principles upon which our Society was founded. This is your association just as much as it is mine; you have merely laid the mantle upon my shoulders for a brief twelve month period. Will each of you be a partner with me in working together for the good of our National Society?
>
> No one need be told that our country faces problems that are truly serious. The "isms" are at work—they have been insidious—now they are boldly brazen. We are not against change — we must not be against change. But it should be progressive, calmly and sanely determined, unselfishly solved, and clearly based upon and consistent with the principles upon which our country was founded and our constitution evolved.
>
> But there is a world trend; it is not in accord, in many phases, with American principles. America must arise from its lethargy. We must throw off the anemic shackles of complacency.
>
> Those who are striving for, and to a marked degree acquiring, a strangle hold upon American institutions and principles are organized and at work. Why should we sit idly by, content with forms and formals, ritual and show? It is time for constructive action, men! It is time for our membership to assert its leadership in the communities where we live and resurrect the love of country and the flag which is emblematic of the principles of true liberty and freedom.
>
> Agreed, you say! What shall I do? Here are some suggestions:
>
> 1. See to it that patriotic, truly American, honest and capable men are elected to all elective positions of trust in your city, your county, district, state and nation. Do more than just vote for him.
>
> 2. See that your Chapter undertakes some constructive worthwhile patriotic project and be more interested in getting the job done than in who gets the credit for it.
>
> 3. Personally busy yourself in helping increase the membership of our Society not as an end in itself but

as a means to an end, that we may thereby increase our influence in carrying out the objects of our organization.

May we all act happily together this year!

Here are some of the accomplishments of the Oliver administration:

Raised sufficient money to pay off the Society's debts*

Obtained many new members.

Endorsed the construction of "The Cathedral of the Pines" in New Hampshire by Compatriot Douglas Sloane. Each state sent a stone.

Initiated move to have the priceless records at Headquarters microfilmed. (It was later done with the exemplary work of George Albert Smith of Salt Lake City for about ten percent of the Washington, D.C. bids.)

The President-General personally wrote and received approximately 4,000 letters during his stay in office.

Obtained proclamations and held appropriate ceremonies and services throughout the nation on Flag Day, Constitution Day, Bill of Rights Day and on any other patriotic occasions.

Supported the California State Society in its aggressive and successful effort to rid the public schools of that state of the use of textbooks openly critical of America and praising the program of the Soviet Union. The President-General was supplied with and has kept a copy of these textbooks. To the California Society belongs the credit for a courageous and successful stand.

Recommended that the Society approve the establishment of a National Memorial Forest Park by the Federal Government in which there would be a living tree for each individual soldier, sailor, wave, wac that wore the uniform, such tree to be marked with his or her name and serial number, with evergreens for those who died in the service.

---

*The debt was liquidated on July 1, 1947 while A. Herbert Foreman was President-General, but the final funds were accumulated to pay it in President-General Oliver's administration.

The President General and his wife travelled approximately 16,000 miles, at this own expense, visiting many State Societies, installing some new chapters; were everywhere cordially received and royally entertained.

At the banquet at the fifty-seventh Congress held at Huntington, West Virginia, the toastmaster was the Honorable Louis A. Johnson, then Secretary of Defense. After brief remarks by President-General Oliver, Mr. Lee R. Pennington, Inspector for the F.B.I., talked to the delegates. The principal address of the evening was by Compatriot the Hon. Colgate W. Darden, Former Governor of Virginia and at that time President of the University of Virginia, who made an inspiring and thought-provoking address.

A. Herbert Foreman was elected PresidentGeneral May 15, 1947.

THE ADMINISTRATION OF A. HERBERT FOREMAN, 1947-1948

Compatriot A. Herbert Foreman was elected President General at Huntington, West Virginia.

One of the first important accomplishments of President General Foreman's administration was the liquidation of the debt on the building. This was paid in full by July 1st, 1947. Wallace C. Hall was the Chairman of the Debt Liquidation Committee.

In the President General's message in the fall of 1947, he called attention to one weakness in the billing procedure of the various state societies and chapters. He pointed out that many chapters and state societies do not send out their annual bills for membership dues until January or February. This does not leave much time for collection of the dues to be paid to the National Society by the end of March. Failure to notify members or to attempt collections of delinquent dues earlier means that many are dropped for non-payment of dues. Throughout the years this has represented a heavy loss of membership each year.

In 1947 Compatriot Douglass G. High, of Ohio, contributed $250.00 to be given as prizes in a contest among high-school students for the best written and best delivered paper on early American History having to do with the founding of our Nation. The President General appointed Clarence M. Smith Chairman of the Committee on Plans and Awards to handle this competition.

One of the unique events of the year was the first anniversary of the dedication of the Altar of the Nation, Cathedral of the Pines*, sponsored by the six New England Societies on Sunday afternoon, September 7th, 1947. The mirrored lakes, the verdant mountains, the beautiful grove, the attractive altar, the column of uniformed veterans of the second World War, the vested choirs, the flags of the states led by that immortal flag, the Stars and Stripes, and about 4,000 in attendance on that beautiful autumnal afternoon created a scene never to be forgotten. Practically all the national officers were present. The address of the day was made by President General A. Herbert Foreman.

In the President General's message, January 1948, he congratulated the California Society in its fight against the subversive text books in the schools. Compatriot George L. Gary, President of the California Society, led this fight. The State Legislature appropriated $10,000 for investigating the entire educational system, the Board of Education, the method of text book selection and the appointment of teachers in the State of California.

The fight of the California Society against the use of the subversive text books in America, in the public schools of that state, was the outstanding achievement of the year.

Another activity of the Society was the work of the basic documents committee. Fifty chapters and 26 states took part in the presentation of these documents during the week of Washington's birthday.

President General Foreman presided at the 58th Congress held at Minneapolis on May 23-26, 1948, at which Charles Bunn Shaler of Pittsburgh was elected President General.

---

*The Cathedral of the Pines and Altar of the Nation, composed of stones and earth from the several states, contributed by the S.A.R. State Societies, is the Memorial created by Compatriot Douglas Sloane for his son, Sanderson, who made the supreme sacrifice in the late war. It is regularly used for Sunday services and other ceremonies by groups throughout the summer months.

The Administration of Charles Bunn Shaler, 1948 - 1949

Immediately after his election, President General and Mrs. Shaler made a plane trip West and visited many groups at points between his home State and the Pacific Coast. The planned membership increase for the whole Society seemed sure of success. No doubt on this western trip Mr. Shaler picked up the virulent germ which laid him low upon his return, for after several weeks of hospitalization he died on the 2nd day of December, 1948.

His record of accomplishments in the Society is noteworthy. In the Pittsburgh Chapter he was successively Treasurer, Vice-President and President and in the Pennsylvania State Society he was National Trustee, Vice-Presiden and President.

In National affairs he served as Chairman of the Constitution Day Committee in 1946, and was a member of various Committees during 1946-1947.

Compatriot Shaler's ability in recruiting members was almost phenomenal—in one year he added over 500 members in his own State of Pennsylvania.

He was personally responsible for the erection of twelve new chapters in his home state, adding approximately a thousand new names to the roster of the Society. One chapter, the Fort Jackson Chapter of Waynesburg, Pennsylvania, was instituted with the largest charter membership in the entire history of the Society—either State or National—a charter membeership of nearly two-hundred.

In 1940, 1945, and 1946, Compatriot Shaler was the recipient of the Florence Kendall Award for the most valuable service rendered the Society.

The great impetus to the nationwide observance of Constitution Day in 1946 and 1947 was the result of his energetic presentation of the matter to the governors of the various states, from all of whom he received flattering commendations for the result obtained.

Mr. Shaler was a great advocate of the teaching of American History in our schools, as one of the means of fighting communism. He felt that the Sons of the American Revolution should and could have a membership of at least 100,000.

His untimely death robbed the Society of one of its most indefatigable workers and the promise of a great administration.

THE ADMINISTRATION OF BEN H. POWELL, 1948 - 1949

After the death of Mr. Shaler, Compatriot Ben. H. Powell, III, agreed, at great sacrifice to himself to assume the Presidency. At the Trustee's meeting held in Washington, D.C. on December 9, 1948 Judge Powel was elected by an unanimous vote, having been nominated by Past-President General A. Herbert Foreman and the nomination seconded by Col. Louis Annin Ames, Clarence F. Shriner, and Albert C. Brand.

President General Powell devoted his administration to carrying out the program which President General Shaler had set out for his administration. He vigorously supported movements for the increase of membership, for the teaching of Americanism in our schools, for the observance of our Constitution and encouraged the celebration of Constitution Day, Flag Day, Bill of Rights Day and I Am An American Day.

Judge Powell travelled extensively, delivered many addresses and conducted much of his work by letter writing, telegrams and long distance telephone calls. He devoted practically all of his time to the interest of our Society. It is pleasant to relate that he had the cooperation of the entire membership and particularly of the various committees. On one trip he attended the Executive Committee Meeting in Cincinnati on February 18, visited the Massachusetts Society and enjoyed a banquet with them in Boston. On this same trip he visited Compatriots in New York City, Baltimore and Washington, D.C. He was the guest of Honor of the Maryland Society on February 22. On his way home he visited the Jacksonville Chapter in Florida. At various times he visited Illinois, California and other places from the Great Lakes to the Gulf.

Judge Powell presided at the 59th Congress held in Jacksonville, Florida May 15-18, 1949. He felt that he could not consider the election for a full term as President General although many compatriots, who appreciated his work in the interim, wanted him to take the office again.

The 59th Congress was held at the George Washington Hotel in Jacksonville, Florida. The delegates spent one afternoon visiting the Castillo de San Marcos National Monument, and St. Augustine.

At this Congress was held the first historical oration contest originated in Ohio by Compatriot Douglass G. High. In the first contest the winner was Robert Wood, representative of the Ohio Society who won his right to enter by winning over fifteen other contestants of that state.

In a morning session almost reminiscent of an old-fashioned Methodist revival, a large amount of money was subscribed from the Congress floor to cover the expenses of the Americanization Committee of its efforts to have subversive textbooks removed from the public schools in the United States.

There was much enthusiasm for the organization of what was to be known as Patriotic Education, Inc., to provide patriotic materials for use in the schools and elsewhere. Compatriot Clarence Shriner had accepted the executive secretarship of the organization, and many compatriots were interested in its formation and program.

At the 59th Congress held at Jacksonville, Florida, Compatriot John W. Finger was elected President General.

THE ADMINISTRATION OF JOHN W. FINGER, 1949 - 1950

The first act of the Finger administration was to restore the practice of the National Society Trustees setting the policy of the Society, and assuming active supervision of its affairs instead of having the Executive Committee make all decisions which were ratified by the Trustees at the close of the fiscal year.

To obtain greater participation in discussion of our national problems it was decided to hold trustees' meetings in New York and St. Louis and to invite all State and Chapter Presidents as well as the Chairman of our National Committees.

The form of the Magazine was increased in size and reduced in cost by obtaining a favorable printing contract in Baltimore, Md.

The Americanization Committee filed its famous "A Bill of Grievances" to the United States Congress which was supported by the brilliant editorial "The Battle of the Books" by E. F. Tompkins, on June 26, 1949 and republished in newspapers throughout the country; 100,000 reprints were distributed by patriotic societies and civic groups interested in halting subversive textbooks and teaching in the schools.

Also in June, 1949, Compatriot Harry F. Morse organized a great Boy Scout Pilgrimage to Lebanon, Connecticut to permit them to become acquainted with the history of the Revolutionary War that was made in this community.

In September, 1949 a posthumous citation was awarded to our Compatriot David Lawrence Pierson, founder of the movement to celebrate Constitution Day.

Compatriot Col. James Dela Watson of Winder, Georgia, constructed a beautiful Chapter House of granite to be used by the S.A.R., D.A.R. and C.A.R.

The Society sponsored a service on Sept. 4, 1949 at the Cathedral of the Pines in Rindge, New Hampshire, which had been created by Vice-President General Douglas Sloane.

The prescribed form of Chapter Institution Ceremony was published and used for the first time.

The Society participated in the tour of the Freedom Train which carried historical documents and their meaning to the people.

At the New York Meeting of the Board of Trustees the emblems of the past presidents general were presented to five past presidents general and arrangements made for the formal presentation of those unable to attend.

The silver gilt emblem for members was discontinued because it became easily tarnished, and gold filled medal was substituted at the same cost.

The Trustees adopted a preliminary form of membership application to enable a chapter genealogist to help applicants satisfy the requirements of the Society.

A bronze grave marker for members was adopted in the form presented.

A form of Charter for State Societies was adopted and ordered printed at the 1950 Congress.

On Sunday afternoon following the Trustees Meeting 533 guests including representatives of other patriotic societies called at the home of the President General and Mrs. Finger to pay their respects to the officers of the Society.

Past President General Messmore Kendall instituted "Coast to Coast" broadcasts observing Bill of Rights Day which included some remarks of the President General.

On January 7, 1950 the Pennsylvania Society adopted a Resolution alerting the National S.A.R. membership to the inherent dangers of World Government.

Vice President General John W. Giesecke organized an excellent program for the meeting of the Board of Trustees in St. Louis, Mo.

Shortly after the meeting, Compatriot Giesecke brought to the attention of the National Society and the President General the infamous decision of the California Land Case in which it was held that the United Nations Charter, having been adopted as a Treaty, became the supreme law of the Land and superceded local State Laws. This alert gave rise to the campaign for the proposal of the Bricker Amendment which was lost by one vote in the U.S. Senate.

At the National Congress of 1950 held at Atlantic City May 14-17 attention was called to the unsatisfactory state of the National Headquarters Building and funds voted to permit its rehabilitation.

An amendment was adopted in support of the activities and the projects of the Children of the American Revolution.

The program of the 60th Congress included a message from the President of the United States of America, a reception for the Governor of the State of New Jersey and Mrs. Driscoll, who were celebrating their 25th Wedding Anniversary; an address by Senator Joseph R. McCarthy; an Historic Fashion Pageant of "First Ladies"; an address by Compatriot Hale Boggs, of the U.S. House of Representatives Ways and Means Committee; an address by the

Hon. Albert W. Hawkes, U.S. Senator from New Jersey; and an address by the Hon. Herbert R. O'Connor, United States Senator from Maryland. Mr. Gardner Osborn, Vice President General of the National Society and President of the American Coalition of Patriotic Societies presided at the banquet.

The sixtieth Congress held in 1950 at Atlantic City was characterized as the "Diamond Jubilee" Congress. Actually it was not the diamond anniversary of the Society, but if we consider that the the first meeting which eventually led to the organization of the Society took place in October 1875, then 1950 was the 75th anniversary of the Society.

In any event, President-General Finger made the most of the idea and played it up in many ways at the Congress.

One of the well remembered events was the Tea Dance given at the Park Lounge of the Hotel Claridge on Monday afternoon. With Mrs. Edgar Williamson and Mrs. John A. Fritchey, II, as co-chairman, The Historic Pageant of First Ladies was presented. The wives of the prominent compatriots represented the wives of the Presidents of the United States.

>Mrs. A. Herbert Foreman represented Martha Washington
>Mrs. Alonzo Newton Benn represented Abigail Adams
>Mrs. Loren Souers represented Martha Jefferson
>Mrs. John Fritchey, II, represented Dolly Madison
>Mrs. Harold M. Blanchard represented Eliza Monroe
>Mrs. Frank Steele represented Sarah Polk
>Mrs. James D. Watson represented Jane Pierce
>Mrs. Ray O. Edwards represented Mary Todd Lincoln
>Mrs. Douglass High represented Eliza Johnson
>Mrs. Clarence Shriner represented Julia Grant
>Mrs. Wallace Hall represented Lucy Hayes
>Mrs. George Robertson represented Lucretia Garfield
>Mrs. John Whelchel Finger represented Frances Cleveland
>Mrs. Reuben Garland represented Caroline Harrison
>Mrs. Van R. H. Sternberg represented Ida McKinley
>Mrs. W. Guy Tetrick represented Edith Roosevelt
>Mrs. William T. Carpenter represented Helen Taft

Mrs. S. Denmead Kolb represented Edith Wilson
Mrs. Robert McNeill represented Florence Harding
Mrs. Edgar Williamson, Jr., represented Grace Coolidge
The Queen of the Jubilee was Mrs. Arthur A. de la Houssaye.

Dressed in the costumes of the period, the procession formed a striking pageant, considered one of the most attractive ever presented in a National Congress.

Wallace Hall was elected President General at Altantic City May 17, 1950.

THE ADMINISTRATION OF WALLACE HALL, 1950 - 1952

Beginning in May 1950 the Society entered a period of drastic change and reorganization, and to many of the Compatriots many of the changes seemed too sudden but soon they became adjusted and a wholesome and revitalized interest in and appreciation of the potential of the National Society manifested itself in a spurt of activity that was most unusual.

The expressed desire of the Secretary General and Registrar General, Frank B. Steele, that he retire at the end of his term in 1950, after 28 years in those offices, having been presented to and approved by the Board at its meeting in New York in October 1949, and an agreement to provide a monthly retirement pay of $200.00 per month for the balance of his life having been approved, the Executive Committee was authorized to secure the services of the best available and most able Compatriot to act as Executive Secretary, to begin his duties as soon as possible.

Fortunately the Executive Committee* was able to convince Compatriot Harold L. Putnam, Past President of the California Society and one of the leaders in the California

---

*One departure from the customary form of holding meetings of the Executive Committee was the novel one conducted by long distance conference telephone when all of the members of the Committee were connected on the same line for 54 minutes to decide certain urgent matters of business and to arrange for the position of Executive Secretary to be filled by Compatriot Harold Putnam.

Top panel—Life membership presented to Col. William T. Carpenter at the annual meeting of the Alabama Society, Birmingham, March 14th, 1954. *Left to right:* Robert P. Gordon, Pres. Birmingham Chap.; Arthur A. de la Houssaye, President General, National Society; Col. William T. Carpenter, Past President, Alabama Society; Hugh W. Stallworth, Vice President General, National Society; Robert C. Garrison, Past Pres. Alabama Society.

Panel above—Meeting of the Alabama Society, January 29, 1950, Birmingham. *Stanling, left to right*: Leon Rayburn, President, Guntersville Chapter and State Vice Pres.; William Blair Jones, Birmingham Chapter; Col. William T. Carpenter, Secretary-Treasurer-Registrar; and Vice President General; Dr. George J. Davis, Jr., newly elected President; John T. Bradford, Retiring President; Dr. George W. Williamson, Board of Managers; *Sitting*: Stephen S. Wilkinson, Pres., Birmingham Chapter.

Below—Dr. Burt Brown Barker, Vice President General Nat'l. Society presented the Society's "Texas Traveling Banner" to the Alaska Society on July 26, 1956 at Anchorage. Receiving the award is A. Letcher Seamands, Pres. of the Alaska Society.

Below—Anchorage Chapter Alaska-Officers for 1957. (Standing, left to right): Karl O. Rozell, Vice President; Rev. Frank J. Walkup, Chaplain; Lawrence Whitehead, Pub. Chrm.; (Seated): James C. Wardlaw, President.

Pres. Malcolm Bayley presents certificate of life membership to Compatriot the Reverend James Rockwood Jenkins, Arizona State Chaplain—April 18, 1958.

Arkansas Society S.A.R. annual meeting Feb. 22, 1958. John E. Hains (seated left) Pres.; Alexander S. Smith, (standing left) Sec-Treas.; James H. Smith (standing right) Vice President; and V. Pres. Gen., Wm. F. Turrentine.

Arizona Society presents first Gold Good Citizenship Medal of the National Society to Lieut. Bernard J. Dunn, Phoenix Police Department, as Outstanding Police Officer of 1958. *Left to right*: Dr. George Hearn Wood, Sr.; Macolm W. Bayley, Pres. and Randall Barton, Chrm. of Award Com. Below—Meeting of the Arizona Society. *Let to right*: U.S. Senator Barry Goldwater; Governor of Arizona, Paul Fannin; Judge M. T. Phelps, Chief Justice Ariz. State Supreme Court; Dean Weldon P. Shofstall, President Ariz. State Society.

Delegates to the 61st Congress at San Francisco, July, 1951. ... —H. Lewis Mathewson, Pres. of Cal. Society (1950-52), Vice Pres. Gen. Society (1960-62).

At left—Board of Managers of the California Society at a meeting in San Francisco January the 10th, 1955. (Back row, left to right): Vice President Charles A. Mersereau; Genealogist, George O. Bordwell; Past President, Aaron M. Sargent; Secretary, H. Lewis Mathewson; Treasurer, C. E. Payne; Nat'l Vice President General, Chas. D. Y. Ostrom; Chancellor, Emmet B. Hayes and Manager, Ellsworth E. Mitchell. (Seated): Chaplain General, Dr. Francis Shunk Downs; Past President General, Howard C. Rowley; President General Milton C. Lory; Manager, Judge Bradford Bosley and National Trustee, Wheaton H. Brewer.

rado Society members and guests at reception of Pres. Gen. and Mrs. Geo. ox, Jr., Cherry Hills Country Club, Denver—Summer 1957.

rt—Judge George H. Bradfield, former Colorado Supreme Court Justice, rded Good Citizenship Medal, Washington's Birthday Banquet of Colo. So-. Left to right: Col. Frank A. Cleveland, President; Judge Benjamin C. ard, Jr., Federal Bankruptcy Referee, who made the presentation; and e Bradfield. Both Judges are Past Presidents of the Colorado Society.

Upper Left: Six members of one family — the Hillyers of Niantic, Conn.—elected to membership in the Nathan Hale Branch at the November, 1953 meeting. *Left to right, seated*: Lawrence Hillyer, Sr., and Ira A. Hillyer, with their brother Walter L. Hillyer. *Left to right, standing*: Lawrence H. Hillyer, Jr.; Frederick A. Hillyer; Ira B. Hillyer; Walter C. Hillyer and Chapter President Harry F. Morse.

Above: The Nathan Hale Branch, No. 6, of the Connecticut Society makes annual pilgrimage to the grave of Samuel Huntington, Signer of the Declaration of Independence.

Below — Officers of Delaware Society elected at annual meeting April 19th, 1960, University Club, Wilmington. *Left to right*: J. Gifford Weaver, Board of Managers; Clarence W. Taylor, Chancellor; Rev. Henry N. Herndon, Chaplain; B. Frank Collins, Secretary-Treasurer; MacSumner Mullin, President; William P. Rheuby, retiring President; Raymond R. Atkins, 3rd Vice President; Lynn D. Sprankle, 1st Vice President; William T. Mahoney, 2nd Vice President; Ellwood A. Davis, Past President and National Trustee.

Above—Connecticut Society honors the President General at Meriden, October 7th, 1954. *Left to right, seated*: Pres. Gen. A de la Houssaye; State President James R. Case; Mrs. de la Houssaye. *Left to right, standing*: Calvin C. Bolles, Connecticut Trustee; Morelle Cook, President, Capt. John Couch branch; Eugene P. Carver, Massachusetts Trustee; Howard E. Coe, Secretary, Connecticut Soc.; Richard P. South, President of Penn. Society.

At Left — Officers of the Delaware Society elected at annual meeting April 20, 1959, at DuPont Country Club. *Left to right*: Clarence W. Taylor, member of board of managers; Raymond R. Atkins, vice-president; Lynn D. Sprankle, secretary-treasurer; William P. Rheuby, president; Mac Sumner Mullin, vice-president; The Rev. Canon Glen B. Walter, chaplain; William T. Mahoney, vice - president; and Dr. Glenn S. Skinner, member of the board of managers.

July 4, 1953, Memorial Services at Grave of Eldridge Gerry, Signer of the Declaration of Independenc, Congressional Cemetery, Washington, D. C. Dr. Chauncy Carly Day, Chaplain, D.C. Society delivering the prayer. Charles T. Macdonald, V.P., D.C. Soc., at left. S.A.R. Colors and C.A.R. Colors at right.

Right—Luncheon at the Statler-Hilton Hotel, Washington, D. C., February 22, 1959, for the Hon. Karl E. Mundt, who delivered the Washington-Birthday-Celebration address. *Left to right:* Robert S. W. Walker (Now in 1962 Librarian General, National Society); Miss Elizabeth Prince Bennett (Now the immediate Past President, the National Society, C.A.R.); Charles T. Macdonald (Past President, District of Columbia Society, S.A.R.); Th Honorable Karl E. Mundt, U.S. Senator, South Dakota; Mrs. Joseph P. Hall, Sr., State Pres.; D.C. C.A.R., and Gen'l. Chrman. Nat'l. Convention; W. Rodney F. Adams (Now Past President, D.C. Society); Miss Patience Veitch, State President, D.C. Society C.A.R.; Hon. E. Y. Berry, U. S. Congressman from S.D.; Col. Thurston H. Baxter, Ret., Past President D. C. Society, and presently Vice-President General—Mid Atlantic District for the S.A.R.; Hon. Wint Smith, U. S. Congressman from Kansas.

Below—Meeting of D.C. Society on April 19, 1962, at Ft. McNair, Officers' Club Dining Room. *Left to right, standing, (rear row):* Robert H. Gravatte, Jr.;Glenn Mayfield Goodman; Grahame T. Smallwood, Jr.; William H. Dumont; Lt. Col. Lee J. Best (part of face showing); Col. Samuel Pierce, Jr., (part of face showing); Simon C. Skells; Louis B. Mainey, Assistant Registrar; Willis Bergen, Chaplain and former Chaplain General, National Society. *Left to right, seated:* Mrs. Wooley; President General Horace Y. Kitchell; Mrs. Kitchell; Col. Thurston H. Baxter, Ret., Past President of D. C. Society and Vice President General Mid-Atlantic District, is placing the Past President's insigne around the neck of General Wooley, the outgoing President.

Below—Members of the D.C. Society held a no-host barbecue and picnic at historic Rippon Lodge, Va., Sunday, October 15, 1956. *Left to right, back row:* Compatriots Hillis Lory, Warren Foster, O. Kenneth Baker. *Left to right, front row, standing:* Harry Byerly, Librarian General; Robert T. Bryan, Jr.; Pres. Gen. Eugene P. Carver; Charles Marsteller, President, D.C. Society; Col. Thurston H. Baxter, National Trustee; Robert S. W. Walker, Registrar D.C. Society.

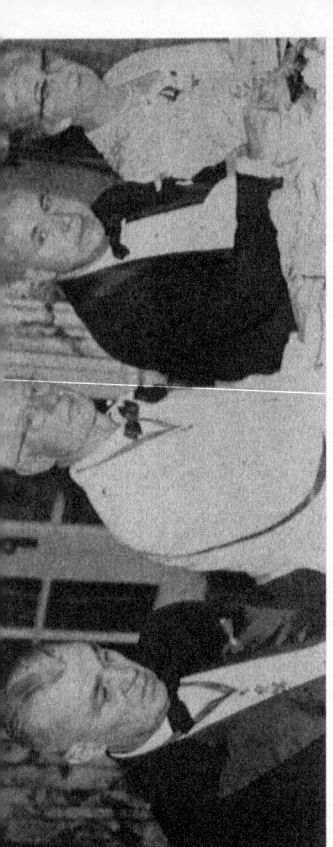

Left to right: Primrose W. Fisher, President Florida State Society S.A.R.; Ralph S. Thompson, President Sarasota Chapter, S.A.R.; Kent S. McKinley, Publisher Sarasota News; Mrs. Fred Freemyer, Regent Sara de Sota Chapter, D.A.R.

Below—Constitution Week, September 17, 1958, was observed in Albany, Ga., by a meeting jointly sponsored by the Thronateeska Chapter D.A.R., and the Rotary Club. *Left to right:* Mrs. J. L. Pittman, defense chairman; P. C. King, past president Georgia S.A.R., guest speaker; Mrs. Wallace Crouch, program chairman; Leo Leader, who presided; and Mrs. Frank Faulk, regent of the D.A.R. chapter.

The four Dame brothers, Members of Wiregrass Georiga Chapter. *Left to right:* Judge Flem C. Dame, County Judge, Fort Pierce, Florida; Mrs. Lula Dame Peagler, Regent of Lyman Hall Chapter, D.A.R., Waycross, Georgia; H. J. Dame, retired attorney; Mrs. Olivia Dame Barnhill, Historian, John Flyod Chapter, D.A.R., Homerville, Ga.; Dr. George A. Dame, President Wiregrass Georgia Chapter; Dr. L. H. Dame, Orlando, Fla. On the occasion of the dedication of the George M. Dame Memorial Park in Homerville, Ga. (Senator Geo. M. Dame was the father of the above).

Insert, left—President General Carver presenting Good Citizenship Medal to Senator George at Albany, Georgia, on December 17th, 1956.

Insert, right—President General Eugene P. Carver, Jr., was guest of honor of the Palm Beach Chapter S.A.R., December 19, 1956. Mayor Maurice Holley presented him with the key to the city. At left is Primrose W. Fisher, President of the Florida Society S.A.R. At far right is John Lanier, President of the Palm Beach Chapter.

Below—Charter Members of the Clearwater, Florida Chapter attended the formal institution ceremonies of the Chapter on January 21, 1952. The officers of the new Chapter: Frederick K. Woodring, president; Joseph Darrell Harvey, vice president; Col. John H. Cochran, secretary-registrar; and Samuel Graham Webb, treasurer.

Ceremony marking Jon Day's grave (Rev. War Soldier), Clark County, Idaho, 7.5 miles northwest of Idaho Falls, July 4, 1953. John Day was buried February 1820. As far as is known he is the only Revolutionary War Soldier buried in the State of Idaho or in the Pacific northwest. *Left to right:* Cy Davis, member of the Committee; Henry W. Hance, Chairman of the Committee; Howard A. Thompson, President of the Eagle Rock Chapter, Idaho Falls; and J. R. Goble, President of the Idaho Society, and Vice President General, National Society.

Compatriot William Stark Hawkins (third from right) was guest of honor of the Eagle Rock Chapter No. 3 Idaho Falls on Nov. 17, 1959 when visiting that city as Grand Exalter Ruler of B.O.P.E. to dedicate a new Elks Lodge building.

Below—Charter members of Fort Sherman Chapter, Coeur d'Alene, Idaho instituted on Feb. 22, 1952. Judge W. F. McNaughton, President; Kenneth D. Spencer, Vice President; and Clement Wilkins, Secretary.

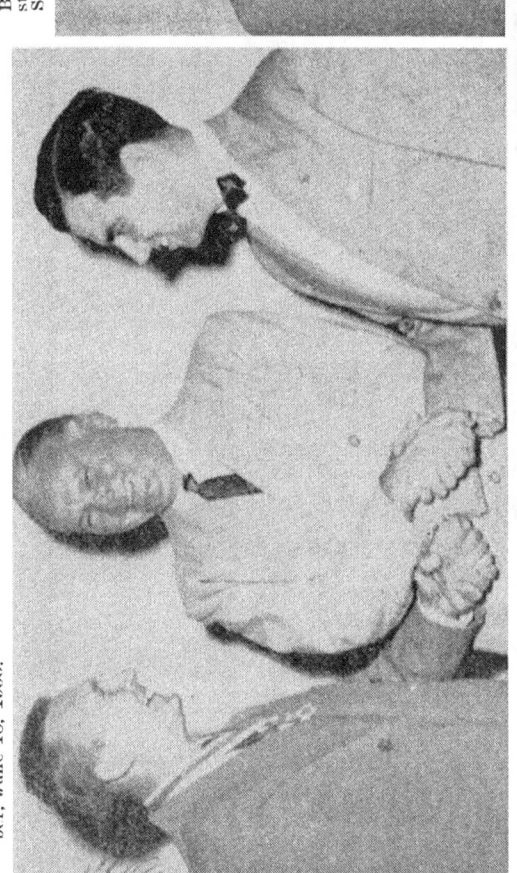

Below—Compatriots Volney A. K. Howard (left) President; Roger Monsarrat (right) Secretary of the Hawaiian Society, greet Norman D. Golbold, new member, June 18, 1953.

Dr. Perry C. Traver, President Alexis Coquillard Chapter, Indiana Society S.A.R., presenting June 7, 1959, R.O.T.C. Medal to Cadet Johnathon R. Ballard of San Marino, Calif., at Culver Military Academy, Culver. Maj. Gen. Delmar T. Spivey USAF (Retired) Supt. of the Academy, stands behind Dr. Traver.

Below—

Illinois Society meeting, Sept. 23, 1955 at Urbana. *Standing:* Prof. H i r a m J. Scovill, Sec.-Treas. Piankeshaw Chapter; Lt. Col. Leonard La Conte, Asst. Prof. Military Science U. of Illinois; Prof. Fred A. Russell, Vice President of Piankeshaw Chapter and 1956 President; Prof. Robert C. Bone, Chrm. P'triotic Education Comm. Piankeshaw Chapter (& asst. provost U. Of Illinois); Charles A. Goodwin-Perkins, organizing president Piankeshaw Chapter and 1956, 2d Vice President Illinois Society. *Seated:* D.A.R. Ladies Alliance Chapter: Mrs. J. B. Andrews, Mrs. F. E. Richart, Miss Emma Jutton, Mrs. Kenneth Stice, Chairman—wife Compatriot Col. Kennth Stice. Standing with men: Miss Lola McClurg.

Above—S.A.R. Medals presented by Col. P. C. Traver (Ret.), Pres. of South Bend Chap. S.A.R. to ROTC students at Notre Dame Univ. June 1957. Army, Edward C. Thompson (highest rated Freshman); Navy, Paul W. Willingahnz; Air Force, David F. Windle.

Below—Annual meeting Illinois Society Dec. 3, 1958. *Left to right:* Charles A. Goodwin-Perkins, elected President; John E. King, Vice-President General of S.A.R.; Dr. Alden J. Rarick, President of Piankeshaw Chapter; and Dr. Harold I. Meyer, Chicago, retiring President of Illinois Society.

Meeting of the Illinois Society on December 6, 1957, at Chicago. Seated at the speaker's table, left to right: Paul B. Teeter, 1st Vice President; Mrs. E. King, Charles A. Goodwin-Perkins, 2nd Vice President; President General George E. Tarbox, Jr., John E. King, retiring President; Mrs. George E. Tarbox, Jr.; Dr. Harold I. Meyer, President-elect; and Judge Floyd E. Thompson, past President.

The National Society of the Sons of the American Revolution Medal presented to Cadet Norman Barkley Gates, outstanding freshman cadet in the 2d Battalion, Army ROTC, University of Kansas at Lawrence, by Charles R. Nagle, President, The Kansas Society, on May 16, 1953.

1t — Officers of Kansas Society a luncheon in 1951 in confer- with President eral Wallace C. (center).

1961 Officers of the Delaware Crossing chapter, Kansas S.A.R. were installed Nov. 1, by president general Herschel S. Murphy and Maj. Joe Nickell, president of the Kansas Society. *Left to right, front:* Judge Frank H. Thompson, secretary; Donald C. Little, president; Col. John W. Breidenthal, treasurer; Wm. Thomas Little, registrar. *Back row:* Gen. Nickell, Dr. Murphy, and Frank L. Gates, chapter chancellor.

1961 Officers of the Kentucky State Society. *Left to right, front row:* Jean A. Auxier, historian, Pikesville; Larry A. Cassidy, Jr., retiring president, Louisville; Thomas Burchett, incoming president, Ashland; David C. Grams, first vice president, Lexington; *back row,* Charles B. Pipes, treasurer, Lexington; P. Demaree, registrar, Lexington; S. W. Hearne, secertary, Ashland, and J. Norman, second vice president, Louisville.

Cadet Basic Wayne R. Barcelo presented ROTC Medal by Lt. Col. Robert Jones, representing La. Society S.A.R., at Awards Day ceremonies, Tulane University, May 17, 1957.

Below — Good Citizenship Medal and Certificate presented to Compatriot J. Blanc Monroe, leading attorney of New Orleans, by the Louisiana Society, May 15, 1958 (At right) *At left*—John St. Paul Jr., Pres. of La. Soc.; *Center*—Arthur A. de la Houssaye, Past President General of Nat'l Society.

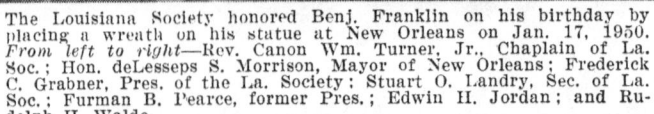

The Louisiana Society honored Benj. Franklin on his birthday by placing a wreath on his statue at New Orleans on Jan. 17, 1950. *From left to right*—Rev. Canon Wm. Turner, Jr., Chaplain of La. Soc.; Hon. deLesseps S. Morrison, Mayor of New Orleans; Frederick C. Grabner, Pres. of the La. Society; Stuart O. Landry, Sec. of La. Soc.; Furman B. Pearce, former Pres.; Edwin H. Jordan; and Rudolph H. Waldo.

Above—Meeting of the Attakapas Chapter Louisiana Society S.A.R. at Lafayette, 1959. *From left to right:* Herbert C. Parker, Guerric G. de Coligny, Charles E. Boudousquie, Mrs. Herbert C. Parker and Mrs. Guerric G. de Coligny.

Below—Meeting on Constitution Day September 17, 1958, in Council Chambers of the City Hall. *From left to right:* Mrs. Marion C. Adams, Regent Vieux Carre Chapter D.A.R. Glenn P. Clasen, President of Council, City of New Orleans, Hale Boggs, U.S. Representative from Louisiana, John St. Paul, Jr., President Louisiana Society S.A.R.

Presentation of "Medal of Appreciation" to Mrs. Allene Wilson Groves, President General of the Daughters of the American Revolution, by the Louisiana Society on November the 12th, 1958. Executive Secretary Harold L. Putnam flew from Washington to make the presentation. Mrs. Henry L. Mayer, Regent of Galvez Chapter D.A.R., Lafayette, also received a medal. *From left to right:* Harold L. Putnam; Mrs. Henry L. Mayer; John St. Paul, Jr., President of the Louisiana Society; Mrs. Allene Wilson Groves; and Horace Y. Kitchell, Vice President General.

Below—Louisiana Society Constitution Day Luncheon at New Orleans (1949). *Left to right:* Compatriots Healy, Grabner and Pearce; Congressman Hebert, and Clem Sehrt representing the Gov. of La.

Above—Henry S. Shryock, Past President of Maryland Society of the Sons of the American Revolution, presents the S.A.R. Medal to Cadets Joseph T. Fletsch, Bruce E. Moats, William H. Taylor and Wayen O. Harris, at John Hopkins University, Baltimore, May 12, 1958.

Upper left—The Honorable Owen Brewster, former U.S. Senator from Maine, was the guest speaker at the Annual Meeting of the Maine Society, April 20, 1957 in Portland. At the speaker's table were: *(Left to right)* Harry K. Torrey, Registrar; Gen. George A. Davis, President; Senator Brewster; George H. Thompson, Secretary; and Herbert S. Hodson, National Trustee.

At left—Mrs. Basil E. Lamb, state regent, Maine Society D.A.R. and Herbert S. Hodson, Past President, Maine Society S.A.R., placing a S.A.R. marker on the grave of Paul Prince, Revolutionary War soldier, in the 1959.

...embers of the Minutemen Chapter S.A.R., Mel-
...se, Mass. attended a testimonial dinner for the
...ayor of Melrose, April 10, 1958. *Left to right,*
...anding: Fred H. Whittemore; George C. Woods;
...rthur J. Flint; U.S. Senator Leverett Salton-
...all; Albert A. Vogt, Jr., chapter president; Fred
... Bryan. *Left to right, seated:* Harold B. Rut-
...dge; Albert W. Keddy; George W. Hemenway;
...aul S. Vaitses and Elliott M. Andrews.

...t right—Meeting Dukes County Chapter, Vine-
...rd Haven, Mass. *Left to right:* Stephen C.
...uce, Jr., Pres. of Mass Soc.; Rev. Samuel R. Har-
...w; Walter C. Ripley, Pres. of the Chapter; Hon.
...bner L. Braley, Secretary of the Chapter; Col.
...ibbard Richter, Past Pres. of Mass. Society; Mrs.
...ark G. Brook, Asst. Sec. of Mass Society.

...ower right—The Massachusetts Society S.A.R.,
...esented a U. S. Flag to the Old North Church,
...oston, November 8, 1956. *Left to right:* Robert
... Needham, Vice President; John C. Wroe, Sec-
...tary; Rev. Howard Kellett, Vicar Old North
...hurch; and Hon. George W. Roberts, President.

...elow—Charter Night, Worcester County Chapter,
...ass. *Left to right:* Color Guard Commander
...lbert Vogt, Jr.; Raymond Harris, Pres. of the
...hapter; State Secretary John C. Wroe; Eugene
... Carver, Jr., aPst Pres. Gen.; Alton Sawin, Jr.,
...hapter Chaplain; Stephen C. Luce, Jr., Pres. of
...ass. Soc.; Vice Pres. Robert F. Needham; Past
...es. Hibbard Richter; Albert Keddy, member of
...olor Guard.

New England Council S.A.R. meeting at the Harvard Club, Boston, April 15, 1950. *Left to right, standing:* Dr. Joseph S. White, Pres. of Me. Society; Harry K. Torrey, Trustee, Me. Soc.; Howard Coe, Trustee, Conn. Soc.; Walker L. Chamberlin, Past Pres. Mass. Soc.; Roger A. Lutz, Sec. Mass. Soc.; Harry Sherwin, Trustee, N. H. Soc.; Col. Hibbard Richter, V.P. Mass. Soc.; Philip R. Arnold, Pres. R. I. Soc. *Left to right, seated:* Eugene P. Carver, Jr., Pres. Mass Soc.; Chester R. Martin, Past V.P.G., R. I. Soc.; John W. Finger, Pres. Gen.; Douglas Sloane, V.P.G., N. H. Soc.; Arthur McCrillis, Past Pres. Gen. (from R. I. Soc.); Col. Harry J. Beardsley, Trustee, Conn.

At left — Officers of Springfield, Mass., Chapter S.A.R. being sworn in Dec. 5, 1953.

Below—Members of the Massachusetts Society S.A.R. witness the signing of the bill on Mar. 12, 1953, by his Excellency Gov. Christian Herter, for the Annual Proclamation of Constitution Day on September 17. *Seated:* Gov. Christian Herter and Representative Hibbard Richter, President of the Mass. Society S.A.R. *Left to right, standing:* Representative William D. Morton, Jr., Charles K. Lawton, Vice President; William B. Lamphrey, Treasurer; John C. Wroe, Vice President; Laird DeVou, Vice President; Harvey T. Pond; John Fisher Robinson; Francis R. Sears; Philip F. Lackey, Secretary; Capt. David G. Maraspin; Hon. George W. Roberts; General Otis Whitney; Representative Gordon C. Boynton; Representaitve Marcus Wright; Charles D. O'Malley, President of Boston Chapter; and Stanley D. Foster.

Meeting of Michigan Society Board of Managers, Hotel Bancroft—Saginaw, Michigan, November 15, 1952. *Left to right, standing:* W. Merrill Stuckey, Samuel C. Root, Frank L. Lowmaster, Neil A. Cameron, Roy V. Barnes, T. Virgil Frantz and Robert B. Frantz. *Left to right, seated:* Lynn S. Gordon, Secretary; John P. Thomas, Treasurer; Charles S. Prescott, First Vice President; Carl O. Moody, President; Barry T. Whipple, National Trustee.

Officers of Michigan Society for 1954-1955. *Left to right:* The late Barry T. Whipple, Vice-President General; Lynn S. Gordon, Secretary; William C. Hudson, 1st Vice-Pres.; Marion H. Crawmer, President; Frank L. Lowmaster, 2d Vice-Pres.; Rev. Grant L. Jordan, Chaplain.

The Board of Managers of the Michigan Society, S.A.R., held its January 1958 meeting at the Michigan Union, Ann Arbor. *Left to right:* Edwin C. Eddy, President, Valley Forge Chapter; Stuart B. Everett, who was sent to Wolverine Boys' State by Michigan Society; Robert H. Peterson, President, Detroit Chapter; RAIM Dr. George A. Parkinson, Vice President General; Frank L. Lowmaster, President Michigan Society; Hugh P. Gaston, President Washtenaw Chapter; Rev. Grant L. Jordan, Chaplain General and Neil A. Cameron, First Vice President of the Michigan Society.

At left—Medals presented to the NROTC Midshipmen at the University of Minnesota, Minneapolis, at the annual Spring Review, May 19, 1955. Col. Robert T. Connor, USA, PMS&T at the University of Minnestoa, was an honored guest at the NROTC Review, and presented the Medals at the request of the Professor of Naval Science. *Left to right*: M/Sgt. M.J.D. Loy, USMC, assists Col. Connor in presenting awards to R. L. Erickson and his twin brother R. A. Erickson; J. R. Forster; R. L. O'Brien; J. P. Valenti; and H. J. Wasik.

The annual meeting of the Southeastern Minnesota Chapter was held in the Kahler Hotel, Rochester, January 15, 1960, when Dr. H. L. Williams was elected for a third term as president of the chapter. *Left to right*: Leslie W. Myers, president-elect of the state society; Dr. Williams; Mrs. F. L. Long, guest speaker, representing the D.A.R.; Dr. George Loomis, re-elected vice president, and Carl Hooper, secretary-treasurer.

At right—President General Jones was the guest speaker at a meeting of the Minnestoa Society held at the Minneapolis Athletic Club, December 5, 1959. *Left to right:* Lt. Col. Edward P. Barrows, state president; Mrs. Jones; president general Jones; and Mrs. Barrows.

At left—The Southeastern Minnesota Chapter organized in Rochester, 1956. *Left to right, front row:* Lt. Col. Wm. B. Howard, State President; Carl A. Herrick, Vice President General; and Senator A. C. Gooding. *Left to right, second row:* Dr. Henry L. Williams of Mayo Clinic, Organizing President; and Dr. G. C. Loomis, Organizing Secretary.

Annual Meeting of the Mississippi Society, February 26, 1959. *Left to right:* L. L. McNees, Secretary-Registrar; Horace Y. Kitchell, Vice-President General, who installed the state officers; Rev. W. L. Philly, Chaplain; R. A. Billups, First Vice-President; Donald R. Fraser, Second Vice-President; Norman C. Brewer, President; E. A. Nichols, Board of Governors; Prof. Cyril E. Cain, Historian; George A. Chamblis, Board of Governors; Dr. J. J. Kyzar, Board of Governors.

Officers elected at the Annual Banquet of the Mississippi Society S.A.R., March 10, 1960, at the Country Club, Greenwood. *Left to right:* Donald R. Fraser, Vice President; Rowell A. Billups, President; Charles A. Jones, President General and guest speaker; Norman C. Brewer, retiring President; Horace Y. Kitchell, Vice President General; and Lucien L. McNees, Secretary-Registrar.

Annual Meeting the Mississippi Society, R. (Below)

Missouri Society meeting September 27, 1957. *Left to right, standing:* Compatriot John M. Dalton, Attorney General for the State of Missouri; K. M. Crossen; John W. Giesecke, National Trustee; Henry F. Chadeayne, Secretary-Treasurer of the Missouri Society; Fred G. Williamson; John H. Dunn; Lucien Erskine; William Pagenstecher, all Past Presidents of the Missouri Society; S. F. Adreon; W. W. Dalton. *Left to right, seated:* J. Alonzo Matthews, Past President; Col. Frederick W. Huntington, Vice President General of the South Mississippi District; Joseph E. Burger, President of the Missouri Society; William S. Cordry.

Members of the Omaha Chapter SAR who were able to appear for the photograph: *Left to right, seated:* Rev. Dr. Earle Van Arsdale Conover, Junior Vice President and Chaplain of the State Society also Secretary-Treasurer and Chaplain of the Omaha Chapter; Ernest Basil Blease, Vice President of the Omaha Chapter; F. Edward Borchers, President of the State Society; Frank H. Binder, President of the Omaha Chapter and Member of the Board of Managers. *Left to right, standing:* Harvey A. Smith, Jr. Gordon Roberts, Wallace Guhl Quest, Wayne McPherren, Stephen M. Sawtell.

At left—Sept. 17, 1953 Constitution Day Dinner—*Left to right:* Robert B. Crosby, Governor of Nebraska; Mrs. Kenneth Lawson, Regent, Deborrah Avery Chapter, D.A.R., Lincoln; L. R. King, President, Nebraska Society.

Anti-Subversive Textbook "Campaign", to leave his lucrative employment in California and become the new Executive Secretary. He arrived in Washington in March 1950 and immediately began his long and fruitful career as Executive Secretary.

The fulfillment of the plans and the hopes of the leaders of the National Society was brought to fruition through the efficiency and dedication of Harold L. Putnam, and they were fully realized after the 60th Congress at Atlantic City, New Jersey, when Wallace C. Hall of Michigan was elected President General.

Among other things authorized at the 60th Congress was the rehabilitation of the Headquarters Building. The officers were directed and authorized to borrow sufficient money up to $25,000.00 to rehabilitate and put the Headquarters Building in good condition, and the work was immediately started and completed late in the Fall of 1950.

It was at this time that the President General's suite was established at the National Headquarters building and furnished by President General and Mrs. Hall as contribution to the Society. Since that time this suite has been widely used by Past Presidents General and the current President General through all the years.

In the process of the rehabilitation of the building, it was necessary to make substantial changes in the structural features of the building, repairing necessary outside damage which had been done through the years. The heating system was obsolete and needed repairing, and it became advisable to change over from coal heat to oil heat. The completion of the rehabilitation work was done at a total of $17,500.00. This proved to be a valuable investment in safety, comfort of our staff and economy of operation.

One of the outstanding measures taken to re-vitalize the Society was the convening of the Board of Trustees in more meetings per year. A total of 5 meetings were held by the Board and it really assumed responsibility for the management and operation of the Society. The Vice-President Generals of the respective districts were also charged with the duty of not only being Vice-President General, but assuming the responsibility of membership activity within their respective districts.

In preparation for the 61st. Congress to be held at San Francisco in July 1951, the work of Compatriot Clarence E. Shriner, Vice-President General from Ohio, as Chairman of the Organization and Membership Committee, in putting on the Golden Gate Marathon Membership Campaign,* produced remarkable results and made a very definite and desirable change in the picture so that the Society showed a substantial net gain in membership during the year.

In connection with this campaign, an experiment was tried which paid off, because the Board of Trustees authorized the giving of certain cash prizes to those who produced the most members during the period up to the time of the Congress. It was astonishing to see how many of the Compatriots entered into the spirit of the contest and how many members resulted from their efforts.

During the first year of the tenure of the Executive Secretary, it immediately became apparent that the organization was on a very much more efficient basis; and the operations of the Headquarters and its staff, in the functioning of the various departments began to show the capable executive ability of Compatriot Putnam. It is a matter of great gratification to those who were responsible for securing his services, for he not only took the full responsibility of his position, but gave to it much more than any organization employing an Executive Secretary can expect, because of his dedication and devotion to the Society. The Society entered upon a strong and healthy period which was continued wherein the Executive Secretary has given of himself unselfishly and shown how dedicated he is to the principles of Americanism and the purpose and objectives of the institution. The Society has been indeed fortunate in being able to keep his services for such a long period of time.

The 61st. Congress at San Francisco in July 1951, was one of the most active and exciting Congresses that had

---

*The winner of the Golden Gate Marathon was Compatriot Arthur de la Houssaye of Louisiana, later to become President General.

been experienced for many years. There was a great deal of enthusiasm and an appreciation of the fact that the responsibility of the members of the Society, was not only to stand militantly for the things best for the United States and the Constitution, but also to do something about it. And so at the Congress in San Francisco, after strenuous argument and debate, a very strong set of resolutions was passed, including the one which has stood from that day to this in connection with the attitude of the Society toward the United Nations. It is quite apparent that this attitude of the Society has never changed.

At the San Francisco Congress there were two special events: a very fine Noon address by former Senator Albert Hawkes of New Jersey, and the awarding the first Gold Medal for Constructive Citizenship to Commentator Fulton Lewis, Jr., of Washington, when he gave his acceptance speech over the coast to coast network of the Mutual Broadcasting Company in response to the presentation by President General Hall.

The attendance was large considering the distance which most of the Compatriots had to cover to get there. It was the consensus after the Congress was over that it had been one of the most worth while and satisfying Congresses ever held.

At the San Francisco Congress Wallace Hall was re-elected president for another term.

Following the San Francisco Congress events once again pointed up the wisdom and the usefulness of having the Board of Trustees assume it's full responsibilities in the management of the affairs of the Society. During 1949 and 1950 the officers had been successful in obtaining passage of a bill through Congress and signed by the President of the United States, which fully exempted the Society from all taxation, both on real and personal property. This gave the Society a freedom from taxation which was very important and worthwhile from a monetary view point.*

---

*In 1934 Congress passed a bill exempting the S.A.R. property from taxation, but this applied only to the real estate. In this last bill all the Society's property is exempt from taxation.

It became apparent that the Headquarters property was going to be hemmed in by large buildings, so the Board authorized the purchase of a twenty-five foot lot immediately adjoining Headquarters Building, in order to give the Society a frontage of 61 feet on 16th Avenue N.W., and it was purchased. However, even then it was obvious that the continuance of the Society in the Headquarters building at that address would not long be tenable, and, while there were many offers made for the purchase of the property, none was accepted because the building had just been rehabilitated and it was ideally suited to the Society's purposes.

The Board of Trustees started work on a program to increase and stimulate assumption of responsibilities for constructive work in their communities on the part of the state societies and it is the opinion of some that during this period, more compatriots took an active part in the affairs of the Society than at any previous time, and because of their taking a more active part, they attracted a great many splendid and high grade new members who joined the Society. The membership production was maintained at a high level.

The 62nd Congress, held at Houston May 18-22, 1952, was a most enjoyable affair.

Among the highlights of the Congress were the establishment of "Recognition Night" and the creation of the "Minute Man Awards", the highest decoration of the Society for outstanding service to the National Society above the State Societies. It is proper to state that this award is a much coveted and appreciated honor.

In his report, President General Hall pointed out that since his election no elected officer has been a paid employee of the Society and that this fact is deemed to be a great step forward by avoiding the problems that such payments necessarily entail. He emphasized that the establishment of the secretaryship had justified itself in the splendid results obtained and the fine cooperation that Headquarters had enjoyed on the part of all state societies and chapters and the improvement of the relationship between the state and local organizations and the National Society. The screening of members became a very definite program and the quality of membership was much improved.

It was a strenuous period for all of the general officers, because there was so much activity and so many demands made upon all of them, but all appreciated the opportunity to be of greater service.

On May 22nd at Houston Compatriot Ray O. Edwards was elected President General.

THE ADMINISTRATION OF RAY O. EDWARDS, 1952 - 1953

In his inaugural address, President General Edwards quoted the words of that great American, Charles Evans Hughes: "You cannot be saved by valor and devotion to your ancestors; to each generation comes its patriotic duty; and upon your willingness to sacrifice and endure as those before you have sacrificed and endured, rest the National hope."

The President General was an ardent advocate of the necessity for securing the younger generation as members of our organization and devoted much activity towards that end. His example should be a beacon to continuously beckon us on to greater efforts in this regard.

He was very active in the fight against subversive interests and advocated and indulged in the dissemination of accurate and authentic evidence to aid in this endeavor.

Compatriot Edwards was very active in establishing personal contacts with the various State Societies and their chapters, and he made a special effort to visit those which distance or other factors had deprived of contact with the President General. He visited all but nine of the forty-eight States.

At the meeting of the Board of Trustees held at Denver, Colorado, on August 2nd, 1952, the appointment of a Special Awards Committee was authorized to make a study of all medals of the National Society and the conditions under which each is to be awarded and by what authority and to report to the Cincinnati Congress.

The appointment of a Committee was authorized to design a new type of Official Grave Marker for Revolutionary Soldiers.

The President General called attention to the plan adopted at the Houston Congress for State Societies to donate chairs to be used by the Trustees at Headquarters, the chairs to contain on the back thereof a suitable credit plate engraved with the name of the donor.

At the third meeting of the Board of Trustees held at Headquarters on November 8th and 9th, 1952, a resolution was adopted urging the Congress of the United States to reestablish September 17th as Constitution Day only. While Congress did not reestablish September 17th as Constitution Day only, it did establish Constitution Week, September 17th to 23rd, included. (U.S.C.A. Title 36, Section 159. August 2, 1956—C. 875, 70 Stat. 952.)

Compatriot A. G. Trimble of the Pittsburgh Chapter donated the "A. G. Trimble" Trophy award, and Mr. Putnam announced that it had been received at Headquarters and he read the regulations for the award. The President General announced that the regulations would be submitted to the "Special Awards Committee" for recommendation to the next Congress.

At the Trustees Meeting of February 14th, 1953, at Jacksonville, Florida, the President General was authorized to send a message to our Compatriot, Honorable Dwight D. Eisenhower, President of the United States, pledging to him the support of the Society.

The National Society of the Sons of the American Revolution, under President General Edwards' leadership, entertained the general officers of other patriotic societies on the evening of April 18th, 1953, at the Society's Headquarters, and the reception was one of the brilliant affairs of the Washington winter season.

Compatriot Edwards presided over the 63rd Congress held at Cincinnati, Ohio, on June 14th to 17th, 1953.

A pleasant feature of the Congress was the appearance of Robert A. Taft, Jr., to bring greetings from our great compatriot, his father who was unable to be present because of illness.

At the 63rd Annual Congress of the Society held at Cincinnati, Ohio, Compatriot Arthur A. de la Houssaye was elected President General. The contest for President General was actively waged between Compatriot George

E. Tarbox, Jr., and Compatriot Arthur A. de la Houssaye. The total votes cast were 193 and one was invalidated. There were 64 votes for Compatriot George E. Tarbox, Jr., and 128 for Compatriot Arthur A. de la Houssaye.

THE ADMINISTRATION OF ARTHUR A. DE LA HOUSSAYE, 1953 - 1954

Among the accomplishments of President General de la Houssaye's administration, were the following:

Increase of income of the National Society by approximately $19,000 by increasing the annual dues $1.00 to $2.50.

The adoption of the policy providing for the annual appropriation of $5,000 in the budget to defray the actual expenses of future Presidents General while travelling on official SAR business.

The adoption of the design for souvenir plates and demi-tasse cups to be sold by the Society.

The issuance of a stamp to be sold to the members, the proceeds of the sale to be used to help finance patriotic projects. 56,000 were sold during the year. (Credit for this design and the idea should be given to Executive Secretary, Harold L. Putnam).

Establishment of the Robert A. Taft Travelling Banner.

The adoption of a plan for the award of the Gold Medal for constructive citizenship; the Florence Kendall Award for the compatriots securing the greatest number of members.

Exchanged correspondence with President Eisenhower and assisted in having him withdraw his resignation and continue his membership in the Society.

During the year, the President General worked with the President General of the Sons of the Revolution in and endeavor to merge the two Societies, and notwithstanding the favorable recommendation of the President General of the Sons of the Revolution, was unable to effect a merger.

The establishment, for the first time, of a Public Relations Committee, headed by a public relations counsellor—a member of our Society.

Secured the services, for the first time, of a President General of D.A.R to serve on a standing committee of S.A.R.

Adopted a plan to present all President Generals with a gavel, with a silver band, suitable for engraving, to be presented each year as the President General receives his badge of office.

The raising of funds to pay the balance due on the mortgage on the Headquarters building. An amount in excess of $10,000 dollars was obtained (6,332.50 was contributed and pledged on the floor of the 64th Congress) and the mortgage was subsequently paid off.

The enrollment of 1458 new members and reinstating of 360 old members. This exceeded the number of enrollment in any one year during at least the preceding five years. Eleven new Chapters were organized —the largest number for any one year.

President General de la Houssaye wrote an inspiring address on the Constitution, which was favorably commended and printed in the S.A.R. Magazine.

The 64th Annual Congress was held at Williamsburg, Va., on May 24-26, 1954. A letter from Compatriot Dwight D. Eisenhower to President General de la Houssaye was read.

There were 282 registered delegates and 239 registered visitors in attendance at the 64th Annual Congress, but it should be noted that there were 620 in attendance at the President General's banquet, the largest attendance on record at any Annual Congress. More than twice as many people showed up as were expected. The weather was fine and the many families who came were given an opportunity to enjoy the sight seeing and visiting of historic shrines. An unusually large number of distinguished visitors were noted. Housing and dining facilities were taxed to the utmost and three different dining rooms had to be pressed into service at the same time to accommodate the banquet crowds. Speeches were transmitted to these auxiliary rooms by loud speakers.

A long-to-be-remembered incident occurred at the Memorial Services which opened the Williamsburg Congress. To the sound of trumpets the color guards in Revolutionary War uniforms, each carrying a state flag, marched impressively into the old Burton Parish church, the oldest in the United States in continuous use.

Standing at attention, awaiting the massing of the flags in the chancel, those in attendance were startled to see the United Nation's flag across the rostrum from the flag of the United States. This sickly blue emblem, patterned after the Russian army flag, aroused no little resentment. There was much stirring and whispering with a few audible non-complimentary comments. After the services the culprit who introduced the U. N. flag—not one of our members—was apprehended and called upon by two regular army colonels and a major, delegates in uniform, who gave him a severe reprimand.

A tribute to one of the Society's most illustrious members, Robert A. Taft, was read in the famous church.

Possibly the locale of this Congress may have had something to do with the patriotic fervor so apparent there at all times. The more than one-hundred resolutions presented taxed to the utmost that hard-working committee. Practically all of these proposals concerned communism and the United Nations' threat to independence and sovereignty.

An outstanding example of patriotic fervor was demonstrated by the work of the Society's Americanism Committee of which Compatriot Lory was chairman. A long row of tables was set up in the Williamsburg Lodge upon which booklets, pamphlets, government documents and other publications of a patriotic and anti-communist nature could could be had at no cost to the recipients. Over 100,000 pieces of printed material were placed on these tables at the opening of the Congress. Large manila envelopes and folders were provided each visitor in which to carry the material. A few hours later more 600 people carried away an average of 100 pamphlets each or 60,000 pieces all told. Tourists visiting Williamsburg and the restorations took much of this literature and expressed appreciation that the S.A.R. was doing such worthwhile work. Many pamphlets were mailed to all parts of the country. When the Congress was over there was hardly a small carton of material left.

At the election, Milton M. Lory was elected President General without opposition.

THE ADMINISTRATION OF MILTON M. LORY, 1954 - 1955

Milton M. Lory was elected President General in historic Williamsburg on May 26, 1954.

After a few days in Washington making committee appointments and transacting other Society business the new President General drove back to Sioux City and then to a much needed vacation. Returning in September he started his long President General's pilgrimage and Society visitation.

It would have been almost a physical impossibility to call upon all chapters or state societies but Compatriot Lory and his wife did travel 28,000 miles and touched 38 states in travel for the Sons of the American Revolution. These journeys took the President General from coast to coast and from the Canadian border to the Gulf. Within one month, January, of 1955, he spoke in Portland, Oregon, and Portland, Maine and carried the greetings of the citizens of the Maine Portland, for the Oregon city which was named after and founded by people from Portland, Maine. He was invited to speak and did before the state legislatures of Massachusetts, Iowa, and New Hampshire—at the latter at the behest of Compatriot Lane Dwinell, Governor of that state.

One delightful break in his travels, as President General Lory wrote, was a week spent in New Orleans at the home of his immediate predecessor in office, Admiral Arthur A. de la Houssaye. It was during the week of Mardi Gras. Adm. de la Houssaye had been a king of one of the important balls and his wife and daughter had been queens, and this assured the President General and his wife access to many Carnival activities.

After Carnival was over, President General Lory gave the address at the S.A.R.-D.A.R. Washington's birthday banquet at the New Orleans Country Club. It did not seem that many would have the strength or desire to attend a banquet right after Mardi Gras. But lo and behold some 450 people turned out filling the dining room. "What stamina those New Orleanians do have," commented Lory. At that dinner, as he often did in his talks, the President General expressed a desire that the U.S. get out of the

U.N. and the U.N. out of the U.S. He was overwhelmed by receiving a standing ovation after that remark with considerable newspaper comment given the incident.

A few days later at Houston, Texas 550 persons crowded the Rice Hotel ballroom to hear the President General. The banquet was also to honor and award a medal to Compatriot Warren S. Bellows, a Houston contractor who erected many of the largest buildings in the city, a hundred million dollars worth it was said. That night he gave membership in the S.A.R. to his five sons who were in business with him.

Some members become angry for one thing or another and resign. This however does not occur with much regularity and probably serves to strengthen the membership. Mr. Lory inherited the first year of the increased dues. Some didn't like that and resigned over the $1.00 increase. When one of the Philadelphia chapters gave Sen. McCarthy a medal there were a few objections. Most members enthusiastically concurred, however.

In the late summer of 1954 a hurricane toppled the steeple of Old North Church in Boston. A resurgence of patriotism and a fervent love for the well-known shrine welled up in the heart of America. No sooner had the winds ceased than efforts were under way to restore the famed church tower.

When millions of citizens heard Fulton Lewis, Jr. ring out over the air, "One if by land, two if by sea" on his 450-station Mutual Network newscast, September 1st, many throats tightened, tears came to many eyes and many pulses beat faster from the emotion of love of country. When Mr. Lewis appealed for funds for the restoration, President General Lory immediately wired him that the Sons of the American Revolution would endorse his move. He gratefully acknowledged this telegram on the next night's broadcast. The S.A.R. played an important financial role by the contributions of compatriots in the restoration of that famous shrine.

Among the incidents the President General long remembered vividly, was that of walking down Sixteenth Street with Gen. U. S. Grant III, grandson of President Grant, and when approaching the Society's former headquarters the General mentioned the enjoyable times he had as youngster playing in and around that building. He had lived there as a small boy.

The Sixty-Fifth Congress was held at the Conrad Hilton Hotel in Chicago, May 22-25, 1955. President General Lory in his report said that things had gone along smoothly and he felt that he had a successful year, that there was considerable evidence that his time, effort, and expense had borne some fruit. The mortgage on the old building was burned with due ceremony. Several new chapters had been chartered including those of Reno, Nev., Tacoma and Bremerton, Washington and three in Pennsylvania. Alaska and Hawaii came into the fold that year. It was announced that 105 attended the Washington's birthday dinner at Anchorage, Alaska in snowy frigid weather. A wealthy Boston man left the Society an inheritance with which was started the Society's educational scholarship fund. A study to investigate the authenticity of Betsy Ross as the maker of the first United States flag was started.

When the Pledge of Allegiance was recited at the opening of the Chicago Congress arrangements had been made for it to be said in all of the public schools of Chicago. It was quite a thrill to the President General to know that 400,000 pupils were saying this pledge in unison with the S.A.R. General Bonner Fellers and Paul Harvey, the radio newscaster, were speakers at the two banquets.

That the Sons of the American Revolution are great talkers—probably due to the large number of lawyers in the membership—is evidenced by the fact that the proceedings of the Chicago Congress filled 375 typewritten pages.

Compatriot Edgar Williamson, Jr., was elected President General at Chicago, on May 25th, and duly installed.

THE ADMINISTRATION OF EDGAR WILLIAMSON, JR.,
1955 - 1956

During this administration, a signal honor was paid the head of the Society. The New Jersey Senate adopted a special resolution honoring President General Williamson —an unusual occurrence.

President General Williamson's term of office was noted for his realization of the importance of a large membership—so necessary to the success of the organization and its aims and purposes. The President General attempted in every way possible to increase membership and particularly to secure young men as members.

The Executive Secretary, Compatriot Harold L. Putnam, made an exhaustive trip at the suggestion of President General Williamson, covering some nine thousand miles to visit many of the state Societies and chapters in the West and Mid-West thereby infusing enthusiasm and vigor into the organization.

With the presentation of a Charter to the Nevada Society on November 17, 1955, the Society became organized in each state of the Union.

A handbook, fulfilling a long felt need, was issued in 1956.

During President General Williamson's administration the Board of National Trustees gave favorable action to a new award, "The President General's Cup". The first presentation thereof was made by President General Williamson.

The plans for the 66th Congress at Bolton Landing, New York, on Lake George warranted the very successful and entertaining Congress which was held on May 27th to 30th, 1956, at the Sagamore Hotel at that resort.

At this Congress, President General Williamson enjoyed the unique distinction of being escorted by a personal honor guard composed of members of the New Jersey Blues in their resplendent new uniforms commanded by Compatriot Dr. C. Malcolm B. Gilman.

At the Bolton Landing Congress, Compatriot Eugene P. Carver, Jr., was elected and installed as President General.

THE ADMINISTRATION OF EUGENE P. CARVER, 1956 - 1957

Eugene P. Carver, Jr., was elected President General on May 30, 1956 and went out of office a year later.

Without doubt the most important occurrence of his term was the entering into negotiations for the sale of the property on 16th Street, which resulted in the purchase of the Patrick Hurley property at 2412 Massachusetts Ave., N. W. The old property was sold for $305,000, less a broker's commission, and the Hurley property was purchased for approximately $160,000.

For the sale of the property on 16th Street, it was necessary to call a special congress. At this congress, the propositions voted on were (1) the sale of the 16th Street property and (2) the purchase of the Belgian Embassy. President General Carver had consistently opposed the sale of the 16th Street property until and unless the Society was able to secure another property at least equally good for a considerable less figure, and a committee had been appointed to search for an appropriate place which could be purchased.

The National Education Association originally had bid about $150,000 for the 16th Street building, which in the President General's opinion was all or more than it was worth, but apparently there was nothing available equal to it, or even near it, for any such figure. The N.E.A. wished to purchase the 16th Street property to incorporate it in their much larger building, so they desired the land and not the building, and strategically the Society was in a very strong position for a sale. Gradually they upped by stages to $200,000, $250,000 and finally $305,000.

The arguments in favor of selling were (1) it was more than the building and land were worth and (2) the Society was faced, within a very few years, with repairs and renovations of the elevators, plumbing, heating and air conditioning which would have probably gone over $30,000. To the President General's dismay, at the Special Congress, the Trustees voted to sell the building but NOT to purchase the Belgian Embassy. In other words, the Society was to become homeless! The vote on the purchase of the Belgian Embassy was not helped by the fact that the Belgian Ambassador insisted that the President General guarantee the deal, which he definitely was not willing to do. Probably the Belgian Embassy would have cost the Society—after repairs, remodeling and fixing up—some $210,000, and considering it in the nature of a swap, the President General felt it would have been an advantageous one for the Society. He was later told that the purchasers of the Belgian Embassy re-sold it at a very handsome profit. The Special Congress having voted NOT to buy the Belgian Embassy, it was necessary for the Society to trade with the National Education Association to insure being able to continue to occupy the building for at least a year. The deal was put through on that basis and the money duly paid over.

Due to the very able efforts of the committee under the leadership of Admiral Furlong, the Hurley House was found to be available, and there is now no question in the then President General's mind but what it was a much better buy than the Belgian Embassy would have been, requiring much less repairing. The actual purchase and remodeling was done under President General Tarbox's regime, but the financial groundwork of the trade was completed during President General Carver's term, though it did require a Special Act of Congress of the United States to unzone the property for the Society's use.

The net result of the deal was that the Society got a much better building, with much more land, and an additional lot which can be sold for a very fancy figure. The location is on a street which, it is believed, will be the last street in Washington to "go" and it received in addition $85,000 in cash! If we consider that the $85,000 remained after a complete renovation of the Hurley House and that the Society was no longer faced with the $30,000 to $40,000 cost of the renovation of the Society's former headquarters which by now perhaps would have become necessary, it is believed that a very good trade was made.

During President General Carver's term of office, the "warmest" reception he received was from Dallas, Texas— they admitted it was 107°!

President General Carver was one of the more active President Generals as far as visits were concerned. He went everywhere he was invited unless the dates conflicted.

May 8, 1957, the President General unveiled a bronze plaque commemorating the death of General Montgomery on Citadel Hill in Quebec. It is not generally known that this was America's FIRST A.E.F., and unlike our others, was a complete failure. Those who urged us to send troops there, promising that Quebic would revolt, later sold us out, and the attempt on New Year's Eve, 1775, to storm Quebec met with a bloody repulse. Practically our whole force was killed, wounded or captured, and General Montgomery himself was killed. There had been a stone plaque placed there some hundred years ago by the school children of the United States, but frost and passage of time had cracked it and chipped it. The Society put a very nice bronze plaque there which certainly should last at least one hundred years, and received some extremely favorable publicity. The exercises were attended by Brigadier J. V. Allard, Second in command of the Canadian Army, and by many important Canadian officials as well as the American Consul.

The President General spoke briefly about the expedition and dilated upon the present wonderful relations between the United States and Canada. However, the President General felt that the Canadian Soldiers, drawn up in parade review, failed to get much from his speech because —with one or two exceptions—they were all French Canadian and did not speak any English.

President General Carver went out of office in Salt Lake City in May 1957 at a very well attended Congress, considering the distance from any large number of our Compatriots. It was an extremely fine Congress, and it was very interesting to note that the Mormon Church certainly rolled out the "plush carpet" for the members of the Society. They could not have been better received had they been Mormons. Perhaps one of the reasons for it was that most of the early Mormons were descendants of Revolutionary patriots.

At the Congress at Salt Lake City, May 29, 1957, George E. Tarbox, Jr., was elected President General.

THE ADMINISTRATION OF GEORGE E. TARBOX, JR.,

1957 - 1958

The administration of President General George E. Tarbox, Jr., was one marked by many "firsts" for the Society. It commenced with the Salt Lake City Congress in May, 1957, when the delegates elected to its highest office for the first time one of their compatriots from the Rocky

Mountain District. At that time the Rocky Mountain District, the largest in area in the Society, was made up of the present Rocky Mountain District and the Inter Mountain District.

A reorganization of some of the operating procedures of the Society was effected early in the year. It can be assumed that these proved beneficial since they have been continued to the present day. These changes included the separation of Program Committees from Administrative Committees with the result that their duties were more clearly defined and better performed. An Associate Editor was named to the Magazine Staff and this additional attention to the Magazine permitted the Editor to give more time to his other duties as Executive Secretary of the Society. An Editorial Board was named to select material appearing in this publication. The regular column on Genealogical Inquiries appeared for the first time in the Magazine during this administration.

A Special Project Committee was named and suggestions and programs having to do with the future growth of the Society were solicited from all compatriots. Prizes of U. S. Savings Bonds were awarded as a personal contribution from the President General.

During this administration tentative arrangements were made for the first S.A.R. Award to any of the Service Academies, the Lieutenant General Burton K. Yount Award at the U.S. Air Force Academy. It received final approval of the Society the following year and was presented to the winning Cadet for the first time in 1959 by Past President General Tarbox at the request of President General Wentworth, during the Individual Awards Ceremonies held at the first graduation exercises of the Academy, and again at the request of President General Jones, during the graduation in 1960.

Past President General Allene Wilson Groves of the Daughters of the American Revolution offered to the Society an annual Americanism Award which was gratefully accepted and approved during this administration. Rules governing the Gold Good Citizenship Medal Award were formulated and approved during this administrative year.

Approval was made of the S.A.R. matched sets of cuff links and tie bar for sale to compatriots.

The President General, with the assistance of the Executive Secretary, was able to secure splendid publicity for the Society with an article entitled "The Valiant Men of the Sons of the American Revolution", which appeared in the pages of the AMERICAN MERCURY in its issue of May, 1958.

The President General at ceremonies in the Rhode Island Historical Society rooms at Providence, Rhode Island accepted for the National Society a very handsome silver punch set as a gift from Mrs. Eloise Brown McCrillis in memory of her late husband, Arthur M. McCrillis, who served as President General in 1933 - 1934.

During this year the President General made the principal address at meetings throughout the country in more than thirty States. These were meetings of our State Societies, except for two and these two were the largest Chapters in the National Society. These visits included the first National S.A.R. Day, a special day set aside for the Society at the Festival celebrating the 350th Anniversary of the Founding of Jamestown; a special meeting of the Alabama Society at the Kate Duncan Smith D.A.R. School at Grant, Alabama; the Florida S.A.R. State Conference at Sarasota; the laying of a wreath on the grave of Andrew Jackson at the Hermitage; the laying of a wreath at the statue of George Washington on the anniversary of his birth at Portland, Oregon; the acceptance by the President General of the presentation to the Society of Compatriot Olzendam's "Declaration Of An American Citizen" and the dedication to the President General of Ralph Chaplin's poem, "Republic of Vigilant Freeman", at Seattle; and a combined meeting of twenty-three Patriotic Societies at Los Angeles, honored by the presence of the then Governor Goodwin Knight, and messages from Vice President Richard M. Nixon and other prominent Americans.

An accomplishment of lasting worth to the Society during this administration was the completion of the sale of the old Headquarters Building at 1227 16th Street, N.W. in Washington and the purchase of the present National Headquarters at 2412 Massachusetts Avenue, N.W. This transaction, before it was finally consummated entailed much planning and occupied much of the time of the President General, the Executive Secretary, members of the Headquarters Committee, and also of the delegates to a Special Congress which it became necessary to convene at Washington in February, 1958. (See the chapter about the S.A.R. building)

After purchasing this property the Society emerged without indebtednes of any kind and at the end of President General Tarbox's term found itself in the best financial position ever held in its entire history up to that time.

The administration of 1957-1958 was a very busy one for the general officers, the Headquarters Staff, the Trustees and for every working member of the Society. It is generally believed that the Society became stronger and grew in its ability to better serve America.

President General Tarbox's administration closed with the 68th Annual Congress at Biloxi, Mississippi, May 12-14, 1958. This was the first Congress ever held in Mississippi.

At Biloxi the Douglas G. High Historical Oration Contest was held for the first time in conjunction with Recognition Night and fitted in so well that it has been the outstanding feature of the opening night of every succeeding Congress.

It developed at the Congress held at Biloxi that Compatriot John St. Paul, Jr., the then President of the Louisiana Society, had devised a "Medal of Appreciation"* for the

---

*The Louisiana Society Sons of the American Revolution, John St. Paul, Jr., President, presented medals of appreciation as follows:

October 22, 1957, Mrs. Herbert C. Parker and Mrs. Robert J. Kuhn, both members of the "Spirit of '76" Chapter, Daughters of the American Revolution, New Orleans.

November 12, 1958, Mrs. Frederic A. Groves (Allene Wilson Groves), President General of the Daughters of the American Revolution, from Cape Girardeau, Missouri, and Mrs. Henry L. Mayer, Galvez Chapter D.A.R., Lafayette, Louisiana. For the occasion of the presentation of the Louisiana medals to Mrs. Groves and Mrs. Mayer, Executive Secretary Harold L. Putnam flew from Washington to make the presentation.

November 19, 1959, Mrs. John S. Weitz, Calcasieu Chapter, D.A.R., Lake Charles, Louisiana.

1960, Mrs. James L. Dudding, Avoyelles Chapter D.A.R., Bunkie, Louisiana.

Louisiana Society to award to those members of the Daughters of the American Revolution who were of conspicuous help to the Sons of the American Revolution in obtaining members. The Louisiana Society had arranged with J. E. Caldwell Company to produce an appropriate Medal for the uses of the Louisiana Society, and it had presented severaly to D.A.R. members. The National Congress then adopted the "Medal of Appreciation" for the use of the National Society. It also authorized state societies to make such awards to members of the Daughters of the American Revolution who rendered particular assistance to the State Society.

THE ADMINISTRATION OF WALTER A. WENTWORTH,

1958 - 1959

On May 14th, 1958 at the 68th Annual Congress held in the Buena Vista Hotel, Biloxi, Mississippi, Walter Allerton Wentworth of Frankfort, Kentucky was elected President General.

The new headquarters having been purchased in the early spring of 1958, one of the first responsibilities of the President General was to arrange for its preparation for use by the National Society. The Trustees had recommended and the 68th Annual Congress approved the expenditure of $60,000 for rehabilitating and modernizing the building, including the installation of an elevator and complete air-conditioning.

A committee of compatriots of the area who were familiar with the Society and its needs and with construction work in the city of Washington was appointed. The compatriots named were: Col. Robert P. Waters of Falls Church, Va., Chairman; Allan B. Hobbes of Arlington, Va.; J. Maynard Magruder of Arlington, Va.; Charles M. Marsteller of Kensington, Md.; William P. Parramore of Arlington, Va.; Harold L. Putnam, Executive Secretary, Washington, D. C.

The committee received bids from local contractors and awarded the contract to Harry W. Goff of Washington, D.C. He proceeded with the work capably and speedily and the house was ready for occupancy in two and one-half months. The Society moved in during the week of August 18th, 1958.

The regular fall meeting of the Trustees was held in the new headquarters on October 4th, 1958, which was followed with an open house and reception that evening.

The first presentation of the Medal of Appreciation by the National Society was made to Mrs. Virginia L. Kagy on October 4, 1958, for twenty-eight years of service to the Society, first as assistant to the Secretary-Registrar General and later as Executive Assistant.

The total cost of the improvements, including some approved landscaping, was $60,127. This left a balance $68,712. on hand from the sale of the previous headquarters. That amount was transferred to the Permanent Fund, which than was $13,000. and a sufficient amount was added from the General Fund to bring the Permanent Fund's total to $85.000.

During Compatriot Wentworth's term as President General, meetings and conferences with State Societies and Chapters were attended in seventeen States and the District of Columbia. One trip to the South and Southeast included Nashville, Jacksonville, Birmingham, New Orleans, St. Petersburg, Tallahassee, Albany (Ga.), and Atlanta. One trip to the West included Phoenix, San Diego, Pasadena, San Francisco, Portland and Salt Lake City. Other meetings attended were held in Massachusetts, New York, West Virginia, Kentucky, South Carolina, Ohio, Illinois and Minnesota.

Each of these meetings and conferences were well attended by compatriots of the area and it is believed that they contributed to the general development of the Sons of the American Revolution.

On February 21, 1959 the Medal of Appreciation was presented to Mrs. George E. Tarbox, Jr., the wife of Past President General Tarbox, for her activities as a D.A.R. member in assisting in enrolling members for the Sons of the American Revolution.

As is customary the greetings of the SAR were extended to the National Society of the DAR at its Continental Congress and to several other patriotic and hereditary societies at their meetings.

A resolution adopted by the 68th Annual Congress directed the President General to appoint a Committee on Amendments to the Constitution and By-Laws, directing that these be brought to a more modern status. The committee selected was made up of the following Compatriots: Chairman, Aaron M. Sargent of California; Harry T. Burn of Tennessee; Arthur A. de la Houssaye of Louisiana; Stanley S. Gillam of Minnesota and Walter Giles Parker of Maryland.

The Committee's recommendations which were adopted by the 69th Annual Congress at Pittsburgh, were as follows:

    1. Made ex-officio members of the Executive Committee; the President General, the Secretary General, the Treasurer General and the Chancellor General. The Executive Committee membership remains at nine and the President General has the authority to appoint the remaining five, subject to the approval of the Trustees.

    2. Authorized the telephone conference method of conducting meetings of the Executive Committee.

    3. Expanded the right of the Trustees to vote by mail in certain instances.

    4. Added to the duties of the Vice Presidents General.

    5. Created and defined the duties of a Permanent Fund Committee and provided for controls of the Society's securities and negotiable assets.

    6. Established procedure for reactivating State Societies when needed.

    7. Made several technical changes, such as: to legally identify the Constitution with the Charter and establish uniformity therewith, revise election procedure, reduce the number of committees required by the By-Laws, create uniformity in the amending provisions of the Constitution and of the By-Laws, define legal notice of meetings, authorize the Executive Committee to determine by a two-thirds vote the existence of disability of the President General, and clarify provisions relative to delegates to, and quorum at a Congress.

A recommendation to create an office of President General elect was not approved by the Congress.

At the 69th Congress these actions were taken:

Adopted rules governing the Gold Good Citizenship Medal Award and for the selection of the annual winner of the Allene Wilson Groves Americanism Award; and made arrangements governing the selection of a recipient for the Air Force Academy Award. (The first award was in June 1959).

Appointed a committee to investigate the possibility and desirability of providing similar awards at the U.S. Military Academy, the U.S. Naval Academy and the U.S. Coast Guard Academy. (These developed later and the first awards were made at the Naval and Coast Guard Academies in June 1960).

Accepted administration of the Edwin S. Graham Trophy, the gift of Compatriot Arthur G. Trimble of Pennsylvania, for recognition of the winners of the annual Douglass G. High Historical Oration Contests.

The Congress awarded the Society's Constructive Citizenship Medal to President General Allene Wilson Groves of the National Society, Daughters of the American Revolution and it was presented to her from the platform of the Continental Congress of that Society.

The 69th Congress gave consideration to the division of the Rocky Mountain District because of its size and resultant difficulty of being adequately served by one Vice-President General. A committee of former Vice-Presidents General of the District was appointed to study and report a solution. (As a result the 70th Annual Congress amended the By-Laws creating the two districts from this great area).

A committee was appointed to study the feasibility of a retirement program for the members of the staff of the National Society. Its recommendations were put into effect by the 70th Congress.

The committee on Revolutionary Graves, under the Chairmanship of Reginald H. Runge and twenty-seven state chairmen, recorded 4,250 graves of Revolutionary soldiers. This brought the total to 9,315 located in 34 states, the District of Columbia, Canada and China.

Two SAR-DAR tablets on the Gateway Center Building in Pittsburgh were dedicated during the 69th Annual Congress. These tablets, provided by the Equitable Life Assurance Society of America, commemorate the defeat of the French and Indians at this site, Ft. Duquesne. They do honor to Col. George Washington, Col. Henry Bouquet, Gen. John Forbes and Gen. John Armstrong.

So many contests and so prolonged debate took place at the last business session of the Congress that time for the annual banquet had almost arrived before the business session could be adjourned. A feature of the nominating speeches was a telegram from United States Senator John W. Bricker, a compatriot, strongly commending the record of Mr. Jones.

At the conclusion of the 69th Congress Charles A. Jones was elected President General.

The Administration of Charles A. Jones, 1959 - 1960

Immediately following his election at Pittsburgh, President General Jones appointed as members of his Executive Committee:

Dr. Charles A. Anderson, Warren, Ohio; Horace Y. Kitchell, Greenwood, Mississippi; Stephen C. Luce, Massachusetts; Walter A. Wentworth. Serving with this Committee Ex Officio were the President General; Robert P. Gordon, Secretary General; Calvin C. Bolles, Treasurer General; and Folks Huxford, Chancellor General.

The President General spent a very active year visiting states societies and local chapters wherever possible. Soon after his election he participated in the Memorial Day exercises at the famous "Altar of the Pines" in New Hampshire, where he placed a wreath in behalf of the Society and met with officers of all the New England state societies save one. During the ensuing months he travelled approximately 25,000 miles, visiting twenty-two states: Alabama, Colorado, Connecticut, Florida, Georgia, Illinois, Indiana, Kentucky, Massachusetts, Minnesota, Mississippi, New Jersey, Ohio, Oklahoma, Pennsylvania, Rhode Island, South Carolina, Tennessee, Texas, Washington, and West Virginia. In most of these states, he attended the annual meeting of the Society; in others he met with groups of compatriots or with chapters as seemed best to officers of the State Societies. In several states he visited more than one Chapter.

This being the 70th year of S.A.R. history, the President General took occasion to contrast the national situation in 1889, the year our Society was formed, with that of a hundred years previously when the nation began with the inauguration of George Washington as President. He emphasized that the developments of this century brought to the founders of our Society, as they look backward, a more complete realization of the fact that our Revolutionary forefathers had achieved something more worth preserving in our world than just liberty; this achievement has been accentuated in these additional seventy years.

The President General in every address emphasized the necessity of patriots, however tired they may become of discusing the theme, keeping keenly alive to the grave danger free countries are facing from the "Permanent Warfare" policy underlying the Communist movement in the world. Quoting Ex-President Hoover's statement to the effect that communism is infiltrating into every form of our government, national, state and local. And that patriots must be continually on guard to understand the forces they must combat; and not be misled by policies, which, from the American viewpoint, are difficult to comprehend. He pointed out that patriots face the difficulty that the American people are complacent and do not like long-continued emphasis on a subject of this character, and that many are disposed to consider as fanatics citizens who do place emphasis on continual watchfulness.

As the Society's representative, the President General cultivated relationships with other patriotic societies. He brought greetings to the National Congresses of the Daughters and Children of the American Revolution. In the fall, he and Mrs. Jones were guests of a special dinner in Washington honoring Mrs. John W. Finger, senior National President of the C.A.R. This was the first dinner at which were present the chief officers of the three societies: S.A.R., D.A.R. and C.A.R.

To President General Jones, as to others in this high office, the membership situation in our Society posed a challenge of supreme importance. In a ten year period the membership had stood almost unchanged. Compatriot Jones' first act was to send a personal letter to the President of each State Society emphasizing this situation and giving comparative figures for the particular state. Shortly thereafter the elected Historian General, Compatriot John E. Dickinson, accepted the chairmanship of the Membership Committee and gave vigorous and devoted service to the cause in the ensuing months. He prepared at his own expense an attractive brochure and other materials, which, under his leadership, turned the trend upward.

Criticism arose from members of the short time allowed for consideration of proposed resolutions under the rules which brought both the resolutions and the annual election on the Annual Congress program at its closing business session, Wednesday morning, led the President General to propose a revision of our procedures. (At the Pittsburgh Congress the final business session had lasted until 4:25 P.M.) The changes were approved by the trustees for submission to the Congress which, after a fairly strenuous debate, adopted the changes providing that:

(1) Delegates might be registered until ten o'clock on Wednesday morning. (Many favored closing registration on Tuesday afternoon).

(2) Nominations for National Officers should be made on Tuesday morning, balloting to begin at 2 P.M. and continue until 5 P.M., then on Wednesday morning starting at 9 A.M. and closing at 12 P.M. under supervision of the Credentials Committee.

(3) Uncontested nominees s h o u l d be declared elected on the closing of nominations.

The new rules provided for a much more satisfactory balloting situation. Only a few delegates remained to vote Wednesday morning and the final ballot was cast at ten o'clock. As a result the Credentials Committee unanimously recommended that the procedure be continued in future years, and in 1961 the trustees recommended continuance to the Annual Congress.

Early in the year distinguished President General Messmore Kendal passed to his reward, leaving to our Society in his will a ring certified as having been the property of General Washington, on condition that the principles he enunciated in his famous Farewell Address should be formulated into a ritual for the installation of each new President General. The Trustees took prompt action to comply with the terms of the bequest. Past President General de. la Houssaye, at the request of the Trustees, confected a special installation ceremony, and the ring came into possession of the Society. On the closing evening at Memphis, President General Jones was the first of our chief officers to wear this distinguished memento.

Among other developments of the year were the following:
1. Division of the former Rocky Mountain District into two districts.
    (a) Section 1 Rocky Mountain District: Arizona, Colorado, New Mexico;
    (b) Inter Mountain District: Idaho, Montana, Utah and Wyoming.
2. Presentation of annual awards to chosen representatives of the military, naval, air force, and coast guard academies.
3. Adoption of a retirement plan for the employees in National Headquarters.
4. Continuation of improvements of the National Headquarters and adoption of a special arrangement under which flags fly every day in front of the headquarters.

Twenty-two resolutions having been adopted at the Pittsburgh Congress, special effort was made to enlist the active support of the Societies throughout the country in their implementations. New rules at the Memphis Congress provided that no proposed resolutions might be recieved after four o'clock on Monday and that the Resolutions Committee should present its report in mimeographed form so delegates might have copies early Wednesday evening. This procedure, together with the amended proceedings changing election procedures, gave most of Wednesday to consideration of the suggested resolutions, thereby reducing criticism of hurried action.

249 delegates were registered at the 70th Annual Congress held in Memphis, Tennessee, at the Hotel Peabody, May 15-18, 1960. Impressive memorial services were held on Sunday afternoon at the Idlewild Presbyterian Church. At luncheon on Monday the speaker was Mr. Ross W. Dyer, administrative assistant to Governor Ellington who was unable to be present. A trip on the Mississippi river was provided for the afternoon, followed in the evening by the Douglass G. High Oratorial Contest and the "Recognition Night Ceremonies".

Mr. Jack Carley, associate editor of the Memphis Commercial Appeal was speaker at the Tuesday luncheon, and the dinner speaker that evening was Dr. Athens Clay Pullias, president of David Lipscomb College, Nashville. The principal speaker at the Wednesday evening banquet was Admiral Felix B. Stump (USA retired), vice-chairman and chief executive officer, Freedom Foundation at Valley Forge.

Mrs. Ashmead White, President General of the Daughters of the American Revolution, honored the Society by attending all the sessions of the Congress.

The election of President General was a close contest between Compatriot Herschel S. Murphy of New Jersey and Compatriot John E. Dickinson of Wisconsin, Dr. Murphy winning by a vote of 128 to 118.

At the President General's dinner on Wednesday, May 18, 1960, Dr. Herschel S. Murphy was inducted as President in the ceremony using George Washington's signet ring. President General Charles A. Jones placed the ring on Dr. Murphy's finger and they went through the ring ceremony together.

The Administration of Herschel S. Murphy, M.D.,
1960 - 1961

After the Memphis Congress was over, Dr. and Mrs. Murphy went to Florida where he inspected accommodations and facilities for holding the May, 1961 Congress at Sarasota and Clearwater. Colonel Herbert C. Roberts, who extended the invitation for the Society to come to Florida, worked with the Doctor on the matter and tentative reservations were made with the Jack Tar Harrison Hotel in Clearwater. Later, during the summer, Executive Secretary Putnam went to Clearwater and made final arrangements for the Congress.

Early in July, President General Murphy attended a meeting of the Virginia Society where a fifty star Flag was presented at Mt. Vernon to the Virginia Society. At a dinner that night in Alexandria, Mrs. Ashmead White, National President General of the Daughters of the American Revolution; Mrs. James H. Summerville, Senior National President, Children of the American Revolution and the President General of the National Society of the Sons of the American Revolution were all present and all brought greetings.

During the year President General Murphy visited the Connecticut Society at East Hadden; the Vermont Society at Burlington; the New Jersey Society at Westfield; the New York Society at Schenectady; the Tennessee Society at Nashville; the Kentucky Society at Lexington; the Nebraska Society at Omaha; the Kansas Society at Kansas City, Kansas; the Missouri Society at St. Louis, where the Missouri Society was re-established by the election of new officers after a lapse of a couple of years. After Thanksgiving the President General and Mrs. Murphy visited the Indiana Society at a meeting in South Bend; the Illinois Society at Chicago and the Minnesota Society at Minneapolis-St. Paul.

In February, 1961, the President General visited and spoke to the Valley Forge Chapter of the Pennyslvania Society; and on February 22nd, he spoke to the District of Columbia Society. On March 17th, he attended a meeting of the Massachusetts Society and the New England Council in Boston. Early in April, he paid an official visit to the Delaware Society. At all of these meetings a forum, or workshop was held in the afternoon, based on getting new members and new chapters and at the evening meetings, the President General usually spoke on "The Program and Activities of the National Society of the Sons of the American Revolution".

These visits stimulated local interest in new members and in new Chapters and the results seem to show that where the wives attended with their husbands, the meetings were the most successful ones.

In the middle of April, Dr. Murphy spent a week in Washington where he attended and brought greetings to the Colonial Dames of the 17th Century, the National Daughters of the American Revolution, the National Society of the Children of the American Revolution, and the National Huguenot Society.

At the begnining of his administration, President General Murphy suggested several projects for a long-range program and made plans for a short-range program to be completed during his year. Under the long-range program a Memorial Auditorium-Library building is planned to be built next door to our Headquarters on Massachusetts Avenue in Washington. Plans were made to revise the membership kit so that there might be a continuing program of enlistment of new members as well as of establishing new chapters in the various States.

The President General worked with the Membership Committee in improving and streamlining our membership kit and drew up for them a leaflet "Ways To Help An S.A.R. Applicant Prepare His Application Papers". This was printed on page 33 of the January, 1961, S.A.R. Magazine.

At the October Trustees meeting a Library Reserve Fund of $5,000 was set up to be expended over the next several years for binding applications and the rebinding of old genealogical books. During this year, almost $2,000 was raised by donations for the book binding campaign under the able leadership of Librarian General S. W. Walker. A complete set of one hundred sixty-six D.A.R. Lineage books was offered for sale to the Society. This permanently-bound set of lineage books, in excellent condition, was bought for a little over Five Hundred Dollars.

Work was started on developing a new certificate of membership of smaller size for future use.

At the October, as well as the February meeting, discussion was given to the publishing of a history of our National Society. Historian General John St. Paul, Jr.'s efforts to gather material for this history were approved.

At the October Trustees meeting, Vice-President General Laurens Hamilton of the South Atlantic District, presented to our National Headquarters an oil painting of Compatriot President Dwight D. Eisenhower, which was accepted with thanks.

During the year changes were made in the format of our National Magazine and a column of "Letters to the Editor" planned for the coming year, also some short historical sketches of outstanding Americans.

Mrs. Tennie Burk retired the first of January, 1961. At the Trustees meeting on February 11, 1961, she was given a medal of appreciation by the Society in recognition of fourteen years of service as Staff Genealogist.

During this year, John E. Diciknson, of Milwaukee, passed away, as well as Past President General Benjamin H. Powell of Texas, and Mrs. Frank Steele, widow of our former Secretary-Registrar.

During President General Murphy's administration a substantial number of new chapters were established in the various States and a very successful membership drive was conducted.

At the Seventy-first (71st) Annual Congress, held in Clearwater, Florida, on May 8th through 10th, 1961, two hundred twenty-four delegates attended and one hundred fifty-eight guests.

At 8:00 P.M., Monday, Recognition Night and the Douglas C. High Oration Contest events were held in the hotel ballroom.

In the oratorial contest, James Leitz of Louisville, Ohio was awarded first prize for his oration on the subject of "Unity". Second prize went to Christopher Rores of New York, and third prize to Charles Rush, of Chattanooga, Tennessee. The contest was outstanding with nine boys as contestants from as many states.

Minute Men Awards were conferred upon Horace Y. Kitchell of Mississippi, Calvin C. Bolles of Connecticut, John St. Paul, Jr., of Louisiana, and Dr. Harold I. Meyer of Illinois for their outstanding service to the National Society during the past year.

Among the speakers were Dr. Kenneth Chorley, who spoke on "Washington and Williamsburg", and H. T. Shulenberger, of Miami who gave a humorous talk about "The Architects of History."

Compatriot Horace Y. Kitchell was elected President General by acclamation on Tuesday Morning.

On Wednesday the 10th, 1961 at 8:00 P.M., a meeting of the National Trustees was called to order by President General Kitchell, where the appointnment of the Executive Committee by the President General was confirmed.

Historian General St. Paul reported on the status of the History of the National Society he had been compiling. He introduced Compatriot Stuart O. Landry of New Orleans who offered two proposals for the printing and sale of the History when completed.

On motion duly made, seconded and carried the Trustees accepted proposal number two which provided for a ten (10%) per cent royalty payment to the National Society on each volume sold and involved no financial obligations on the part of the National Society.

On Wednesday night was held the President General's banquet.

The speaker was Dr. George S. Benson, President of Harding College, noted for his support of American traditions and ideals. He gave an inspiring address entitled "Our American Heritage".

Following this address, the George Washington Ring Ritual Installation Ceremony took place, in which the ring of General George Washington was transferred by Past President General Murphy to the finger of Compatriot Horace Y. Kitchell, the newly elected President General.

THE ADMINISTRATION OF HORACE Y. KITCHELL, 1961-1962

During the administration of President General Horace Y. Kitchell, Compatriot Donald Snider, National Trustee from the Louisiana Society of the Sons of the American Revolution, developed the idea of encouraging patriotism in our Country through the great medium of advertising.

He conceived a billboard campaign of extraordinary scope at small expense.

The secret weapon he had was the knowledge that there was a period when each of the thousands of billboards in this Country was vacant between one advertisement and the next; and the knowledge that the billboard industry was most charitable and patriotic; and that they permitted any reputable charitable or patriotic organization to use these billboards for the period of its vacancy without any cost other than the furnishing of appropriate posters.

Mr. Snider thereupon drew the design for a poster, a representation of which graced the front page of the January, 1962, issue of the Magazine, and coupled with the design the motto "KEEP U.S.A. FIRST."

The executive committee of the National Society and the Board of Trustees adopted the idea for use as a nationwide continuous campaign to encourage in the American public a resurgence of patriotism.

Past President General Arthur A. de la Houssaye was appointed National Chairman of the "KEEP U.S.A. FIRST" Committee by President General Kitchell.

The design was also produced for use in streetcars, busses, automobile windshields, store windows, office doors and as miniature replicas of billboard panels to place on desks and counters.

On June 6th, 1961, President General Kitchell and Mrs. Kitchell experienced one of the most exciting and colorful days of their lives. In the company of Admiral William R. Furlong and Col. Robert P. Waters they drove to Annapolis to witness the Naval Academy Awards Day and watch Admiral Furlong present the S.A.R. achievement prize, this year a very fine watch, to Midshipman Gary Gilbert Herzberg.

During the year President General Kitchell and Mrs. Kitchell visited Birmingham, Alabama and Indianapolis, Indiana. At Denver, President General and Mrs. Kitchell were the honored guests at the Constitution Day dinner of the Colorado Society.

At Pocatello, Idaho, a special meeting of the Idaho Society was held on September 12, 1961, to greet President General Kitchell and Mrs. Kitchell. The buffet dinner meeting was attended also by members of Wyeth chapter, Idaho, D.A.R., and a message of greeting was delivered by Mrs. Harly Mathisen, of Nampa, representative of the state regent, Idaho, Daughters of the American Revolution. Following an interesting program of folk songs by a trio of high school girls, Compatriot Kitchell delivered an inspiring message.

At Salt Lake City, plan to return to basic Americanism was voiced by President General Kitchell in his address before the annual dinner meeting of the Utah Society, September 14, 1961. President General and Mrs. Kitchell met the governor George D. Clyde and President David C. McKay of the Latter Day Saints Church.

From here President General and his wife flew by jet to Boston to attend the New England Conference, and then back again to Utah to pick up their car and continue their journey. At Reno they attended a banquet on September 21, with compatriots of the Nevada Society and the Nevada Society, Daughters of the American Revolution.

In California, President General Kitchell and Mrs. Kitchell were the guests of the California Society at five gatherings in various parts of the state—Oakland, San Francisco, Los Angeles, Pasadena and San Diego.

Heading east, the President General visited Phoenix, Arizona. Then to Albuquerque to a dinner meeting of the New Mexico Society on October 10, 1961.

From there President General Kitchell flew to Washington for the meeting of the Executive Board and Trustees. While there, he was the guest of the District of Columbia Society at an evening meeting October 17, 1961, at the Cosmos Club.

In Tulsa, President General Kitchell presented a gold Medal of Appreciation to Mrs. Harold J. Hepp, regent of the Bartlesville chapter of the Daughters of the American Revolution, for her successful efforts in the organization of a new Sons of the American Revolution chapter in Bartlesville. A delegation of the newly formed S.A.R. Bartlesville chapter was present with their president, William F. Logue, and the secretary Darall Hawk.

The fall meeting of the Kansas Society was held jointly with the Kansas Society Daughters of the American Revolution, at Fort Leavenworth, Kansas, on October 30, 1961.

Seven Army staff officers, composing the board of governors from the Fort Leavenworth Historical Museum, were present at the luncheon which they sponsored. Honor guest and speaker at the meeting was President General Horace Y. Kitchell.

With 18,000 miles of strenuous travel behind them, President General Kitchell and Mrs. Kitchell arrived in St. Louis, Missouri, to attend a dinner meeting of the Missouri Society. He was the principal speaker. Compatriot William S. Cordry, president of the St. Louis chapter, presided. Other honored guests included past president general Allen Oliver, and Mrs. F. S. Haeberle, vice regent, D.A.R., St. Louis chapter. Later, to Chattanooga, to attend the annual convention of Tennessee Society on November 4, 1961.

President General Kitchell and Mrs. Kitchell were guests of honor at the 68th annual dinner meeting of the Louisiana Society, held November 16, 1961, at the New Orleans Country Club. It was on this occasion that the President General officially unveiled the "KEEP U.S.A. FIRST" billboard poster.

On December 3rd, President General and Mrs. Kitchell reported to the Freedoms Foundation at Valley Forge where President General Kitchell served through the Seventh, on the Awards Jury representing the Sons of the American Revolution.

On the night of December 7th, the President General and his wife flew to Chicago for the meeting of the Illinois Society. President General Kitchell was the speaker of the evening at the dinner given by the Illinois Society on December 8, 1961, at the Union League Club in Chicago. He spoke on "The American Heritage—Or why I am Proud to Be a Member of the Sons of the American Revolution."

After visiting Milwaukee, from there President General and Mrs. Kitchell went to Detroit, where he presented Compatroit Frank Lowmaster with the Minute Man Award that he was to ill to receive at Clearwater, Florida.

The 72nd Congress was held at Philadelphia, Pa., from May 27th to 30th, at which President General Kitchell presided. In his report to the membership he stated that he had travelled some 50,000 miles on behalf of the Society. At the Congress there were 299 elected delegates and a total registration of 504 including guests. Dr. Charles A. Anderson of Warren, Ohio was elected President General.

VII
THE FRUITFUL YEARS

(In compliance with the request of the editors of the history of our Society, I have endeavored to review some of the salient features of the past twelve years during which time I have served as Executive Secretary of the National Society—Harold L. Putnam)

Perhaps the first development which led to my appointment to the office I have held since 1950 was the presentation of the report of the Americanization Committee (now known as the Americanism and American Sovereignty Committee), made at the Annual Congress held in Jacksonville, Florida, in May 1949. The Committee, composed of Aaron M. Sargent, Wheaton H. Brewer and the writer, reported the results of a detailed study of the degree of infiltration of radical and ultra-liberal teaching methods and materials in the public schools of our Nation. These findings had been filed in the form of a petition for the redress of grievances (entitled "A Bill of Grievances"), with both Houses of Congress of the United States by the Committee just prior to the convening of the Annual Congress of our Society.

The report of the Committee was received with enthusiasm by the delegates, and there was a demand for copies of the now famous document. When it was pointed out that the printing and mailing would entail a substantial sum, the delegates pledged some $6,400.00 on the floor of the Congress to defray the costs of printing and distributing the petition.

This event marked the turning point in the history of our Society. From that day forth, the Society became a more militant patriotic organization.

One year later, at the Sixtieth Annual Congress in Atlantic City, New Jersey, the delegates voted overwhelmingly to adopt the amendments to the Constitution and By-laws which created the office of Executive Secretary and defined his duties and powers. At the same meeting, the President General, Wallace C. Hall, and the Secretary General, Edgar Williamson, Jr., were authorized to borrow a sum not to exceed $25,000.00 for the purpose of making urgently needed repairs and improvements to the Headquarters Building, and to initiate a program of microfilming the application papers on file.

There were numerous changes made in the operation of our National Headquarters resulting from the amendments to the Constitution and By-laws. It must be fairly stated that there was increased efficiency of operation, and the readjustments were accomplished wtihout serious difficulty. The retirement of Compatriot Frank B. Steele was the cause of sincere regret on the part of hundreds of Compatriots, who had acquired a genuine affection for him during his many years of service to the Society. The newly appointed Executive Secretary, who replaced him as the administrative officer of the Society, was faced with the difficult task of establishing cordial relationships with many of the veteran officers of the state and chapter organizations.

The most dificult task faced by the Executive Secretary was that of implementing plans to rehabilitate the National Headquarters. In order to eliminate the loss of time and the resultant stagnation which would develop if the operations were suspended during the work on the building, it was determined to carry on "business as usual." Despite the physical discomfort suffered by the Headquarters staff, operations were conducted in the midst of plaster dust, dirt and the sound of saws and hammers. The task, as far as the building itself was concerned, was completed in January 1951, and the event was celebrated by a brilliant reception attended by National officers and representatives of the various patriotic societies.

A near tragedy occurred at 3:00 A.M. on February 6, 1951, when a fire originated in the partially completed building abutting our Headquarters. The flames swept up the north side of the building, and it was only by fortuitous circumstances that the Executive Secretary and Mrs. Putnam were awakened in time to save themselves and prevent the destruction of the Headquarters and its contents. Prompt action by the fire department prevented serious damage to the structure itself, but broken windows and smoke damage to walls and furnishings amounted to more than $10,000.00 in claims paid by the insurance carriers.

The prompt settlement of claims by the insurance carriers enabled the Executive Committee and the Executive Secretary to undertake the task of redecorating the building. The work did not require as much time as was the case in the original rehabilitation program. Upon completion, the National Headquarters was in excellent condition, and visiting Compatriots expressed a justifiable pride in the building, furnishings and added equipment.

One of the most significant features of the Sixty-first Annual Congress, held in San Francisco, California, was the presentation of the first gold Constructive Citizenship Medal, which was awarded to Fulton Lewis, Jr., in recognition of his relentless fight against the radical-communist propaganda which was infecting our Nation. The presentation ceremony was broadcast over the Mutual Broadcasting network. Numerous requests for information regarding membership in the Society were received during the weeks immediately following the broadcast.

The Sixty-second Annual Congress in Houston, Texas, will be long remembered as the occasion which marked the first presentation of a new award, the Minute Man Award, given by the National Society to Compatriots who had rendered exceptional and invaluable service to the Society. The ceremonies were held, fittingly enough, on the grounds of the San Jacinto battlefield. Twenty-six Compatriots who had records of distinguished service to the National Society were honored in this first awards ceremony. The Minute Man Award has since become the most valuable and highly prized award in the entire list of awards, and now the recipients are recognized by their fellow Compatriots as members of an elite corps of patriots.

Until 1953, the Society consisted of an organization of state societies in each of the states (plus District of Columbia and France) with the exceptions of Alaska and Nevada. The Alaska Society was organized in October of 1953, with offices in Anchorage.

On November 17, 1955, the officers of the newly organized Nevada Society were installed in an impressive ceremony held at the Prospector's Club in Reno. The Executive Secretary and Mrs. Putnam were the guests of honor, and the installation and presentation of the charter were performed by the Executive Secretary. The visit to Nevada was part of an extensive tour of the state and chapter organizations made by the Executive Secretary and his wife. During the trip, units of the Society were visited in fourteen states. The schedule comprised forty-two meetings within a period of six weeks. Several new chapters were organized in places visited during the tour. With the organization of the Nevada Society, the National Society became a "National" Society in fact as well as in name, with a total of 52 state societies, the District of Columbia and the Society in France accounting for the additional units.

For the first time in the history of the National Society, a handbook of information was made available to officers and members of state and chapter organizations. The handbook met with a most favorable reception, and several thousand of the first edition were sold. The first edition was published in 1956, and a second and somewhat revised edition was published in 1961. The revised edition contained changes which were based on experience derived from actual use of the handbook in the field.·

As a result of the extensive increase in the construction of new buildings in the neighborhood of the Society's National Headquarters, offers to purchase the property were received from a number of potential buyers. In comparison with appraisals made just a matter of a year or two earlier, the initial offer of $185,000.00 seemed attractive. However, the National Trustees, acting upon the recommendation of the Executive Secretary, rejected the offer. Shortly before the Sixty-sixth Annual Congress convened at Bolton Landing, New York, another offer of $250,000.00 was received. Despite the urging of a number of influential Compatriots, this offer was not accepted.

Prospective purchasers of our Society's Headquarters property continued their efforts, and in January, 1957 the offer of $305,000.00 made by the National Education Association was deemed worthy of serious consideration, in view of the fact that it was substantially in excess of the most generous appraisals of the market value. A Special Congress held in Washington, D. C. on February 16, 1957 voted, almost unanimously, to sell the property and to authorize the President General, Eugene P. Carver, Jr., the Secretary General, Charles A. Jones and the Executive Secretary to execute the legal documents necessary to complete the transaction.

A proposal to purchase the Commerical Counselor's building of the Belgian Embassy, at 1780 Massachusetts Avenue, N. W. was defeated by the votes of a majority of the delegates to the Special Congress. It then became necessary for the President General to appoint a Special Headquarters Committee for the purpose of surveying the available properties for purchase by the Society for use as Headquarters. President General Carver appointed R. Adm. William Rea Furlong, USN (ret.), Col. Thurston Baxter and Charles A. Marsteller as members of the Special Headquarters Committee, and later added Glenn M. Goodman and Robert H. Overstreet. The President General and the Executive Secretary were named as Ex Officio members of the Committee.

After inspecting some thirty or more properties, the Special Headquarters Committee unanimously recommended the purchase of the residence of former Secretary of War, Gen. Patrick Hurley, at 2412 Massachusetts Avenue, N. W. for use as the Headquarters of our Society. The delegates to the Sixty-seventh Annual Congress, meeting in Salt Lake City, Utah, on May 28, 1957 approved, after a thorough discussion, the recommendations of the Special Headquarters Committee, and authorized the General Officers to take the necessary steps to purchase the property at 2412 Massachusetss Avenue, N. W., Washington, D. C. for use as the Headquarters of the National Society. In accordance with the action of the Sixty-seventh Annual Congress, steps were taken to acquire the new Headquarters property.

Before completion of the purchase of the site, it was necessary to secure the passage of a special bill by the Congress of the United States, which would authorize the National Society of the Sons of the American Revolution to occupy the building and use it as the Headquarters of the Society. The bill, H.R. 9271, was passed and signed by President Eisenhower on March 18, 1958. The pen used to sign the bill is on display at National Headquarters. The passage of this special piece of legislation was made possible through the combined efforts of a great number of members of our Society, including those who were Members of the United States Congress. If any one individual should be singled out for commendation it is R. Adm. William Rea Furlong, whose tireless efforts in contacting key Members of Congress resulted in the favorable action. His invaluable services to the Society were recognized at the meeting of the National Trustees on October 4, 1958, when a handsome hand-engrossed and emblazoned certificate was presented to him, together with a rising ovation by all present.

One benefit accruing from the sale of the former building and the purchase of the new property was the establishment of a Permanent Fund of $86,000.00 created from the surplus after purchasing and remodeling the new Headquarters. Thus, for the first time in the history of the S. A. R., the National Society was in a strong financial condition. The new building was free and clear of all debt, and substantial operating funds were available in addition to the previously mentioned Permanent Fund.

On the evening of October 4, 1958, the new Headquarters was the scene of a reception to which Past Presidents General, General Officers, National Trustees, and their wives were invited. In addition, officers and members of the District of Columbia, Maryland and Virginia Societies were issued invitations. One of the highlights of the occasion was the first use of the handsome sterling silver service of punch bowl and cups, the gift to the Society of Mrs. Arthur M. McCrillis, widow of Past President General McCrillis.

The task of moving our Headquarters from the building on Sixteenth Street, which had been occupied for nearly thirty years, was an undertaking of sizeable proportions. There was a tremendous accumulation of material of all descriptions, which had to be inspected, evaluated, and the useless items disposed of. There were more than three hundred cartons of books in the library to be packed, labelled, and replaced on the shelves in the new Headquarters. This task imposed a heavy burden on the Librarian General, Robert S. W. Walker, and his assistant, William M. Cain, both of whom spent many hours on numerous weekends in reorganizing the shelves in the new Headquarters. The transportation of furniture and equipment by a commercial moving organization required a full week of strenuous work.

One of the advantages of the new Headquarters is the increased efficiency of operations. The rearrangement of offices provided vastly improved working conditions for the Headquarters staff. The installation of central air conditioning has proved to be a profitable investment, as it permits the Headquarters staff to work in comfort during the hot, humid days of July, August and part of September. The elevator which was installed as a part of the remodeling program has long ago demonstrated its value and justified the expenditure.

A development which has been something of a surprise is the totally unexpected growth of the National Society library. When the new building was acquired, a great amount of additional shelf space was installed, and it was believed that provision was being made for many years in the future. That estimate has proved to be too conservative. Constant additions to the library have used all of the available space, and the Librarian General and his assistants have been forced to dispose of some of the material not directly related with the objectives of our Society.

The demands of a growing organization, more and more dependence on National Headquarters, and the requirements for more facilities for the library, have made it obvious that more space must be provided in the near future. With this in mind, the Executive Secretary proposed that consideration be given to the possibilities of constructing a memorial library-auditorium on the vacant property owned by the Society. This proposal was acted on favorably by the National Trustees at the meeting held in St. Louis, Missouri, February 15, 1959. A committee, of which R. Adm. William Rea Furlong is chairman, and which includes Compatriot George Morris Whiteside, Col. Robert P. Waters, the President General and the Executive Secretary, has been working on preliminary plans for the proposed building.

Before definite plans could be prepared, it was necessary to request the Congress of the United State to amend the charter issued in 1906, which placed a limit on the amount of real and personal property the Society might hold. Thanks to the splendid cooperation accorded the Executive Secretary by Compatriots Senator Strom Thurmond of South Carolina, and Senator Samuel J. Ervin, Jr. of North Carolina, a bill entitled S2239 was introduced in the Senate on July 12, 1961. It was passed by the House and signed by the President of the United States on September 8, 1961. This legislation cleared the way, in a legal sense, for making definite plans for the construction of the memorial library-auditorium. Once more, the members of our Society became deeply indebted to Admiral Furlong for his effective assistance in securing prompt and favorable action by the House of Representatives on the bill passed by the Senate.

Any review of the past twelve years would be incomplete and somewhat lacking in accuracy without a tribute to the members of the Headquarters staff, whose unfailing efforts have made possible the progress achieved. Our Society is especially indebted to Mrs. Virginia Kagy, whose loyalty and devotion to the Society has been so thoroughly demonstrated during the past thirty years. It was proper and fitting that the Medal of Appreciation should be presented to Mrs. Kagy at the meeting of the National Trustees in Washington, D. C. on October 4, 1958, and at the same time she was officially named as Executive Assistant.

Another member of the Headquarters staff was honored with the Medal of Appreciation at the meeting of the National Trustees held in Headquarters on February 11, 1961, when Mrs. Tennie Burk received the medal from the hands of President General Herschel S. Murphy, M.D. It was fitting recognition of Mrs. Burk's years of service as Genealogist, and came at the conclusion of her employment and at the beginning of her well earned retirement. Mrs. Burk became the first of the Headquarters staff to benefit by the Retirement Plan, established by the Socity two years earlier.

Viewed in retrospect, the past twelve years have been eventful years, filled with interesting experiences. Changes have been made which have affected the course of the Society, and it is believed that the majority of the changes have been improvements. There has been a marked improvement in the format and the contents of the Sons of the American Revolution Magazine, and additional improvements will be made from time to time.

Now that the Society is in a sound financial condition, the full attention of the officers of the organization can be given to developing plans and programs, such as the "Keep U.S.A. First" campaign, which will enable the Sons of the American Revolution to accomplish the objectives for which the Society was created. Using the past as a foundation upon which to build, we can now erect a strong patriotic Society which can lead the way in protecting the priceless heritage bequeathed us by our forefathers.

VIII

CONSTITUTION OF THE NATIONAL SOCIETY
OF THE
SONS OF THE AMERICAN REVOLUTION

ADOPTED APRIL 30TH, 1890

ARTICLE I NAME

The Name of this Society shall be the:
SONS OF THE AMERICAN REVOLUTION

ARTICLE II OBJECTS

The objects of this Society are, to perpetuate the memory and the spirit of the men who achieved American Independence, by the encouragement of historical research in relation to the Revolution and the publication of its results, the preservation of documents and relics, and of the records of the individual services of Revolutionary soldiers and patriots, and the promotion of celebrations of all patriotic anniversaries; to carry out the injunction of Washington in his farewell address to the American people, "to promote, as an object of primary importance, institutions for the general diffusion of knowledge," thus developing an enlightened public opinion, and affording to young and old such advantages as shall develop in them the largest capacity for performing the duties of American citizens; to cherish, maintain, and extend the institutions of American freedom; to foster true patriotism and love of country; and to aid in securing for mankind all the blessings of liberty.

ARTICLE III MEMBERSHIP

SECTION 1. Any man is eligible for membership, who is of the age of twenty-one years, and who is descended from an ancestor who, with unfailing loyalty, rendered material aid to the cause of American Independence, as a soldier or as a seaman, or a civil officer in one of the several Colonies or States, or of the United Colonies or States, or as a recognized patriot; provided that he shall be found worthy.

SEC. 2. For the purpose of making more nearly perfect the records of our Revolutionary ancestors and their descendants, any woman of Revolutionary ancestry may file a record of her ancestor's services and of her line of descent with any Registrar, who shall send a duplicate to the Registrar-General.

SEC. 3. Any person is eligible for honorary membership subject to the limitations as to age and descent established in the case of active members.

SEC. 4. The National Society shall embrace all the members of the Societies of the SONS OF THE AMERICAN REVOLUTION now existing or which may be established under this Constitution. Such Societies shall regulate all matters relating to their own affairs, shall judge of the qualifications of their members, and of those proposed for membership, subject to the provisions of this Constitution.

ARTICLE IV OFFICERS

SECTION 1. The General Officers of the National Society shall be a President-General, three Honorary Vice-Presidents-General, five Vice-Presidents-General, a Secretary-General, Treasurer-General, Registrar-General, Historian-General, Surgeon-General, and Chaplain-General, who shall be elected by ballot by a vote of the majority of the members present at the annual meeting of the National Society and shall hold office for one year and until their successors shall be elected, and who together with the Presidents of the State Societies, *ex-officio*, shall constitute a general Board of Managers, of which Board seven shall constitute a quorum.

Sec. 2. An Executive Committee of seven, of whom the President-General shall be the Chairman, may be elected by the Board of Managers, which Committee shall, in the interim between the meetings of the Board, transact such business as shall be delegated to it by the Board of Managers.

ARTICLE V Dues

Each State Society shall pay annually to the Treasurer-General twenty-five cents for each active member thereof. All such dues shall be paid on or before the opening of each annual meeting of the National Society, in order to secure representation therein.

ARTICLE VI Meetings and Elections

Section 1. The annual meeting for the election of the General officers and for the transaction of business, shall be held on the 30th day of April or on the first day of May in every year. The time and place of such meeting shall be designated by the Board of Managers.

Sec. 2. Special meetings shall be called by the President-General when directed so to do by the Board of Managers, or whenever requested in writing so to do by twenty five or more members representing at least five State Societies, on giving thirty days' notice specifying the time and place of such meeting and the business to be transacted.

Sec. 3. The following shall be members of all such general or special meetings, and shall be entitled to vote therein:

(1) All the officers, the ex-Presidents-General and the ex-Vice-Presidents-General of the National Society;

(2) The President, and Senior Vice-President of each State Society;

(3) One delegate at large from each State Society;

(4) One delegate for every one hundred members of the Society within a State and for a fraction of fifty or over.

The following named officials shall be Honorary Members of the National Society, provided they are eligible to membership in the Society, but shall not be entitled to vote:

(1) The President, the Vice-President, and the Chief Justice of the United States;

(2) The President of the Senate, the Speaker of the House, the Secretary of War, and the Secretary of the Navy of the United States;

(3) The Governors of the State and Territories of the United States;

AND ALSO the Senior officer of the Army, and the Senior officer of the Navy of the United States.

ARTICLE VII BY-LAWS

The Board of Managers shall have authority to adopt and promulgate the By-Laws of the National Society, to prescribe the duties of the general officers, to provide the seal, and to designate the insignia.

ARTICLE VIII AMENDMENTS

Amendments to this Constitution may be offered at any meeting of the National Society, but shall not be acted on until the next meeting. A copy of every proposed amendment shall be sent to each member, with a notice of the meeting at which the same will be acted upon, at least thirty days prior to said meeting.

A vote of two thirds of those present shall be necessary to its adoption.

This Constitution was signed by Delegates as follows:

Alexander S. Webb, New York	Lewis L. Morgan, Conn.
Lucis P. Deming, Conn.	Horace N. Strong, Conn.
George B. Abbott, Illinois	Ebenezer J. Hill, Conn.
Edwin S. Barrett, Mass.	C. H. McDowell, Indiana
Wm. Henry Arnoux, New York	Albert Edgerton, St. Paul, Minn.
William E. English, Ind.	Henry Hall, Calif.
S. E. Merwin, Conn.	Charles E. Briggs, Mo.
Alfred R. Lightfoot, Ala.	John W. Buchanan, Ky.
John Jackson Hubbell, N.J.	William Lindsay, Ky.
Wilson R. Parsons, Ohio	Luther L. Tarbell, Mass.
Don J. Whittemon, Wis.	C. B. Fairchild, N.J.
W. C. Stamfors, St. Louis, Mo.	Edward A. Hill, Ill.
L. Backus, Columbus, Ohio	Morrill Moores, Ind.
W. H. Brearley, Michigan	J. C. Pumpelly, N.J.
Charles King, Wisconsin	Wm. Francis Cregar, Md.
	Wm. O. McDowell, N.J.

REPORT OF THE SPECIAL COMMITTEE ON THE NATIONAL CHARTER

To The National Society of the Sons of the American Revolution:

At the meeting of the General Board of Managers and Executive Committee, at the Bellevue-Stratford Hotel, Philadelphia, on December 6, 1904, inquiry was made as to whether the Society was legally incorporated and the subject was discussed at some length. A committee was thereupon appointed to consider and report on the incorporation of the National Society.

This Committee reported at the Sixteenth Annual Congress, held at Philadelphia in 1905, that although at two separate times attempts had been made to incorporate the Society under the laws of Connecticut, the proper steps had not been taken in either case, and that we were simply a voluntary association.

It was then voted that a committee of two be appointed to secure incorporation of the Society under the laws of the District of Columbia; that the same committee be instructed to secure a special charter from the Congress of the United States, and we were appointed such committee.

We prepared the proposed act, submitted it to the Board of Managers, and secured their approval of it.

During the first session of the 59th Congress, January 26, 1906, Hon. E. J. Hill, of Connecticut, our compatriot, introduced the bill in the House of Representatives and on February 26, 1906, it passed the House.

May 23, 1906, it passed the Senate, with a slight amendment. June 5, 1906, it passed the House as amended, and on June 9, 1906, was finally approved by the President, also our compatriot.

We wish to acknowledge our indebtedness to Congressman Hill, who introduced the bill in the House; to Mr. Olcott, of New York, who had charge of the bill on the District Committee, and to Mr. Wiley, of New Jersey, who was chairman of the District Subcommittee at the hearing on the bill and materially aided in its passage through the House; also to Senators Blackburn, Bulkeley, Brandegee,

Dillingham, Frye, and Depew, who assisted its passage in the Senate.

The first meeting of the Corporation, duly called pursuant to Section 5 of the charter, was held at the New Willard Hotel, in the City of Washington, D. C., on November 17, 1906.

At this meeting the charter was accepted, and it was directed that a certificate of its acceptance be filed in the office of the Secretary of State.

This certificate has been duly filed.

A temporary Constitution and By-Laws were also adopted and officers elected to serve until the annual meeting.

A plan has been prepared whereby the incorporated Society and the voluntary association may be consolidated at this Congress, thus carrying out the purpose for which your Committee were appointed and being the final act of the commission entrusted to us, which we beg leave to submit herewith.

MORRIS B. BEARDSLEY,
JOHN PAUL EARNEST,
Committee.

MR. BEARDSLEY (continuing): In connection with this report, I am very happy to be able to present to you, Mr. President General and compatriots, a beautiful engrossed copy of our new charter. I felt as if there ought to be something official that could go among the archives of the Society. This has been gotten up in the State Department, and the certification bears the original signature of the Secretary of State, Honorable Elihu Root.

NATIONAL CHARTER

H. R. 15332
FIFTY-NINTH CONGRESS
OF THE
UNITED STATES OF AMERICA;
At the First Session,
Begun and held at the City of Washington on Monday, the fourth day of December, one thousand nine hundred and five.

AN ACT
To Incorporate the National Society of the Sons of the American Revolution

Be it enacted by the Senate and House of Representatives of the United States of America in Congress assembled, That Francis Henry Appleton, of Massachusetts; Lucius P. Deming, of Connecticut; William Seward Webb, of Vermont; Horace Porter, of New York; Joseph C. Breckenridge, of Washington, District of Columbia; Franklin Murphy, of New Jersey; Walter S. Logan, of New York; Edwin Warfield, of Maryand; Edwin S. Greeley, of Connecticut; James D. Hancock, of Pennsylvania; Morris B. Beardsley, of Connecticut; John C. Lewis, of Kentucky; Henry Stockbridge, of Maryland; Nelson A. McClary, of Illinois; A. Howard Clark, of Washington, District of Columbia; Isaac W. Birdseye, of Connecticut; William K. Wickes, of New York; J. W. Atwood, of Ohio; J. W. Whiting, of Alabama; Ricardo E. Miner, of Arizona; Joseph M. Hill, of Arkansas; Alexander G. Eells, of California; Clarkson N. Guyer, of Colorado; Jonathan Trumbull, of Connecticut; Thomas F. Bayard, of Delaware; William H. Bayly, of Washington, District of Columbia; William S. Keyser, of Florida; Charles M. Cooke, of Hawaii; Inman H. Fowler, of Indiana; Eugene Secor, of Iowa; John Meade, of Kansas; Peter F. Pescud, of Louisiana; Waldo

Pettengill, of Maine; James D. Iglehart, of Maryland; Moses G. Parker, of Massachusetts; Rufus W. Clark, of Michigan; James C. Haynes, of Minnesota; Ashley Cabell, of Missouri; Ogden A. Southmayd, of Montana; Amos Field, of Nebraska; Daniel C. Roberts, of New Hampshire; J. Franklin Fort, of New Jersey; William A. Marble, of New York; Isaac F. Mack, of Ohio; Henry H. Edwards, of Oklahoma; Thomas M. Anderson, of Oregon; William L. Jones, of Pennsylvania; John E. Studley, of Rhode Island; Theodore G. Carter, of South Dakota; J. A. Cartwright, of Tennessee I. M. Standifer, of Texas; Fred A. Hale, of Utah; Henry D. Holton, of Vermont; Lunsford L. Lewis, of Virginia; Cornelius H. Hanford, of Washington; J. Franklin Pierce, of Wisconsin; Trueman G. Avery, of New York; William W. J. Warren, of New York; Henry V. A. Joslin, of Rhode Island; John Paul Ernest, of Washington, District of Columbia; A. S. Hubbard, of California, and all such other persons as may from time to time be associated with them, and their successors, are hereby constituted a body corporate and politic, in the city of Washington, in the District of Columbia, by the name of the National Society of the Sons of the American Revolution.

SEC. 2. That the purposes and objects of said corporation are declared to be patriotic, historical, and educational, and shall include those intended or designed to perpetuate the memory of the men who, by their services or sacrifices during the war of the American Revolution, achieved the independence of the American people; to unite and promote fellowship among their descendants; to inspire them and the community at large with a more profound reverence for the principles of the Government founded by our forefathers; to encourage historical research in relation to the American Revolution; to acquire and preserve the records of the individual services of the patriots of the war, as well as documents, relics, and landmarks; to mark the scenes of the Revolution by appropriate memorials; to celebrate the anniversaries of the prominent events of the war and of the Revolutionary period; to foster true patriotism; to maintain and extend the institutions of American freedom, and to carry out the purposes expressed in the preamble to the Constitution of our country and the injunctions of Washington in his farewell address to the American people.

SEC. 3. That said corporation shall have the power to receive, purchase, hold, sell, and convey real and personal estate, so far only as may be necessary or convenient for its lawful purposes, to an amount not exceeding at any one time in the aggregate five hundred thousand dollars; to sue and be sued, complain and defend in any court; to adopt a common seal, and to alter the same at pleasure; to make and adopt a constitution, by-laws, rules, and regulations for admission, government, suspension, and expulsion of its members, and from time to time to alter and repeal such constitution, by-laws, rules, and regulations, and to adopt others in their places; to provide for the election of its officers and to define their duties; to provide for State Societies or Chapters with rules for their conduct, and to regulate and provide for the management, safe-keeping, and protection of its property and funds; *Provided always*, That such constitution, by-laws, rules, and regulations be not inconsistent with the laws of the United States or any of the States thereof.

SEC. 4. That the property and affairs of said corporation shall be managed by not more than sixty or less than forty trustees, who shall be elected annually at such time as shall be fixed in the by-laws, and at least one trustee shall be elected annually from a list of nominees to be made by each of the State Societies and submitted to this Society at least thirty days before the annual meeting, in accordance with general provisions regulating such nominations as may be adopted by this Society.

SEC. 5. That the first meeting of this corporation shall be held on a call issued by any fifteen of the above-named corporators by a written notice signed by them, stating the time and place of meeting, addressed to each of the corporators personally named herein and deposited in the post-office at least five days before the day of meeting.

SEC. 6. That this charter shall take effect upon its being accepted by a majority vote of the corporators named herein who shall be present at said meeting, or at any other meeting specially called for that purpose; and notice of such acceptance shall be given by said corporation by causing a certificate to that effect signed by its President and Secretary to be filed in the office of the Secretary of State.

SEC. 7. That Congress reserves the right to alter, amend, or repeal this act.

J. G. CANNON,
Speaker of the House of Representatives.
CHAS. W. FAIRBANKS,
*Vice-President of the United States
and President of the Senate.*

Approved, June 9, 1906.
THEODORE ROOSEVELT.

IX

THE STORY OF THE HEADQUARTERS OF THE NATIONAL SOCIETY

For many years the subject of a National Headquarters had been discussed by the delegates of the Congress and on several occasions special committees had been appointed to investigate the possibilities of acquiring a building from which the work of the Society could be carried on and to meet the demands of the growing organization.

It was not until the Richmond Congress in May, 1927, that a specific proposition was brought before the organization, and after a rather prolonged discussion, but with practically no opposition, the S. A. R. Congress of that year voted to purchase the private residence of the late Mrs. Norman Williams at 1227 Sixteenth Street, Northwest, in Washington.

The story of the carrying out of the mandate of the Congress is interesting, and rather remarkable, for the Society, which was at that time in excellent financial condition, had practically no funds available to apply to such a large purchase. The price of the building and all the furniture including handsome and valuable rugs and bric-a-brac, a grand piano and other items of value, was reduced to $145,000.00, the original price being $175,000.00. However, there were forward looking men at the head of the Society; and they set about raising the amount of the first substantial payment, $25,000.00, which was to be made on August 26, 1927.

This took some hard work on the part of the men who were responsible. The Chairman of the Headquarters Committee was Mr. Henry F. Baker, of Baltimore, later

Past President General, and the then President General, Mr. Ernest E. Rogers of New London. who had been elected at Richmond in May. These two men with the assistance of a number of devoted compatriots, raised the $25,000.00, which was to be paid on the date of transfer from the Williams estate to the Society.

On August 26, 1927, Mr. Rogers, Mr. Baker, and the Secretary General, Mr. Steele, met in Washington and the $25,000.00 was paid and the transfer made to these three gentlemen, who, because of a legal condition imposed by the Society's Constitution, took the property over in their own names and gave their personal notes for $120,000.00. Later, when this legal restriction was cleared up, the property was transferred to the National Society of the Sons of the American Revolution, at a dignified and impressive ceremony held at the new Headquarters Building in October of that year, 1927.

The building was then occupied by the Society and a campaign was started to raise the balance of the amount due upon the indebtedness. Within the first year more than half of the sum was raised by voluntary subscriptions through the efforts of the committee.

However, there was still a substantial amount to be raised and at the Congress held in Washington in May, 1928, a plan was evolved by a committee appointed at that Congress headed by Past President General Colonel Louis Annin Ames, which was substantially as follows: There were to be three hundred donors who would each contribute $500.00, which would make an amount more than sufficient to pay the original cost and form the nucleus of an endowment fund. Those who had already paid the sum of $500.00 as well as all who later made this contribution were to be considered donors. There were two other classes, "Sustaining Members", who would contribute $100.00 or more, and "Contributing Members" who would subscribe any sum whatever up to $100.00*.

More than 200 donors were secured.

---

*One of the conditions made in the original plan of Colonel Ames and his committee was that a bronze tablet should be erected at the Headquarters upon which the names of all Donors should be inscribed.

Then came the financial disaster of October, 1929, and it became difficult to secure further donors. But comparatively few pledges were unfulfilled. The Society's financial situation was relieved in 1934 by the U. S. Congress passing an act giving tax exemption to the Society's property in Washington, D. C.

How the Mortgage on
The National Headquarters Building Was Cleared

During the administration of President General Arthur M. McCrillis the refinancing of the indebtedness of the Headquarters Building was undertaken to reduce the interest charges.

Following the adjournment of the Congress of 1933, President General McCrillis requested the Finance Committee headed by Compatriot John L. Walker of Pittsburg to prepare a refinancing plan. The plan providing for the payment of the indebtedness of approximately $50,000 was submitted to and approved by the Executive Committee and the Board of Trustees and by the Baltimore Congress of 1934. The plan called for Certificates of Indebtedness being issued to subscribing members, and the yearly payment of $2000 on the principal. Because of the excellent security and good rate of interest, although a reduction of the former carrying charge, the certificates were a good investment. It was necessary in December, 1934, to call a Special Congress of the National Society at the Headquarters in Washington to meet certain legal requirements. President General McCrillis presided and some sixty members was present from many States.

While the refinancing was first considered in May, 1933, it was not ready for presentation to the membership until January, 1935. President General McCrillis then organized a selling campaign. Hundreds of letters were written from his office in Providence to the officers of State Societies and Chapters urging them to underwrite the refinancing. He made an extensive trip to the middle west and interviewed many State and Chapter officers personally. At the Louisville Congress he reported that the subscriptions secured were nearly enough to effect the refinancing. At the Congress in Louisville other subscriptions were also received. By August 26, 1935 the original mortgage note was paid and the original guarantors released from their obligation Certificates of Indebtedness were issued to the subscribing members for approximately $30,000.00. By July 1, 1947 these certificates were called for redemption.* Here is the Treasurer General's report for March 31, 1957:

> Probably the outstanding information regarding the finances of your Society is the fact that on July 1st all the Certificates of Indebtedness, which were issued in 1934 and 1935, will have been called for redemption. At the present moment there are $6,000.00 worth of these Certificates outstanding and they will all be retired on July 1st, 1947.
>
> The final retirement of the Certificates has been brought about by the work of the Debt Liquidation Committee which has earnestly worked throughout the year to secure voluntary contributions so that this small amount of indebtedness of our National Society could be paid off; and, although at the time this report is being written the total amount has not been subscribed, it is sincerely hoped that by the time of the Congress, and certainly prior to July 1st, the entire amount will be in the hands of the Treasurer General for the redemption of these Certificates.
>
> George S. Robertson,
Treasurer General

In 1950 the Trustees authorized the expenditure of $25,000.00 for repairing the Headquarters building. The money was obtained by a mortgage on the property. The repairs were finished in the Fall of 1950. However, instead of the full $25,000.00 being used, the repairs cost only about $20,000.00.

The mortgage loan was liquidated in 1954. This was accomplished by the contributions of individuals, and those of Chapter and State Societies. Under President General de la Houssaye the drive was instituted to collect funds to

---

*It is of especial interest to note that the final payment on the mortgage note was completed during the administration of President General Henry F. Baker, who had been the original Chairman of the Headquarters Committee which had undertaken the purchase of the building and raised the first $25,000.00.

liquidate the indebtednes. Before the 64th Congress at Williamsburg cash contributions and pledges amounting to $6,332.50 were made.

Before the meeting of the 65th Congress at Chicago in May 1955 enough money was raised to pay the mortgage in full, and at that Congress one of the highlights of Recognition Night was the burning of the mortgage.* Those who took part in the burning of the mortgage were President General Lory, Past President General de la Houssaye and Executive Secretary, Harold Putnam, who applied the match.

The first headquarters building at 1227 16th Street was one the Society was always proud of. It was substantially constructed and beautiful in appearance, and it was one of the buildings in Washington that was pointed out to visitors and mentioned in information bulletins issued by the various hotels of the city. The interior of the building was very pleasing, and the proportions of the rooms were harmonious and dignified.

There were some interesting features also on the grounds outside. The lovely noble elm in front of the house had historic significance in that it is a "grandchild" of the famous Cambridge Elm under which General Washington took command of the army.

This tree was planted in 1928, as a very small sapling, and this was taken from a slip that came from the original Cambridge Elm in 1875, many years before it was destroyed. It was the gift of Mrs. John R. Dorsey of Baltimore who had personally nurtured the slips. The beautiful tree grew to lovely proportions and gave inspiration to those working at the Sons of the American Revolution Headquarters.

The New Building

Because of the splendid location of the Society's building at 1227 16th. Street, N. W. Washington, there were continous offers being made to buy the property. In 1956 the National Educational Association made an offer of $250,-

---

*The burning of the mortgage of the Headquarters was actually a facsimile because the original had to be filed in the record office in Washington.

000.00 for it. The 66th Congress confirmed the report of the Board of Trustees that the building be not sold. In the meantime the Executive Secretary was empowered to have an appraisal made of the property.

The pressing offers to buy the building at a favorable price were so insistent that the Officers and Trustees finally thought it advisable to sell.

On February the 16th, 1957, a special Congress was called to authorize the sale of the building and the purchase of the Belgian Embassy building. The special Congress authorized the sale of the building on 16th Street for $305,000.00 less the real estate agent's commission of $10,500.00, but the Congress voted not to buy the Belgian Embassy building.

The building was sold to the National Educational Association with the privilege of staying in the building until July 1st, 1958 at a rental of $100.00 a month for the first four months, and $750.00 a month up until July 1st, 1958.

At one time there was a suggestion that the headquarters be moved to Philadelphia, but the Chancellor General ruled that the Society is legally required to maintain its headquarters in the District of Columbia.

Then arose the problem of buying another building for the headquarters of the Society.

The project to locate a new national headquarters for the Sons of the American Revolution continued through two administrations. The first was under a committee appointed by Past President General Carver consisting of Admiral William Rea Furlong, Charles Marsteller, Thurston H. Baxter, Glenn M. Goodman and Robert H. Overstreet.

This Committee located a satisfactory building at 2412 Massachusetts Avenue, Northwest, owned by General Patrick Hurley. The 67th (SAR) Congress voted in favor of buying the Patrick Hurley home and an additional lot for a price of $165,000.00.

While the Congress under Past President General Carver was in session at Salt Lake City, the Zoning Board of Washington was hearing General Hurley's petition to permit the Society to occupy his building. On the last day of the SAR Congress the Board denied the petition.

The new President General, George E. Tarbox, Jr., appointed a new Committee to continue the work of the mandate of the Congress, which was to the effect that the Society should obtain the Hurley House if possible. The members were: Compatriots Louis J. Hiezmann, Reading, Pa.; Alan B. Hobbes, D.C.; Denmead Kolb, Salisbury, Md.; Stewart James, Gloucester, Va.; Charles M. Marsteller, Silver Springs, Md.; Col. Robert P. Waters, Falls Church, Va.; and *ex officio* President General George E. Tarbox, Jr. and Executive Secretary Harold L. Putnam; and Adm. Wm. Rea Furlong, Chairman.

The Society appealed to the Zoning Board for a rehearing and a law firm specializing in zoning cases was employed. The Zoning Board denied the request for the rehearing. The Committee then had no recourse other than to ask the Congress of the United States to authorize the Society to occupy No. 2412 on Massachusetts Avenue as a National Headquarters. This is a procedure commonly followed in Washington as the District Committee in Congress is the last body of appeal on zoning matters.

As the First Session of the 85th Congress of the United States closed in this same month of August, there was little time left to have a Bill passed.

The Bill authorizing the Society of the Sons of the American Revolution to occupy the Hurley Property was introduced in the Senate by Senator Case of New Jersey; and in the House by Representative Howard W. Smith, of Virginia, and Representative Carrol D. Kearns of Pennsylvania.

The First Session of the 85th Congress closed without the Bill coming to the Committee for a vote. However, since the Bill already had been introduced, this gave members of the Society an opportunity to contact members of the Senate and House before the Congress reconvened the Second Session of the 85th Congress in January 1958.

The response of the members of the Society to the President General's letter requesting them to urge their Senators and Representatives to support the Bill was overwhelming and most effective. The Bill was passed in the House on February 10, 1958. It was passed in the Senate on March 18, 1958; and was approved by Compatriot President Eisenhower on March 28, 1958.

Few realize the immense effort required to get a bill through Congress. Chairman Admiral Furlong not only wrote letters to the Senate and the House Committee but he appeared before them to urge the passage of the bill. The help of many Compatriots was needed. Dr. Herschel Murphy through his contact with Senator Case of New Jersey, got him to consent to introduce the bill in the Senate. Two senators who are Compatriots were most helpful— Senator Byrd of Virginia and Senator Thurmond of South Carolina. Past President General Foreman, through his friendship with Senator Byrd was able to get his help. Senator Byrd in turn requested Representative Howard W. Smith to introduce the bill into the House and push it through.

The Chairman of the Committe, Rear Adm. William Rea Furlong, USN, contacted Compatriot Harry Sherwin of New Hampshire who was able to get in touch with Sherman Adams, Assistant to President Eisenhower, and who had been President of the New Hampshire Society. When the District Commissioner refused to permit the Society to locate on Massachusetts Avenue because it was solely reserved for first class residences and embassies, Sherman Adams helped in presenting the Society's plea to various members of the Senate and House.

There were no objections on the floor of the House when Representative Smith brought the bill to the floor for a vote. But in the Senate when the bill came up, there were two objections. Both of these were overcome particularly through the efforts of Senator Thurmond. He obtained the withdrawal of the objections by the two senators, and its passage was thus assured.

The acquisition of the Hurley property provided the Society with a headquarters in keeping with the dignity and prestige of the organization. It is well suited for the purpose and permits the operation of the executive office on an efficient basis. The building is located on one of the most important avenues in the city and is surrounded by embassies and chanceries of foreign governments. It is four and a half blocks west of Dupont Circle, three blocks west of the headquarters of the Society of the Cincinnati and Cosmos Club, and two blocks west of Sheridan Circle. There is convenient bus transportation with a bus stop just a few feet from the driveway entrance.

The building is of smooth cut stone on the front and part of the sides with cement over brick on the remainder. It is of handsome proportions, set back 40 feet from the street. The lot extends 100 feet deeper to Rock Creek Park.*

The building, including a two-car garage, occupies 90 feet of the width of the property, leaving an adjacent vacant lot of 75 feet frontage, which can be used by the Society for future development or sold for an estimated price of at least $30,000.00.

The exterior dimensions of the house are 58' x 56'. The combined height of the two lower stories is 32 feet. The third floor, which is set back from the outside wall is 8 feet high.

A wide circular driveway affords easy access to the main entrance and the paved parking area leads to the two car garage. There is ample room to provide parking space for more cars than normally are found at the meetings held at Headquarters.

In the rear of the house is a paved veranda, some lawn area and a garden all of which is enclosed with a well constructed fence.

The rear of the property abuts on Rock Creek Park.

The vacant portion of the property is partially planted in lawn with some shrubbery and a number of shade trees.

Original Cost of the Property at 2412 Massachusetts Avenue, N.W., Washington, D. C.

The square number is 2507 and the house is built on lot #806. The original owner of the house was Frederick Atterton and he got permission to build the house in 1930. The builder was R. W. Bolling and it cost to build the house $105,000.

General Patrick Hurley purchased Lots #806, 807, 808 and 816 on October 6, 1943 for $100,000. He bought Lots #809, 810 and 811 on May 10, 1949 for $28,000.

The house on Lot #806 in 1957 was assessed at $73,500 and the grounds assessed for $41,250, making the total amount of the assessment $114,750.

Annual Meeting of Nebraska Society, Lincoln, Nebraska, February 22, 1960. *Left to right, seated*: ...t Egan (guest speaker), Compatriots Moseley (Nat'l. Trustee), Turner (State President), Mutz ...ast President General), Likes, Cox (State Secretary-Treasurer). *Left to right, standing*: Compatriots Wood, Hatten, Bodenbach, John M. Hale, Gilpin, George F. Smith, Robert P. Smith (President, Lincoln Chapter), Merle M. Hale, Henninger, and a prospective member.

...evada Society September 1961 Banquet in honor of President General Horace Y. ...tchell and Mrs. Kitchell.

At left, Dr. Olin C. Moulton, President of the Nevada Society presents the Nevada State Flag to the National Society at the 1959 Congress. *At right*, President General Wentworth accepts the Flag.

Below — Officers of Nevada Society S.A.R., inspect the Society's banner at formal installation ceremony, Reno, on Nov. 17, 1956. *Left to right*: Dr. David Lambird, Secretary; Dr. Olin C. Moulton, President; Dr. Lawrence Parsons, Treasurer; and Harold L. Putnam, Executive Secretary.

Above — Members of the New Hampshire Senate and House Members of SAR—1951. *Left to right, first row*: Leroy E. Godding, John H. P. Chandler, Carl C. Spofford, C. Murray Sawyer, Treas.; Harry E. Sherwin, Secy., Capt. Emory P. Eldredge, Arthur H. McAllister, Col. John Brown. *Left to right, second row*: Col. John B. Evans, Holland S. Wheeler, Eralsey C. Ferguson, Robert English, Lawrence W. Rathbun. *Left to right, third row*: Lane Dwinell, Speaker of the House; Blaylock Atherton, President of the Senate; Richard F. Upton, immediate past Speaker of the House. There were forty-three active SAR members located in the State House, including the Governor, President of the Senate, Speaker of the House, twenty-six members of the Legislature, seven State commissioners and seven state employees.

Below — Meeting of three New England State Presidents at Concord, N. H., April 29, 1959. *Left to right*: John P. H. Chandler, Jr., Vice President, New Hampshire Society; Robert Needham, President Massachusetts Soc.; Col. Carroll H. Clark, President, Maine Soc.; Blaylock Atherton, President, New Hampshire Soc.; Paul G. Richter, Sec'y, New Hampshire Soc.

Above — State Highway Commissioner Frank D. Merrill presented a membership in the New Hampshire Society, S.A.R., at State House. *Left to right*: Rep. Harry Sherwin of Rindge, Society Secretary; Rep. C. Murray Sawyer of Concord, treasurer; Governor Adams; Commissioner Merrill, and Dr. J. Duane Squires of New London, Society President. Major Gen. Merrill won fame in the Far East where he first served as Chief of Staff to Gen. Joseph Stilwell in China and later participated at Saipan and Okinawa.

At left — New England Council meets at Harvard Club, April 15, 1950. *Left to right, standing*: Compatriots White, Lutz, Torrey, Sherwin, Coe, Richter, Bauer and Chamberlin. *Left to right, seated*: Compatriots Carver, Martin, Finger, Sloane, McCrillis and Beardsley.

Delegation of eleven Compatriots of New England District met at the Cathedral of the Pines on Memorial Day, May 3, 1959. President General Charles Jones (from left) presided.

Morris County Chapter, New Jersey Society, S.A.R., meeting, March 26, 1950, at Washington's headquarters, Morristown, N.J. *Left to right, sitting*: Frank R. Pingry, State Registrar; Paul S. Lewis, Glenn K. Carver, Past State President; Arnold Saunders; L. C. Derbyshire; James H. Bruen. *Left to right, standing*: Edgar Williamson, Jr., Secretary General, National Society; John D. Alden, State Historian; Dr. William R. Ward, State Past President; John G. Coleman, Melvin J. Weig; Carroll B. Merritt; Dr. Herschel S. Murphy, President State Society; William H. Rinkenbach, Wood Vance; Senator David Young III; F. F. Vogt; Carl Scherzer; J. P. Wardlaw; Leon A. McIntire; A. N. Phillips; Berry Potter; Harold Farrand; Stanton T. Lawrence, 1st Vice President State Society; and William Y. Pryor, State Secretary and Chairman of New Chapters Committee.

Below — Meeting of compatriots at Newark, N.J., January 1954. *Left to right*: Dr. Herschel S. Murphy, Vice President General North Atlantic District; Judge Stanton T. Lawrence, National Trustee; Compatriot Harry F. Byrd, U.S. Senator from Va.; Compatriot William F. Halsey, Fleet Admiral (Ret.); Harvey B. Nelson, Jr., President New Jersey Society, S.A.R.

Above — Board of Managers reception for the New Jersey Society at the Abraham Clark Chapter House, Roselle, on Feb. 9, 1955 in honor of President General Milton Lory. *Left to right, seated*: Edgar Williamson, Jr., Executive Com. National Society; Harvey B. Nelson, Jr., Pres. N.J. Society; President General Lory; Clement D. Asbury, Vice Pres. General; Dr. George J. Deyo, Secretary N.J. Society. *Standing*: Rev. Frederick P. Mudge, Chaplain N.J. Society; William Y. Pryor, 2nd Vice Pres. N.J. Society; Ross K. Cook, 1st Vice Pres. N.J. Society; Harold L. Maryott, Pres. Abraham Clark Chapter; Stanton T. Lawrence, National Trustee; Joseph Ash Baxter, Registrar N.J. Society. *Standing in rear*: J. Neal Arrington, Board of Managers N.J. Society; and C. Alan Phillips, Chancellor N.J. Society.

Left — Dr. C. Malcolm Gilman of Monmouth County Society S.A.R. presented with 150 yr. old American Flag by the American Legion and its Auxiliary, for "his outstanding patriotic and civic work." *Left to right*: Pres. of Legion Auxiliary, Pres. the Legion, Pres. Dutcher of the Monmouth Old Guard, and Dr. Gilman.

Below — The New Jersey Society's luncheon honoring President General Charles A. Jones at Newark, Jan. 15, 1960. *Left to right, seated*: Dr. George J. Deyo, National Trustee; Edgar Williamson, Past President General; President General Jones; Wilbur A. Stevens, Pres. N.J. Society; and Dr. Herschel S. Murphy, Surgeon General National Society.

Upper left — Installation of officers of New Mexico Society, 1956. *Left to right*: Clinton M. Roth, President State Society; Robert G. Norfleet II, Vice President General, Rocky Mountains District; and Edward K. Elder, President, Albuquerque Chapter.
Upper right — The assemblage in Albuquerque, New Mexico, for Chapter Institution ceremonies on January 11, 1951.
At left — New Mexico Society, 1958. *Left to right*: Ernest W. Hall; Marshall S. Hester; Col. Burton N. Pinkham, President; Howard Bryan; Horace R. McDowell, Nat'l Trustee; George E. Tarbox, President General.

Below — The Rochester chapter of the Empire State Society awarded its gold medal to Dr. Howard Hanson, Director of the Eastman School of Music. *Left* — Chapter president Roger A. Ruth presenting medal; Dr. Howard Hanson, and *right* — Dr. A. C. Parker, past president of the Rochester chapter.

Right — Costume pageant presented at the New York Chapter's 25th anniversary Colonial Ball held Feb. 26. George Washington, impersonated by George Field Pearson, escorts his sister Betty Washington Lewis, played by Miss Louise Gruber *left*, and his sweetheart from New York, Mary Philipse Morris, played by Miss Elizabeth McD. Harris *right*.

Below — Regents of local chapters D.A.R. guests at conference of western New York chapters S.A.R., Watertown, October 24, 1959. *Left to right, seated*: Mrs. A. C. MacKenzie, regent Lowville chapter; Mrs. J. D. Bernard, regent LeRay de Chaumont chapter; Judge Abram Zoller, vice president general S.A.R.; Mrs. G. E. Green, regent Silas Towne chapter, and Mrs. W. H. Kelsey, regent Sylvia De Grasse chapter. *Left to right, standing*: Ralph D. Johnson, past vice president general S.A.R.; James B. Gardiner, secretary Empire State S.A.R.; E. Fred Daugherty, president Empire State S.A.R.; Charles Sneil, Rochester chapter S.A.R.; and Phillip C. Myers, historian Empire State S.A.R.

...emonies on April 28, 1950, anniversary of Washton's inauguration, (1789) at Federal Hall Memorial, sponsored by the New York Chapter S.A.R. retary Douglas McKay, Dept. of the Interior, delivered the principal address. Left to right: Past sident General John W. Finger; Secretary Douglas Kay; Robert Pierce, President, New York Chapter.

Above — Committee for organizing Colonial Ball for the Empire State Society in New York City, February 20, 1959. Left to right, standing: Ralph M. Barton, general chairman of the ball; Frederick M. Winship, vice chairman. Seated: Miss Kitty Coburn, vice chairman; Mrs. William Beecher Hambright, chairman of patrons' committee; Miss Louise R. Gruber, general co-chairman.

Below — Wreath-laying ceremony at Trinity Church grave of Alexander Hamilton, January 11, 1950. Great-Great-Grandson Alexander Hamilton (left), Past President New York Chapter S.A.R.; American Legionnaire with American Flag and New York Chapter Flag held by Compatriot Nelson Tower; Col. Montgomery Schuyler descendant of Gen. Phillip Schuyler; Spencer C. Young, New York City Treasurer; and Hon. George McAneny.

...ve — Reception in honor of President General Ray Edwards at home of Past President General John Finger, on Constitution Day, 1951. Left to right: ...bert G. Johns, President, Pa. Society, S.A.R.; Dr. ...schel S. Murphy, Vice Presilent Genl.; President ...eral Ray O. Edwards; Senator Albert W. Hawkes; Genl. Willis D. Crittenberger.

...it — Officers of New York chapter elected Oct. 1961. Left to right: Frederick M. Winship, assist-secretary; George F. Pearson, secretary; James Gardiner, 2nd, first vice president; Brig. Gen. Don B. Adams, president; Edmund F. Smith, treas...; and Ansel E. Talbert, second vice president.

Left — Dedication of reconstruction of Fort Delaware by Empire State Society, Binghampton Chapter July 25, 1959. Left to right: Philip C. Myers, State Historian; Leland Post, Committee Member; Donald C. Hotchkin, Chapter Registrar; Roger C. Underhill, Binghamton Chapter President; Charles D. Snell, Sr., Empire Society Treasurer; E. Fred Dougherty, Empire Society President; James B. Gardiner, Empire Society Secretary; Walter V. Irving, Committee Member, Past President Binghamton Chapter, formerly State Historian.

Above — Members of North Carolina Society in observance of founding of the Greensboro Historical Museum, Greensboro, October 28, 1954. *Left to right*: A. Earle Weatherby, McDaniel Lewis, Dr. Archibald Henderson, Karl E. Prickett, Charles Alderman and Maj. William Oliver Smith, President of N.C. Society.

At left — North Carolina Society S.A.R. at Washington's Birthday Banquet at Woman's Club, Raleigh, February 22, 1954. *Left to right*: Major William Oliver Smith of Raleigh, President of the State Society; National Trustee James E. Henderson of Canton, N.C.; Mrs. William B. Umstead, wife of the Governor of North Carolina; Dr. Robert B. House, Chancellor of the University of North Carolina, Chapel Hill; and Lt. Col. Jeffrey F. Stanback of Montgomery County, Vice President of the North Carolina Society.

At left — Secretary Harry C. Northrup, extreme left, assembling (1950) Mecklenberg Society S.A.R. at Charlotte, North Carolina, to examine freshly cleaned monument to the Mecklenberg Declaration of Independence. Others in group: Kenneth Whitsett; Jerre C. Whitsett; Attorney Henry Strickland; C. B. Asbury, Empire State Society; Russell S. Henderson; Francis Clarkson; David Henderson; Osmond Barringer; Commissioner Sidney McAden. In center: John McDowell VIII, whose family still lives in the original homestead built in 1727.

Below — Officers of the North Dakota Society with wives of officers and members present at the meeting held in the Gardner Hotel, Faro, May 2, 1953. *Left to right, front row*: Mrs. M. E. McCurdy, Washburn; Mrs. O. A. Stevens, Fargo; Mrs. Milton M. Lory, Sioux City, Iowa; Mrs. N. B. Knapp, Grand Forks; and Mrs. W. E. Davenport, Grand Forks. *Back row*: H. L. Chaffee, Third Vice President; M. E. McCurdy, National Trustee; Eldon Lum, Chaplain; O. A. Stevens; N. B. Knapp, Secretary-Treasurer; W. B. Shotwell; Fred A. Irish, Second Vice President; B. E. Groom, Historian; Milton M. Lory, Vice President General, Sioux City, Iowa; and W. E. Davenport, Pres.

ing of the Ohio Society October 4, 1957. *Left to right*: DeWitt well; Rex Ford Bracy; James J. Tyler, M.D.; James R. Izant; Louis dgway, Past Registrar General, The National Society; John A. Tal- J. Boyd Davis; Charles A. Anderson, M.D.; Ruth Partridge; Wil- C. Burbank; Charles A. Jones, Secretary-General, The National ty; Miss Martha Jenkins; Samuel K. Houston; Virgil T. Bogue; S. ard Scott; Norman W. Adams; J. Wayne Rush; Elmer W. Schelhase.

—Lima (Ohio) Chapters S.A.R. and D.A.R. in ceremony November 54, dedicating a marker for the final resting place of Elijah States, utionary soldier and Lima pioneer. *From left to right*: Morris H. , President, Lima Chapter, S.A.R.; Mrs. Marshall Bixler, State Re- Ohio D.A.R.; Mrs. James A. Howenstine, Regent, Lima Chapter, .; Lima Mayor William L. Ferguson; Richard Denman of the Allen y Lumber Co.

Left — Dr. Warren G. Harding, 2d., nephew of President Warren G. Harding, was installed on January 20, 1951, as president of Benjamin Franklin Chapter, Columbus, Ohio. *Left to right*: Dr. Harding being congratulated by Clare E. Cook, his predecessor as president of the chapter; J. Boyd Davis, 1st vice president; Dr. Paul Dingledine, 3rd vice president, and Charles A. Jones, secretary-treasurer.

Left — Senator John W. Bricker presented with the National Society's gold "Good Citizenship" medal by Ohio Society at State Conference in Columbus, April 12, 1958. Presented by Edwin J. Taylor, President, while Past President General Loren E. Souers looks on.

Above — Constitution Day Meeting, Lafayette Chapter, S.A.R., Akron, September 17, 1958. *Left to right*: Carlos E. Pick; President General Walter Wentworth; Sam Houston, President Ohio Society; Charles A. Anderson, M.D., Vice President Central Dist.

elow — Membership certificates were presented to twenty new members of the Cincinnati, Ohio, hapter at the dinner meeting February 19, 1954, at which President General General Arthur A. la Houssaye was guest speaker. The famous sword, a personal gift from George Washington to e Chilley family, of Cincinnati, rests on the small table in front of the speaker's table.

Above—Vice President General Dr. Burt Brown Barker and Compatriot Herbert Hoover, at Newberg, Oregon, August 10, 1955, celebrating the former President's birthday at the dedication of the Minthorne House.

At left—Portland Chapter, Oregon State Society and Friendship Masonic Lodge place wreath on statue of Washington in Portland, February 22, 1957. *Left to right*: Compatriot Col. Owen R. Rhoads; Wor. Mas. Harry W. Evans; Ernest C. Potts, President Oregon Society (placing wreath); Compatriot Ray B. Fryer; H. Stockton Boyd, Chapter President, who gave eulogy.

Pennsylvania Society, S.A.R., Annual Meeting at Williamsport, October 29, 1955. *Left to right*: John R. Kauffman, III.; Mrs. Morris W. Hazel, Past Regent Col. John Procter Chapter, D.A.R.; Myer Solis-Cohen, M.D., Past President Penna. Society; William H. Heffner, Sr.; Edwin B. Graham, Trustee and Member Executive Committee, National Society, S.A.R.; Morris W. Hazel, President-elect Penn. Society; Mrs. Thomas Henry Lee, Recording Secretary General National Society, D.A.R.; Edgar Williamson, Jr., President General National Society, S.A.R.; H. Ryerson Decker, M. D. President Penn. Society, S.A.R.; Mrs. Edgar Williamson, Jr.; Hon. Charles S. Williams, Judge Lycoming county Court, Guest Speaker; Louis J. Heizmann, Vice President General National Society, S.A.R.; Mrs. Melvin C. Donkle, Regent Lycoming Chapter, D.A.R.; Clyde R. Flory, M.D.; Mrs. Charles S. Williams; M. Elward Toner, Chancellor Penn. Society.

Right — Unveiling of a plaque to the memory of General Arthur St. Clair, September 24, 1954, by the Pittsburgh Chapter at the St. Clair Memorial Hospital. *Left to right*: John M. Russell, Franklin Blackstone, James L. Taylor, Jr., Arthur G. Trimble, Richard C. Trimble, Charles E. Dinkey, Jr. *Second row*: Ansley A. Izenour, John W. Cost, Stephen C. M. Goodnough, Henry Rockwood, Edwin B. Graham, Walter L. Moser, George M. Bogue, Malcolm Macpherson. *Back row*: William J. Titzel, H. Ryerson Decker.

re—Pensylvania Society, Sons of the American olution Annual Meeting October 27, 1951, Schenley Hotel, Pittsburgh.

ow — Officers of the Mount Pleasant, Pa., Chapter Instituted April 2, 1955. *Left to right, front row*: ph Oliver Hunter, James Russell Wood, Charles ert Freed, Harry Chambers Gettemy, Shannon W. Inbrook. *Left to right, back row*: Joseph W. O. el, Robert William Stahl, Luther Jennings Grimm, a Herman Hamel, Carl D. Lauffer, Howard D. irer.

Above—The Board of Managers of the Penn. Society (1953), Altoona, meeting. *Left to right, seated:* Morris W. Hazel, vice president; Fred Schenk; A. G. Trimble, registrar; James L. Taylor, Jr., president of Pittsburgh Chapter; Richard Blough, president of Cambria Co. Chap.; Gene Davidson. *First row, standing:* Dr. Lewis E. Theiss, historian; Dr. Gerald Groskin; Dr. G. H. Miles; E. M. Schroder, vice president; and Edwin B. Graham, secertary-treasurer. *Second row, standing:* Floyd G. Hoenstine, president of Blair Co. Chap.; James Mathers, secretary of Blair Co. Chap.; Dr. H. R. Decker, vice president, and Richard P. South, president of the Penn. Society.

At left — Meeting of Rhode Island Society, February 22, 1955. *Seated, left to right*: Philip M. Shires, Vice President; Herbert A. Crowell, President; Richmond H. Sweet, Secretary; *Standing, left to right*: William M. Muncy, Poet; Philip R. Arnold, Registrar; Lewis A. Waterman, Treasurer.

Below, left—Members of Rhode Island Society, S.A.R., receive Constitution Day Proclamation in the office of the Governor of the State. *Left to right*: Philip M. Shires, President, R. I. Society; Walter R. Martin, 1st Vice Presilent; Col. Benjamin Franklin Tefft, M.D., National Trustee; Richmond H. Sweet, Secretary; Governor Dennis J. Roberts; Henry G. Jackson, Past Presdent R. I. Society; Stuart H. Tucker, Vice President General; Lewis A. Waterman, Treasurer, R. I. Society; F. Rickmond Allen, President, Kent County Chapter; George L. Fales, Sr., 2nd Vice President, R. I. Society.

Below, right — The annual meeting of the Rhode Island Society was held in the John Brown House Feb. 22, 1956. *Left to right*: Walter R. Martin, Vice President; Arthur M. McCrillis, Past President General; Chester R. Martin, National Trustee; Eugene P. Carver, Jr., National Trustee (Massachusetts), and Philip M. Shires, President, Rhode Island Society.

Above — Dr. Boyce M. Grier of Greenwood (extreme right) elected President of the South Carolina Society S.A.R., annual meeting, April 27, 1957. Other officers, *left to right*: Joseph A. Pippin, Secretary; Dr. Joseph H. Cutchin, Treasurer; and Col. Arthur P. McGee, Registrar. Harold L. Putnam, Executive Secretary, National Society, guest speaker, and Mrs. Matthew W. Patrick, State Regent, D.A.R., a guest.

Upper right — On January 17, 1959, 178th Anniversary of battle of Cowpens, members of Daniel Chapter, S.A.R., Spartanburg, S. C., met at the Daniel Morgan Monument. *Left to right*: Dr. Patrick B. Bowles; John D. McCravy, Vice President; Lieut. Col. Samuel S. Wood, Army Res.; Maner L. Tonge, President; Alfred L. Price; Joseph E. Bolt, Sec.-Treasurer; Dr. Moore R. Blackstock.

Above left — At Meeting of South Carolina Society, April 11, 1959, Senator Thurmond was awarded gold Good Citizenship Medal. *Left to right*: Vice President General C. D. Baucom; Executive Secretary Harold L. Putnam; President General Walter A. Wentworth; National Trustee, Senator J. Strom Thurmond; State President Dr. Boyce M. Grier.

Above right — Officers of South Carolina Society elected April 11, 1959. *Left to right*: Maner L. Tonge, Treasurer; Col. Arthur P. McGee, President; E. Allison Farlow, First Vice President; Joseph E. Bolt, Historian; Dr. Joseph H. Cutchin, Second Vice President; Paul H. Leonard, Genealogist; Joseph A. Pippin, Secretary; and Dr. Boyce M. Grier, Retiring President.

Above — The Tennessee Society, S.A.R., awarded at Biloxi Congress the "Colorado Trophy" for 1958 for greatest percentage increase of new members. Ernest Clevenger accepts the plaque from President General Walter A. Wentworth. *Left to right*: Martin Nunnelley, State President; Wentworth, head of the National Society; Elbert Hays, Pres. of John Sevier Chapter; Past Pres. Clevenger; and Harry Burn of Rockwood, National Trustee.

Above — Tennessee Society Officers — 1954.

Tennessee Society, S.A.R. Annual Banquet, December 6, 1955.

At left—Tennessee Society officers elected at annual meeting, Oct. 31, 1959. *Left to right*: Adolph Shelby Ochs; Sidney W. Rawlings, Vice President; Hugh M. McCain, Chaplain; A. Paul Brown, Vice President; Horace Y. Kitchell, Vice President General; H. Martin Nunnelley, Past President; B. H. Webster, M.D., Surgeon; Earle L. Whittington, President.

Below — Officers of the Andrew Jackson Chapter elected Oct. 11, 1954. *Left to right, seated*: Littell Rust, vice president; Dr. John Youmans, president; anl A. Paul Brown, vice president. *Standing*: H. Martin Nunnelley, vice president; Alex E. Hart, treasurer; Don MacDonald; and Sims Crownover, retiring president.

Left — Officers of the Tennessee Society elected Nov. 4, 1961. *Left to right*: State President, A. Paul Brown; Vice Presidents, O. M. Wilson and John Rawlings; retiring President, Col. Harrison W. Gill; state treasurer, George H. Rhea. President General, Horace Y. Kitchell, extended his congratulations.

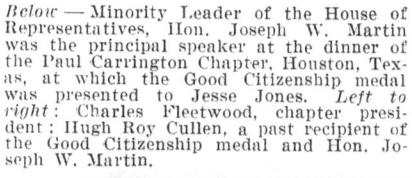

Below — Minority Leader of the House of Representatives, Hon. Joseph W. Martin was the principal speaker at the dinner of the Paul Carrington Chapter, Houston, Texas, at which the Good Citizenship medal was presented to Jesse Jones. *Left to right*: Charles Fleetwood, chapter president; Hugh Roy Cullen, a past recipient of the Good Citizenship medal and Hon. Joseph W. Martin.

ow — Members of Major White Chapter, town, Texas, received (1957) certifi-s of membership from Compatriot ien F. Drouihlet. *Left to right, seated*: ton Pearce Connally; Nat Pace; Dr. ert Worth Pipkin. *Left to right, stand*: William Macklin Douglas and Adrien ncois Drouihlet.

Washington's Birthday Banquet on February 22, 1960, by the Paul Carrington Chapter, Houston, Texas, at the Houston Club. More than 800 attended, one of the largest gatherings of its kind. Charles A. Jones, President General, was guest of honor.

Carrington Chapter, Houston, Texas, observed Constitution Week September 17, 1958. Discussion panel: *Left to right:* Joseph Reynolds; Paul E. Wise; Robert J. Sonfield; Joseph F. Blanton and Charles E. Gilbert, Jr.

Robert B. Overstreet, President Paul Carrington Chapter, Houston, presents the Good Citizenship Medal to Francis Marion Law at annual meeting, Houston, Feb. 22 1954.

Vermont Society, S.A.R., summer outing and picnic August 23, 1958, at East Highgate, residence of Compatriot Oscar Rixford.

Left—Another outing of Vermont Society, S.A.R.

Installation of officers, Utah Society, S.A.R., Feb. 22, 1961, Alta Club, Salt Lake City. *Left to right, seated:* Dr. T. Earl Pardoe, Vice President General, and Jed F. Woodley, newly elected president. *Standing:* Emerson C. Willey, past president, and William F. Bulkley, secretary.

Below—The George Mason Chapter's Christmas party (1961) honoring President General Horace Y. Kitchell. *From left to right:* Ben Rucker, president of Virginia Society, C.A.R.; L. Ralston Curry, treasurer, Va. Society; Virginia Cottrell; Joseph H. Cottrell, Va. Society; Robert S. W. Walker, Librarian General; chapter president Claude H. Smith; Mrs. Smith; Mrs. Kitchell; President General Horace Y. Kitchell; Robert P. Waters; chapter secretary, Col. Robert P. Waters; Mrs. Weaver; Col. John C. Weaver, President Elect; Mrs. Morgan; Col. Irving Morgan, George Mason chapter; and James F. Hayes, chapter chaplain.

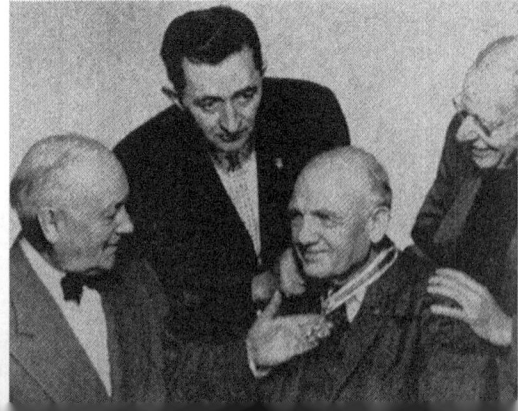

The Richmond Chapter, Virginia, S.A.R., honored in summer of 1961 its twenty-eight "old" members — members with state numbers below 500 — ten of the 28 pictured here. Jesse T. Fontaine, president of the chapter, presents emblem to William Macfarlane Jones (since deceased), oldest member of the Society, for many years its secretary-registrar, one-time genealogist general and historian general of the National Society. Others, *left to right*: S. Peachy Ryland, Dr. G. MacLaren Brydon, Joseph S. Potts, Jr., Thorpe L. Purcell, R. McC. Bullington, Dr. William H. Parker, James F. Ryland, P St. George Cooke, and William D. Duke.

Left — S.A.R. Charters — Fred W. McWane (left), of Lynchburg; Colonel Robert P. Walters, of Falls Church; Harry M. Pearson, of Remington, and Walter E. Sanford, of Alexandria, receive charters from Kenneth C. Patty (right), retiring president of the Va. Society.

Below — The George Mason Chapter, Falls Church, Va., won (1961) the President General's Cup for the second consecutive year. *Left to right*: Lt. Col. Robert P. Waters, past president; President General Murphy; Claude H. Smith, chapter president, and Capt. Robert A. Abernathy, president of the Virginia Society S.A.R.

Left — Officers of Bremerton Washington Chapter S.A.R., March 15, 1955. *Front row, seated, left to right*: Charles C. Casad, Vice President; Alfred March Peeler, President; J. A. Hibbard, President, Washington Society. *Rear row, standing, left to right*: Alfred B. Richards, Chaplain; Herbert M. Atherton, Treasurer; Henry E. Larkin, Historian; John Henry Short, Secretary; Richard I. Sampson, Secretary; Ben Henry Smith, Chaplain.

[Lower] — On January 26, 1957, at Yakima, [Wash]ington, the Yakima Valley Chapter was [insti]tuted. At banquet, Compatriot J. A. Hib[bard], National Trustee, installed: Ottis F. Kel[ley, P]resident; Robert A. McMahan, Vice Presi[dent]; E. V. Lockhart, Jr., Sec.-Treas.; Frank [ ]y, Historian; and James A. Macdonald, [Chap]lain.

Insert — Silver Distinguished Citizenship medal presented to Past President of Washington State Society S.A.R., Merton C. Lane, by Marcus Whitman Chapter Walla Walla, Washington Society President, John N. Wilson (right), witnessed by Clarence Gordon, National Genealogist General (left).

The West Virginia Society annual meeting at Huntington, April 28, 1956, with wives of officers and members as guests. *Left to right, seated:* Col. John W. Hollister, chaplain; Mrs. C. A. Walworth; Mrs. Warren M. Reeser; Mrs. C. Leon McIntosh; Mrs. V. Eugene Holcombe; and Mrs. C. J. Stagg. *Left to right, standing:* Dr. C. H. Moffat, guest speaker; P. O. Duncan, retiring state president; Will H. Daniel, past president; C. A. Walworth, secretary-treasurer; C. Leon McIntosh, president-elect; Kenneth C. Mastin, secretary, Gen'l. Andrew Lewis Chapter; Warren M. Reeser, board member; Dr. V. E. Holcombe, national trustee, and Dr. C. J. Stagg.

W. Va. Society—*Left to right:* Dr. Charles A. Anderson, Vice President General; Walter A. Wentworth, President General; Samuel K. Houston, president of the Ohio Society; Edwin J. Taylor (standing) National Trustee from Ohio; and Charles A. Jones, Secy-Registrar Ohio Society. Extreme right: Chester A. Walworth, President-Elect W. Va. Society receives gavel from Kenneth C. Mastin, retiring President.

Dinner at the Milwaukee University Club on November 28th, 1958, honoring U. S. Sen. Alexander Wiley who received the Good Citizenship Award. *From left:* John E. Dickinson; U. S. Sen. Alexander Wiley; Gov. of Wis., Vernon Thomson; Rev. Hansen Bergen, National Chaplain of the S.A.R. and President of Wisconsin Society. *Seated, from left:* Mrs. Thomson; Mrs. Berger; Mrs. Wiley; Mrs. Dickinson.

Above—Charleston, W. V. S.A.R. officials are shown as they gathered to welcome president general, Wallace C. Hall at a special dinner meeting of the Daniel Boone chapter, 1951. *Left to right, seated:* State Supreme Court Judge Frank C. Haymond, president of the West Virginia Society; Mr. Hall; Col. J. H. Long, Honorary Life Presidnet. *Left to right, standing:* Will H. Daniels, state secretary; Rev. John W. Hollister, chaplain; Dr. V. E. Holcombe, chapter president; Harold Hutchinson, state vice president; and Buford Tynes, vice president general.

Below—Col. Horace M. Seaman, honored by officers of the National Society. A 50 year member and Past President of the Wisconsin Society. Also honored was Henry C. Fuller, (left), President of the Wisconsin Society. Arthur A. de la Houssaye, New Orleans, President General, spoke at the dinner-meeting (1953).

President General Milton M. Lory, (left), at Milwaukee, Dec. 2, 1955. *Left to right:* Henry Fuller, Vice President General Col. Hansen Bergen, Preident of the James Morgan Chapter; Read E. Widrig, former National Trustee; and John E. Dickinson, President of the Wisconsin Society.

Below—President General George E. Tarbox, Jr., guest speaker at the annual Constitution Day dinner of the Wyoming Society, September 17, 1957, Cheyenne. *Left to right:* Daniel C .Leach, Secretary; Mrs. Wood Wormald; Wood Wormald, Vice President General Rocky Mountain District; President General Tarbox; Mrs. George Tarbox, Jr.; Dr. Paul Emerson, National Trustee and Leo Deuel, President.

Photograph of the Star Spangled Banner that flew over Ft. McHenry in 1814 during the bombardment. This flag is now in the possession of the Smithsonian Institution at Washington.

The Bennington Battle Flag used at the Battle of Bennington Aug. 16, 1777 is considered by authorities to be the oldest Star and Stripes flag in existence. It was made by the women of Bennington of linen from locally grown flax and was flown over the Continental supplies stored there. The original flag is now in the possession of the Bennington Museum and is flown every Aug. 16th.

Left—Copy of the Ft. McHenry Flag which Compatriot Rogers Clark Ballard Thruston had made and presented to the National Society at the Louisville Congress in 1911. Making the presentation is General Simon Bolivar Buckner to the President General.

George Washington's Seal Ring now used in ceremony of induction of Presidents General.

Former Headquarters of the National Society of the Sons of the American Revolution at 1227 16th. Street N. W., Washington, D. C.

The Monument erected on the battle site of the Battle of Cowpens, one of the decisive battles of the Revolutionary War. The scene is looking East North-East across the battlefield. At left is the inscription on the monument. (Photographs by Wm. M. Cain)

CONGRESS OF THE UNITED STATES CAUSED THIS MONUMENT TO BE ERECTED ON THE SITE OF THE

BATTLE OF COWPENS

A TESTIMONIAL TO THE VALOR AND APPRECIATION OF THE SERVICES OF AMERICAN TROOPS ON THIS FIELD IN BEHALF OF THE INDEPENDENCE OF THEIR COUNTRY

Delegates to the annual Congress of the Sons of the American Revolution held at Independence Hall, Philadelphia, on May the 2nd, 1905.

Delegates to the Congress held in Boston in 1906.

General officers and guests of the S.A.R. at the Boston Congress 1906. *First row, left to right*: Warren, Green, Ames, and Marble. *Second row, left to right*: Battis, McClary, Wickes, Satcheller, Lawrence, Hancock, Joslin, Beardsley, Worcester, Butler, R. W. Clark, and A. H. Clark. *Third row, left to right*: Stockbridge, Atwood, Gov. Guild, Lewis, Appleton, Greeley, Pugsley, and Parker.

S.A.R. Banquet at Iroquois Hotel, Buffalo, 1908.

Above—Six Presidents General at the Baltimore Congress, 1909, on a visit to Annapolis. *Left to right*: Nelson A. McClary, Edwin Warfield, Edwin S. Greeley, Morris B. Beardsley, Henry Stockbridge, and Cornelius A. Pugsley.

Below—The Louisville Congress, 1911. Delegates at the Louisville Country Club.

Group of S.A.R. Delegates at the Syracuse Congress, 1914.

At Left—Officers at the Syracuse Congress, 1914. *Left to right:* Chaplain General Whitaker; Ex-President Parker; Ex-President General (1889) Deming; President General Thruston; Ex-President General Stockbridge; Ex-President General Beardsley; Secretary General Clark; Ex-President General Hancock.

Delegates and guests at the 1923 Congress.

At Right — President's Party at a stopover at Louisville, 1925. *Left to right, first row*: Frank B. Steele, Secretary General; Chancellor L. Jenks, Past President General; Hon. Harvey F. Remington, President General; Col. Marvin H. Lewis, Past President General; Lewis B. Curtis, Director Geenral; R. C. Ballard Thruston, Past President General. *Left to right, second row*: Rulef C. Schanck, Director General; Wilbert H. Barrett, Director General; G. A. Jewett, Secretary Iowa Society; R. T. Durrett, II., Vice President Kentucky Society; Chauncey P. Overfield, Past Director General; James M. Breckenridge, Vice President General. *Left to right, third row*: George Albert Smith, Vice President Gen.; Brainard Lemon; Frank M. Mills, National Trustee, So. Dak.; George Danforth Caldwell, President Ky. Soc.; Dr. Frank Ward Holt, Past President Michigan Society; Alex W. Tippett, Treas., Ky Soc.

Above — Executive Committee and General Officers, 1939. *Left to right*: Frank B. Steele, Sterling F. Mutz, President General Kendall, Clarence A. Cook, Louis A. Ames, Clarence H. Wickham, George S. Robertson.

Above, left—National officers 1925. *Left to right top*: James H. ...kenridge, Linn Paine, W. H. ...ett, Marvin H. Lewis, Harvey ...emington, Lewis B. Curtis, W. ...Adams, George A. Smith. *Left ...ght, lower*: F. W. Millspaugh, ...Overfield, R. C. Schanck, F. ...eele, B. H. Wiggin.

...t—National Officers, Executive Committee and local officers, ...s of President General Bar... at luncheon at the Book...llac, October 19, 1926. *Left ...ight, standing*: Henry F. ...r, President of Maryland So...; Dr. Frank Ward Holt, Na...l Trustee from Michigan; ...ence W. Dickerson, President ...etroit Chapter; Francis C. ...pbell, Vice President of Mich... Society; Raymond E. Van Syckle, Secretary of Michigan Society; *Left to right seated*: George S. Sage, ...y F. Brewer, Rev. Joseph A. Vance, President of Michigan Society; Harvey F. Remington, Chauncey ...verfield, Wilbert H. Barrett, President General; Marvin H. Lewis, Frank B. Steele, Frederick W. Mills-...h, Milfred Mattoon, Alfred E. Driscoll.

Above — Delegates and guests at at the Congress held in Richmond, Va., May 19, 1927.

At left — Group of Compatriots with Mr. Hoover on occasion of his induction into membership. *Left to right*: Hon. George Gosser, Postmaster of Pittsburgh; J. Howard Johnson, Pittsburgh; John L. Walker, President of the Pennsylvania Society S.A.R.; Hon. Willima Tyler Page, Clerk of the House of Representatives; Mr. Hoover; A. W. Wall, Treasurer of the Pennsylvania Society S.A.R.; Hon. Josiah A. Van Orsdel, Director General, S.A.R.; Dr. Mark F. Finley, Past President D.C. Society; Frank B. Steele, Secretary General.

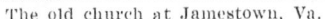

The old church at Jamestown, Va.

Above—The Nelson house at Yorktown, Va., Cornwallis' headquarters. The home of the former Governor of the colony.

Above, right—Greenway Court, the seat of Lord Thomas Fairfax. The mansion was burned about 1840 but two of the original buildings remain, one a stone building known as Washington's office, where he kept his surveying instruments and the records of his surveys.

Right—The Moore house at Yorktown, Va. Here the Articles of Capitulation of Cornwallis were prepared and signed.

X

FINANCES OF THE SOCIETY

The National Society of the Sons of the American Revolution is in excellent financial condition. On January 31, 1962 its statement showed:

Cash in Banks in Washington, D. C.	$25,585.75
Deposited with Building Association in Washington at interest	10,000.00
Cash deposit air travel credit card	10,000.00
Treasury Bonds and Treasury Bills	25,720.19
Total	$61,730.94
Permanent Fund, U.S. Treasury Bills and Bonds	86,022.50
Total Worth	$147,753.44

In addition the building and property at 2412 Massachusetts Avenue, Washington, D.C. is worth at least $250,000.00. It must be seen that the National Society of the Sons of the American Revolution has a net worth of approximately $400,000.00.

The Treasurer General's report through January 31, 1962 shows receipts of $73,340.20 with disbursements of $71,237.33. Let us compare this with the Treasurer General's report of April 30, 1892:

RECEIPTS:

On Hand May 1, 1891	62.50
From annual dues	259.75
Sale of Certificates	1,029.30
Rosettes and Blanks	163.95
	$1,515.50

DISBURSEMENTS:

Expenses — Printing Blanks		$243.81
Printing Certificates		864.64
Cash on Hand		407.05
		$1,515.50

The Permanent Fund

The Society years ago endeavored to build up a reserve fund to be known as a "Permanent Fund." It was never very large. For instance, the Treasurer's report of March 31, 1947 showed $327.08 in the fund. On September 30, 1958 the profits arising from the sale of the old building, after deducting the necessary amount for repairs on the new building, left some $76,000.00 which the Board of Trustees placed in the Permanent Fund, increasing it to $85,000.00 with an addition from the General Fund. The Permanent Fund now stands at $86.022.50. It is invested in Treasury Bills and Treasury Bonds.

The Permanent Fund is well safe-guarded. The by-laws of the National Society provide that it can only be used or diminished as recommended by the Executive Committee, approved by the Board of Trustees and ratified by a three-quarter majority vote at an annual or special Congress.

National Society Dues

The dues paid the National Society by each member were at first 25 cents annually. It is interesting that at the Congress held in 1904 there was a debate and considerable discussion about raising the dues from 25¢ to 40¢. No change was made.

At the Congress of 1921 on May 16th the annual dues were raised to $1.00 per member and the initiation fee to $5.00

The dues were later raised to $1.50 per member, and on May 26, 1954 the Constitution was amended to authorize the collection of $2.50 annually from each member as dues to the National Society.

The initiation fee was made $10.00 instead of the former fee of $5.00.

XI

AWARDS AND HONORS

MINUTEMAN AWARD

The National Society of the Sons of the American Revolution, acting through its Board of Trustees, may award to its compatriots in recognition of distinguished and sustained service of an exceptional character to the Society on the national level, the MINUTEMAN AWARD.

This award, which is the highest that the National Society bestows exclusively upon a compatriot, can be earned but once by a compatriot.

The National Society may bestow not more than twelve of these awards at each annual Congress.

RULES GOVERNING THE AWARD

Only compatriots of the Sons of the American Revolution, in good standing, are eligible to receive this award.

Nominations for this award must be made by a State Society, and be accompanied by a detailed written statement of the record of the nominee. This information must be received by the Executive Secretary ninety (90) days prior to an Annual Congress of the National Society.

The Executive Committee will review these nominations, and will in turn, submit its recommendations to the Board of Trustees, for their approval.

MEMBERS OF OUR SOCIETY HONORED WITH THE MINUTE MAN AWARD

1962—Charles A. Anderson, M.D. Ohio
1952—Babb, John H., Illinois
1961—Bolles, Calvin C., Conn.
1952—Brewer, Wheaton H., California
1954—Bennett, William S., New York

1956—Blackstone, Franklin, Pennsylvania
1958—Bulkley, Dr. William F., Utah
1959—Ballord, John G., Minnesota
1953—Cook, Clarence A., Indiana
1962—Cook, Ross K., New Jersey
1954—Coe, Howard E., Connecticut
1955—Carver, Eugene P., Massachusetts
1955—Carpenter, Col. William T. Alabama
1955—Cole, Redmond S., Oklahoma
1956—Cole, Arthur F., New Jersey
1957—Cain, Cyril E., Mississippi
1960—Cecil, James G., Indiana
1952—de la Houssaye, Arthur A., Louisiana
1958—Dickinson, John E., Wisconsin
1952—Edwards, Ray O., Florida
1952—Eubank, H. Ragland, Virginia
1955—Elder, Charles Burke, Illinois
1952—Foreman, A. Herbert, Virginia
1952—Furlong, Rear Adm. William Rea, District of Columbia
1953—Finger, John W., New York
1955—Fritchey, Dr. John A., Pennsylvania
1952—Gobble, John R., Idaho
1954—Gilbert, Charles E. J., Texas
1954—Gillam, Stanley S., Minnesota
1955—Graham, Edwin B., Pennsylvania
1959—Gordon, Robert P., Alabama
1953—Hall, Edward M., Ohio
1952—Hall, Wallace C., Michigan
1959—Hawkes, Albert W., New Jersey
1958—Hibbard, Jean A., Washington State
1952—High, Douglass G., Ohio
1962—Samuel K. Houston, Ohio
1958—Huntington, Col. F. W., Texas
1953—Huxford, Folks, Georgia
1956—Jones, Charles A., Ohio
1953—Kolb, S. Denmead, Maryland
1953—Kendall, Messmore, New York
1956—King, John E., Illinois
1960—Kitchell, Horace Y., Mississippi
1952—Lory, Milton M., Iowa
1954—Ladd, Col. J. B., Minnesota
1955—Landry, Stuart O., Louisiana
1962—Lanier, John F., Fla.
1957—Lawrence, Stanton T., New Jersey
1959—Luce, Stephen C., Jr., Massachusetts
1961—Lowmaster, Frank L., Michigan
1952—McCrillis, Arthur M., Rhode Island
1962—Martin, Chester R., Rhode Island
1952—Mathewson, H. Lewis, California
1952—Mitchell, Mason E., Arkansas
1953—Miller, James Francis, Kentucky
1953—Mutz, Sterling F., Nebraska
1954—McNeill, Robert H., District of Columbia
1954—Murphy, Dr. Herschel S., New Jersey
1960—Milligan, Edward W., **Colorado**

1961—Meyer, Harold I., Illinois
1952—Oliver, Allen L., Missouri
1955—Osborn, Gardner, Empire State
1956—Ostrom, Brig. Gen. Charles, California
1952—Powell, Ben H., III, Texas
1952—Putnam, Harold L., California
1959—Pardoe, T. Earl, Utah
1952—Ridgway, Louis F., Ohio
1952—Robertson, George S., Maryland
1952—Rowley, Howard C., California
1955—Rogers, Crawford S., Virginia
1958—Roan, Augustus M., Georgia
1962—Rudd, Augustin G., Empire State Soc.
1960—Runge, Reginald H., (legally changed to Metcalf), Empire State
1952—Sargent, Aaron M., California
1952—Sherwin, Harry E., New Hampshire
1952—Shriner, Clarence E., Ohio
1952—Smith, Lewis A., Washington
1953—Sellers, Randolph F., Ohio
1953—Souers, Loren E., Ohio
1953—Smith, Robert H., Alabama
1954—Summerall, Gen. Charles P., South Carolina
1958—Sawyers, Rev. Mott R., Minnesota
1958—Scott, Samuel Hubbard, Ohio
1961—St. Paul, Jr., John J., Louisiana
1952—Torrey, Harry K., Maine
1957—Taylor, Warren M., Ohio
1959—Trimble, Arthur G., Pennsylvania
1962—Walker, Robert S. W., D.C.
1959—Waters, Robert P., Virginia
1953—Watson, James D., Georgia
1953—Wight, Oliver B., Maryland
1955—Wentworth, Walter A., New York
1952—Williamson, Edgar, Jr., New Jersey

THE CONSTRUCTIVE CITIZENSHIP GOLD MEDAL

This gold medal, the highest award given by The National Society of the Sons of the American Revolution, is to be awarded only to citizens who have proven, and have distinguished themselves by their steadfast loyalty and devotion to the principles and ideals of the Constitution, and the Bill of Rights, of the United States of America as CONSTRUCTIVE CITIZENS, and who have consistently rendered conspicuously outstanding and invaluable patriotic service to their state and nation.

RULES GOVERNING THE AWARD

One gold medal, only, may be awarded annually, by the National Society of the Sons of the American Revolution, and it shall be presented with proper decorum, at an annual Congress. Because of the exceptional nature of this award and the honor and prestige that accompanies it, only citizens who have rendered outstanding and distinguished patriotic service, on a National level, can be considered. Recipients for this award may be nominated or recommended by any State Society.

The first recipient of this award was Fulton Lewis on July 9, 1951 at San Francisco.

THE FLORENCE KENDALL AWARD

This award, which consist of an official insigne of The National Society of the Sons of the American Revolution, is made possible by the establishment of a fund by Past President General Messmore Kendall. *A gold bar engraved with the words "Florence Kendall Award" and the year.*

RULES GOVERNING THE AWARD

This award will be made annually, and shall be presented preferably at an annual Congress, to the compatriot who secures the greatest number of new members during a contest year. The compatriot whose name appears as the first sponsor on a new application will be given the credit for securing that member.

The contest year shall begin on April first, and shall end at midnight of March 31st of the following year. Applications must be postmarked prior to midnight of March 31st to qualify.

1950—Treasurer General George S. Robertson
1950—Secretary General Frank B. Steele
1950—Furman B. Pearce of the Louisiana Society (Posthumously)
1951—Arthur A. de la Houssaye, Louisiana
1952—
1953—
1954—H. Lewis Mathewson, California
1955—Edward M. Hall, Ohio
1956, 1957, 1958—Jean A. Hibbard, Washington
1959—J. Van Valkenburg, Illinois
1960—H. Lewis Mathewson, California
1961—James Francis Miller

THE PRESIDENT GENERAL'S CUP

On February 25, 1956 the Board of Trustees of the National Society instituted an award of "The President General's Cup" to be given annually to the chapter which during the year had the best all-around record of activity based on the recommended programs contained in the Handbook. The award is a gold cup on which the name of the winner is inscribed. It is a perpetual trophy and the winning chapter has it for display during the interval between congresses. The winners up to date:

1956—Paul Carrington Chapter, Houston, Texas (First winner)
1957—George Mason Chapter, Falls Church, Va.
1958—Gen. Andrew Lewis Chapter, Huntington, West Va.
1959—The Chapter at San Diego, California
1960—George Mason Chapter, Falls Church, Va.
1961—George Mason Chapter, Falls Church, Va.
1962—George Mason Chapter, Falls Church, Va.

COLORADO BANNER

Awarded to the State Society which enrolls the highest percentage of new members among the state societies with more than 100 members.

1950—West Virginia	1957—South Carolina
1951—Michigan	1958—Tennessee
1952—Georgia	1959—Colorado
1953 and 1954—Mississippi	1960 and 1961—South Carolina
1955—Oklahoma	1962—Kansas
1956—Alabama	

SEN. ROBERT TAFT BANNER

Awarded to the State Society which enrolls the largest number of new members during the current year.

1954—Pennsylvania	1958—Massachusetts
1955—Ohio	1959, 1960 and 1961—Ohio
1956 and 1957—Ohio	1962—Empire State Society

TEXAS BANNER

For largest percentage of increase in membership among the State Societies with membership less than 100.

1950—Alabama	1958—North Dakota
1951—Arizona	1959—
1952—Idaho	1960—Hawaii
1953 and 1954—Hawaii	1961—Arkansas
1955, 1956, 1957—Alaska	1962—Vermont

OHIO BANNER

Awarded to the State Society enrolling the largest percentage of new members under the age of thirty.

South Carolina	1958—Kansas
1951—Oregon	1959—Connecticut
1955—Kentucky	1960—Kentucky
1956—Arkansas	1961—Vermont
1957—Maine	1962—Empire State Society

THE ALLENE WILSON GROVES AMERICANISM AWARD

Donated by Mrs. Frederic A. Groves, President General of the National Society of the Daughters of the American Revolution, this award is designed to stimulate greater activity on the part of individual chapters in carrying on a program of Americanism. It is a handsome plaque of special design, bearing the insigne of the Sons of the American Revolution, with space for the names of the winning chapters.

1960—Paul Carrington Chapter, Houston, Texas (First winner)
1961—Paul Carrington Chapter, Houston, Texas
1962—Sarasota Chapter, Florida

MEMBERSHIP AWARDS AND CITATIONS

The National Society of the Sons of the American Revolution, in recognition of the efforts of its compatriots to increase the membership of the Society, presents to its compatriots, Membership Awards and Citations.

RULES GOVERNING THESE AWARDS

The Membership Awards and the Citations will be presented by the National Society, preferably at an annual Congress.

The Membership Award, which consists of gold enameled lapel button, will be presented to those compatriots who secure twenty-five new members during a contest year.

The Citation, consisting of a citation duly authenticated by The National Society, will be presented to those compatriots who secure ten new members during a contest year.

Members who secure a minimum of five (5) new members during a contest year will receive S.A.R. China, plate or cup and saucer.

The contest year shall begin on April first, and shall end at midnight of March 31st of the following year. Applications must be postmarked prior to midnight of March 31st to qualify.

The compatriot whose name appears as the first sponsor of a new application will be given credit for the member.

The Chairman of the Membership Committee, of the National Society, together with the Executive Secretary, shall prepare a complete tabulation of new members secured by individual compatriots. This tabulation will be submitted to the Medal Awards Committee thirty (30) days prior to the Annual Congress, for its review and final action.

THE ARTHUR G. TRIMBLE AWARD

This trophy is made possible through the generosity of Compatriot Arthur G. Trimble, of the Pittsburgh Chapter, Pennsylvania Society, S.A.R. It is awarded annually, and presented at the annual Congress, to the State Society having the greatest calculated increase in membership over a twelve month period.

In order to assure the greatest possible equity, between states of large and small populations, it must be assumed that there are so many men eligible for membership in the National Society of the Sons of the American Revolution, as there are women eligible for membership in the Daughters of the American Revolution. Therefore, the active DAR membership in each state will be used as the standard for comparison, for that state.

RULES GOVERNING THE AWARD

Each annual contest shall begin on April 1st, and shall end at midnight of March 31st of the following year. Applications must be postmarked prior to midnight of March 31st to qualify.

1954—Hawaii
1955, 1956, and 1957—Alaska
1958—Utah
1959—Alaska
1960—Hawaii
1961—

EDWIN G. GRAHAM TROPHY
DOUGLASS G. HIGH
NATIONAL HISTORICAL ORATION CONTEST

1949—Robert Wood, Ohio Society
1950—Ronald Hengen, New York Society
1951—Thomas Hamilton—Ohio
1952—*No Contest*
1953—James C. Mounie, Virginia
1954—William P. Lynch, Jr., New Jersey
1955—John Haywood, Ohio
1956—John White, Virginia
1957—Thomas Ing, Washington State
1958—Leif Lohbauer, Florida
1959—Julien Calvin, Florida
1960—Herbert Schwartz, Illinois
1961—James Lutz, Ohio
1962—Ralph Milone, Jr., Florida

XII
ORGANIZATION OF STATE SOCIETIES

Alabama—June 2, 1903—General T. W. Whitting, Pres.
Arizona—June 13, 1896—General H. F. Robinson, Pres.
Arkansas—Feb. 11, 1890—Col. Samuel W. Williams, Pres.
California—Oct. 22, 1875—Col. A. S. Hubbard, Pres.
Colorado—July 4, 1896—Joseph F. Tuttle, Jr., Pres.
Connecticut—April 2, 1889—Lucius P. Deming, Pres.
Delaware—Jan. 29, 1889—Thomas F. Bayard, Pres.
Dist. of Columbia—July 25, 1890—Adm. D. D. Porter, USN, Pres.
Florida—Mch. 14, 1896—Lt. James H. Bull, USN, Pres.
France—Sept. 16, 1897—Lt. Walter J. Sears, USN, Pres.
Hawaii—June 17, 1896—Peter Cushman Jones, Pres.
Illinois—Jan. 14, 1890—Gen. George Crook, USA, Pres.
Idaho—April 8, 1909—M. W. Wood, Lt. Col. USA, Pres.
Indiana—Jan. 15, 1890—Col. Samuel Merrill, Pres.
Iowa—Sept. 5, 1893—Henry E. Boardman, Pres.
Kansas—Mch. 31, 1892—Avery Washburn, Pres.
Kentucky—April 8, 1889—Judge Lindsay, Pres.
Louisiana—May 16, 1890—William H. Jack, Pres.
Maine—Mch. 14, 1891—John De Witt, Pres.
Maryland—April 20, 1889—Edward Whyte LeCompte, Pres.
Massachusetts—April 19, 1889—Charles H. Saunders, Pres.
Michigan—Jan. 18, 1890—H. B. Ledyard, Pres.
Minnesota—Dec. 26, 1899—Albert Edgerton, Pres.
Mississippi—May 10, 1909—Gordon Garland Lycee, Pres.
Missouri—April 23, 1889—Josiah Fogg, Pres.
Montana—June 5, 1891—Rev. C. C. Bateman, Pres.
Nebraska—April 26, 1890—C. S. Chase, Pres.
Nevada—Feb. 19, 1910—Robert Martin Price, Pres.

New Hampshire—April 24, 1889—C. R. Morrison, Pres.
New Mexico—Dec. 25, 1908—Dr. John W. Elder, Pres.
New Jersey—April 30, 1889—William C. Stryker, Pres.
Oklahoma—Feb. 22, 1905—Col. Henry H. Edwards, Pres.
So. Carolina—April 18, 1889—J. P. Richardson, Pres.
North Carolina—Mch. 31, 1911—Stephen C. Brogaw, Pres.
New York—Feb. 11, 1890—Chauncey M. Depew, Pres.
North Dakota—Feb. 4, 1911—Burleigh F. Splading, Pres.
Ohio—April 22, 1899—Rev. Wilson R. Parsons, Pres.
Oregon—June 6, 1891—Gen. Thomas M. Anderson, Pres.
Pennsylvania—Nov. 23, 1893—Col. W. A. Herron, Pres.
Philippines—Feb. 17, 1911—Judge Chas. Sumner Lobringier, Pres.
Rhode Island—Feb. 1, 1890—Elisha Benj. Andrews, Pres.
South Dakota—April 24, 1899—
Tennessee—April 21, 1899—Rev. D. C. Kelley, Pres.
Texas—Dec. 8, 1896—Ira H. Evans, Pres.
Utah—Jan. 27, 1895—Ira H. Evans, Pres.
Vermont—April 2, 1889—Edward A. Chittenden, Pres.
Virginia—July 7, 1890—William Wirt Henry, Pres.
Washington—June 17, 1895—Col. Simon W. Scott, Pres.
Wisconsin—Jan. 14, 1890—Don J. Whittemore, Pres.
Wyoming—Mch. 28, 1908—Timothy Farrar Burke, Pres.

MEMBERSHIP

1892—3rd Congress	3,505		1914—	13,178
1893—4th Congress	4,100		1915—	13,748
1894—5th Congress	4,592		1916—	14,045
1895—6th Congress	5,878		1918—	15,422
1896—7th Congress	7,783		1919—	16,201
1897—8th Congress	8,996		1921—	17,121
1898—9th Congress	9,141		1927—	19,195
1899—	9,690		1928—	20,024
1901—	9,909		1929—	20,815
1902—	10,351		1930—	20,658
1803—	10,820		1931—	20,005
1904—	11,152		1932—	18,956
1906—	11,284		1933—	16,213
1907—	11,118		1938—	13,301
1908—	11,493		1939—	13,500
1909—	11,515		1941—	14,368
1910—	11,952		1942—	14,518
1911—	12,421		1946—	17,965
1912—	12,626		1947—	18,728
1913—	12,753			

XIII

MISCELLANIES

FREQUENT MEETINGS OF EARLY BOARD

In 1890 the Board of Managers met eight times:

May 1st, 1890—Louisville	Dec. 11th, 1890—New York City
May 31st, 1890—New York City	Jan. 17th, 1891—New York City
Aug. 20th, 1890—New York City	July 29th, 1891—New York City
Sept. 24th, 1890—New York City	April 30th, 1891—Hartford

THE CALIFORNIA SOCIETY CHANGES ITS NAME

The change of the name of the California Society—Sons of Revolutionary Sires—to Sons of the American Revolution was made on March 22, 1890, and a new Constitution in conformity to the National Society S.A.R. was adopted October 19, 1891.

FLAG DAY AND FLAG LAWS

Flag Day, June 14th, was first observed in 1890 when the Connecticut Society of the Sons of the American Revolution adopted a resolution calling attention to the honoring of the flag.

One of the activities of the National Society has been the institution of Flag-day laws in every state.

At the Congress of St. Louis, the World's Fair in June 1904, a movement was begun to influence the states of the Union to pass flag laws. These laws concerned the desecration of the flag. It should not be used for advertising, printed on paper napkins, boxes tickets, etc. Thus began the effort for the enactment by Congress of a bill to protect the flag.

THE SOCIETY'S PUBLICATIONS AND BULLETINS

The first magazine or bulletin sent to the members was *The Spirit of '76*. This was edited for the Sons of the

American Revolution and the Daughters of the American Revolution as well as other patriotic societies. In 1897 the S.A.R. Congress appropriated $500.00 to print the proceedings of the Congress in that magazine.

In 1902 the National Society of the Sons of the American Revolution issued the National Register which listed all the names of its members together with the names of their ancestors.

In 1908 the Society began mailing the *Official Bulletin* free to each member. It was a quarterly publication which appeared in May, October, December, and March. The number of pages in the first issue was 138.

At the Congress in Buffalo in 1921, it was decided to discontinue the Year Book of the National Society which had been issued in a limited edition since the organization was formed, and to enlarge the Quarterly Bulletin to the status of a Magazine. The Quarterly Bulletin had been for many years ably edited by A. Howard Clark and his successors, but it was felt that something more should be given to the membership at large, as this was the only contact of the members in general with the functions of the National Society. The Year Book edition had been limited to about 200 copies and distributed only to the General and State Officers.

The Secretary General was instructed to carry on this publication with the assistance of the Registrar General. Accordingly, since 1921, the present quarterly Magazine of the Society has been issued, first under the name of *The Minute Man*, and now as the *S. A. R. Magazine*.

GENERAL WINN
A PAST PRESIDENT GENERAL

At the Congress held in New York on April 30, 1892, a resolution was passed that the name of General Albert M. Winn, the first President of the California Society, should be carried on the rolls as a past President of the Sons of the American Resolution. At the banquet held at the Delmonico's, Chauncey M. Depew presided. Among the speakers, besides Compatriot Depew, were Thomas Bayard, of Delaware; Charles Dana, of the New York Sun; and General Horace Porter.

MARKERS ON THE GRAVES OF REVOLUTIONARY SOLDIERS

In 1893, the Society began the placing of a marker on every grave of the soldiers and sailors of the American Revolution.

CALVIN COOLIDGE'S SON WINS THE S.A.R. GOLD MEDAL

John Calvin Coolidge, while a student (Senior) at Amherst in 1895, was awarded in national competition a prize gold medal by the National Society of the Sons of the American Revolution given for the best essay on the American Revolution. His essay printed in Society's Vol. XXVII S.A.R. Magazine, July 1932.

THE SOCIETY'S BANNER ADOPTED

At the meeting in New York of the 11th. Congress on April 30 to May 1st, 1900, a national banner of the Sons of the American Revolution was adopted. Joseph Jefferson, the famous actor, addressed this Congress.

THE MCKINLEY MEMORIAL

In 1902 the President General of the Sons of the American Revolution, in accordance with a resolution of its Congress, appointed a committee in Washington to prepare a Memorial to the martyred president.

On January 29, 1903, an elaborate memorial consisting of nine pages printed on Vellum was presented to Mrs. McKinley at a banquet in Washington. President Theodore Roosevelt attended the banquet and made an address. A copy of the Memorial was sent to all 12,000 members of the Sons of the American Revolution.

MEDALS TO MEMBERS SERVING IN THE SPANISH AMERICAN WAR

In 1901 the Congress of the Sons of the American Revolution authorized the presentation of a medal to all of its members who served in the Spanish-American war.

SOLDIERS UNDER GALVEZ ELIGIBLE TO MEMBERSHIP

In 1903 the Board of Management of the Society ruled that the descendants of Spanish soldiers and the Louisiana

Militia who fought under Galvez in 1789 in the capture of Baton Rouge and Pensacola from the British were eligible to become members of the Sons of the American Revolution.

CARDINAL GIBBONS GIVES THE INVOCATION

At the 20th Congress held at Baltimore on April 30, 1909 the invocation was delivered by His Eminence James Cardinal Gibbons.

A COPY OF THE ORIGINAL STAR-SPANGLED BANNER

At the Congress held in Louisville on May 3rd, 1911, General Simon Bolivar Buckner presented the Society with an exact copy of the flag of the United States that flew over Fort McHenry when it was bombarded by the British on Sept. 12, 1814, and which inspired Francis Scott Key to write "The Star-Spangled Banner." The original flag, which had fifteen stars and fifteen stripes, is now kept at the Smithsonian Institution. The copy was made under the supervision of Ballard Thruston.

THE NATIONAL ARCHIVES BUILDING

At the Congress of the Society held in 1914 it was advocated that there be erected by the National Government a building to store the records and documents pertaining to our history. By resolutions and other efforts the Congress of the United States was urged to enact a bill to establish the Archives building. This was finally accomplished.

THE APPLICATION PAPERS OF THE MEMBERS OF THE SOCIETY

The first 72,000 application papers of the Society of the Sons of the American Revolution have been microfilmed. The negatives are stored in a fire-proof, bomb-proof, temperature-and-humidity-controlled vault, 1000 feet under ground in the vicinity of Detroit, Michigan. Thanks to the cooperation of past President General Wallace C. Hall, the cabinet containing these microfilms is stored in the vaults of a Detroit Bank without cost to the Society.

PRESENTATION OF FLAG TO SULGRAVE MANOR

On June 21, 1921 the National Society of the Sons of the American Revolution presented to Sulgrave Manor in

England, the ancestral home of the Washingtons, a handsome silk United States flag, trimmed and mounted according to United States regulations. The flag was accepted by the Honorary President of Sulgrave Manor, Col. George Harvey, U.S. Ambassador to the Court of St. James.

INTERESTING NOTES BY HOWARD E. COE, SECRETARY OF THE CONNECTICUT SOCIETY

In 1934, a steamship was chartered for the Congress. She lay off Yorktown, and the delegates went ashore for trips. Everyone enjoyed that Congress; I am sorry I did not go but I was new to the Society (1928).

The 1936 Congress at Portland, Maine, was largely attended. It was my first Congress. I was on Credentials. The Chairman was a Mr. Hall and he was quite a chap. He still had funds in his war chest. He took us to Boone's for a lobster dinner on Thursday after a boat trip on Casco Bay.

Mr. Henry F. Baker of Baltimore was the retiring President General. Connecticut President Tomlinson and I took the Bakers north to Passamaquoddy on the way home. The D.A.R. National Regent, a Mrs. Becker, still lives in Florida (then—in New Jersey).

The next Congress was at Buffalo (1937) and I must say that about the only thing I remember about it was a most interesting trip to Fort Niagara. Again I was on the Credentials Committee.

In 1938 at Dallas, it was a small Congress. Messmore Kendall was President General. No member of the Texas Society had ever attended a Congress. Their Chairman had a heart attack about six weeks before it was to start and a friend of Mr. Kendall's, a Col. Lindley (not a Compatriot, I believe) took over, and his very capable secretary and the writer "ran" the Congress. They'd never seen one, so I was their source of suggestion. At this Congress a fine old editor of a Kansas paper was to have become President General, but because of the part he promised to assume at the New York World's Fair, Mr. Kendall was again elected—at the hands of Past Presidents General Ames and McCrillis. (This is the only time "the group" committed an injustice—and it wasn't the present group).

As usual, I had to stay in the hotel to help run things; I'd been drafted! This Congress was notable for the presence of Compatriot Senator Tom Connelly, his son—young Tom, and Howard Hawks. Mr. Kendall had arranged a special train from New York. The Missouri Society took us around St. Louis while we awaited another group from Chicago. From Dallas a number of Compatriots and their wives took a trip to Mexico. At the Dallas Congress, I invited the Society to hold its 50th in Connecticut. New York spoke for it on account of the Fair.

In 1939 the Society's Golden Anniversary Congress was held at the Hotel Griswold, New London, Connecticut over Decoration Day. We had exclusive use of this beautiful structure. This was, we believe, the largest Congress to that date. For the Banquet we had 460. There was some bitterness. Compatriot Sappington (later he became President General), a Baltimore professor was very unhappy to have been defeated by Messmore Kendall. P.P.G. Ernest Rogers of New London was Chairman. I was Secretary of this Congress (and on Credentials again). Of interest at this Congress was the parade of submarines past the hotel morning and night on their way to and from training in Long Island Sound. With the exception of a thunder shower during the luncheon Monday night, we had beautiful 70° weather the whole four days.

THE OFFICE OF EXECUTIVE SECRETARY

The office of Executive-Secretary was created in 1950 by amending the Constitution and the By-Laws at the Congress held at Atlantic City. So far, there has been only one Executive Secretary, namely, Harold L. Putnam.

XIV

THE SOCIETY IN FRANCE

The French Society of the Sons of the American Revolution was organized on September 16, 1897 under the regime of President General Edward S. Barrett of Massachusetts. The first president was Lt. Walter J. Sears, U.S.N.

In 1901 the Society in France had 30 members.

According to Steele, during Col. Ames' administration (1918) the custom was inaugurated by the French Society of flying the American flag continuously over the grave of the Marquis de Lafayette in the Picpus Cemetery in Paris. This practice of keeping the American flag flying over the French flag has always had the full sanction of the French authorities. Each year on July 4th in a simple ceremony a fresh flag is flown and the old one used during the preceding year is taken down.

The old, worn, soiled flag is then sent to National Headquarters in Washington each year and presented to some patriotic organization or museum. One recipient, for instance, was the Lafayette College Library at Easton, Penn. where the "American Friends of Lafayette" maintain an interesting collection of Lafayette memorabilia. Another was General Pershing. Latest among the recipients of the used flag is ex-president Eisenhower.

But, according to Count Rene de Chambrun, President of the Society of the Sons of the American Revolution in France, the flag of the United States has been flying over Lafayette's tomb in the Picpus Cemetery since 1834. Count de Chambrun not only wrote this in an article for *This Week Magazine* (June 30, 1957) but in 1960 he repeated this statement at the ceremony held at Lafayette's tomb.

The Picpus Cemetery in the heart of Paris was established by Lafayette's wife in 1800. She moved to the cemetery 1306 victims of the French revolution, among them being her mother and sister. Mrs. Lafayette and her husband are both buried there. When Lafayette died the State of Virginia shipped to France soil which was put over his grave so that "he might lie eternally under American soil."

During the two world wars the American Flag was flown serenely over Lafayette's grave. Of course during World War II the French Society was inactive, the last ceremony at the grave having been held on July 4, 1939.

In the October 1945 issue of the Society of the American Revolution magazine in a remarkable letter from Benoit de 'Azy, Secretary-Treasurer of the Society of the Sons of the American Revolution in France. It reads as follows:

5 rue Copernic, Paris, 24th July 1945

Dear Mr. Steele,

It has been a long time since I had the pleasure of writing to you, and I am sure that you must be wondering what has happened to our Society in France during this endless war and trying occupation.

Thanks to the efforts and sacrifices of our Allies, we are at last free again, and this freedom allows me today to write this letter to you, in which I shall endeavour to give a brief account of these last five years.

On July 4th 1939, we had our last official ceremony on General de Lafayette's Grave, at Picpus Cemetery. Ambassador Bullitt was present, together with the representatives of the usual Franco-American Societies of Paris.

In August 1939, I joined my regiment as Captain commanding the Anti-Tank Battery of the Morrocan Division. We had unfortunately to fall back on Dunkirk and back to France through England. The 1940 Armistice found me with the remainder of my outfit near Toulouse, where I was demobilized.

In 1941, the Marquis de Rochambeau, our vice-president general, died, and, with Edward de Neveu, then in charge of an American Ambulance Unit, we went to Chitray to lay a wreath on his grave in the names of the Sons of the American Revolution. I am enclosing herewith a brief report and photographs of this ceremony.

I remained as long as I could in the free zone, but received the news that the Germans had been very worried about our past activities, and decided to quench their curiosity thirst by raiding my Paris apartment and removing most of our files, which, of course, I never found back.

Nevertheless, during the entire German occupation, the American flag flew over Lafayette's Grave every day and was changed twice to a new one on my orders by the cemetery warden, Monsieur Bernieres who must be complimented for his courage.

On several occasions German Officers came to the Grave, and saw the American flag, but we were lucky not to be reported.

I believe that this American flag was, at the time, the only one that flew in Paris in the open. At our last July 4th ceremony, one of these flags was presented to the American Ambassador to France, Mr. Jefferson Caffery; another one to Brigadier General Pleas Rogers, Commanding Seine Section Com Z of the U.S. Army; the third was left at the disposal of the American Ambassador for further distribution.

On July 4th 1944, before liberation, I was back in Paris and together with my Mother, my Sister, and my Daughter, went to Picpus at the usual time, convinced that the next year, we would greet there again an official representative of the United States of America. Our prayers were answered. Our president, the Marquis de Chambrun, renewed the tradition this year by receiving, at the foot of the Grave, His Exc. Mr. Caffery, General Rogers, many American Officers and Diplomats, and the Delegations of numerous French and American Societies in Paris.

I tried to bring our members together, and this was not an easy job, for many of them, mostly Americans, have not yet returned to France, or have decided never to come back. I am sending you, herewith, a list of our members, according to our 1939 files. On that list I made a cross in front of those that have not replied to my query. You may be able to help me out for some of the names.

I am sending this letter to you through the American Embassy, and trust that it will find you in good health.

I had the visit of several members of other State Societies, presently members of the American Armed Forces, and, among them, Commander Davis Goodwin Maraspin, who belongs to the Massachusetts Society, and I wish I could have done more for them. As you might easily conceive, things are not yet very much settled over here, and it is hard to organize dinners or receptions when everyone is scattered and homes and restaurants void of food.

With all my best compliments to you, I wish to extend, to all members of the S.A.R., the greetings of their Compatriots in France.

Very sincerely yours,
CH. BENOIST D'AZY
Secretary-Treasurer
S.A.R. Society in France

On May 25, 1945 the Society was reorganized. Every year since the ceremony has been held at the grave of Lafayette on the 4th of July.

The Society attended with its colors on November the 11th, 1947 at Notre Dame Des Victories, a ceremony in the presence of Mr. J. Caffery, Ambassador of the U. S., to inaugurate an inscription offered by Mrs. Theodore Roosevelt, Jr., in memory of General Theodore Roosevelt, Jr., and Lieutenant Pilot Quentin Roosevelt, killed in action. Our President, Count Charles de Chambrun, the Duke de Broglie, and the Marquess de Rochambeau, Members of our Committee; Viscount Benoist d'Arcy and General Azan, our Vice Presidents, and several members of our Society were present, as well as members of the D. A. R. and the Military Order.

On July 4, 1952 past President General Ray Edwards attended the celebration in Paris at the grave of Lafayette. C. Douglas Dillon, the American Ambassador to France, delivered the principal address.

In 1958 the annual Fourth of July Ceremony at the grave of Marquis de Lafayette was conducted by the Sons of the American Revolution Society in France. Every year for many years (except the four years of German occupation in World War II) this ceremony has taken place during which the American Ambassador places a wreath over Lafayette's grave.

This year the flag was taken down and presented by Count de Chambrun to Dr. Brandt, the delegate of Lafayette, Indiana, to be placed in the new City Hall of that city.

A new flag was placed on the tomb by General W. B. Palmer, Deputy Commander in Chief of United Forces in Europe, who renewed the gesture made by General Pershing in 1917,* Ambassador Herrick in 1946, and General Eisenhower and General Patton in 1944. More than 200 leading Franco-American personalities attended, among whom were the former French ambassadors in Washington, Government representatives and former Ambassador John Hughes, who as General Pershing's aide de camp, came to Picpus in 1917.

On July 4, 1960, the French Society organized a very moving ceremony at Lafayette's tomb in Picpus cemetery. It was attended by the American Ambassador; General Palmer, Commander of the American Forces in Europe; the President of the Municipal Council of Paris; the French Minister of Defense; and many other Franco-Americans.

The American flag, which has constantly flown over Lafayette's tomb ever since 1834, was changed for the seventh time. When presenting the new fifty-star emblem to General Palmer, Count Rene de Chambrun, President of the French Society said:

> General, you are standing here exactly where General Pershing, Ambassador Herrick and General Eisenhower stood years ago . . . This is the only spot on the globe where night and day, despite the wars, revolutions, political upheavals of both countries, the Stars and Stripes have flown for more than a century and a quarter. Indeed, during the stormy years of your civil war, when two Americans were at arms, here stood the only remaining symbol of a United America: that

---

*It was then that Gen. Pershing gave utterance to the famous phrase that fired the imagination of the world, "Lafayette, we are here!"

America he loved and prayed for—the America that finally survived.

In handing you this new emblem of your country I say what I believe he would have said: "God bless these stars and stripes and the State for which they stand! God bless and forever protect the American people!"

The old forty-eight star flag was placed in the Anderson House Headquarters of the Society of Cincinnati as a memento of the Triennial Convention they held in Paris last year.

XV

RESOLUTIONS PASSED BY THE CONGRESSES OF THE NATIONAL SOCIETY OF THE SONS OF THE AMERICAN REVOLUTION

At every annual Congress resolutions are adopted pertaining to affairs of state and concerning national and international problems.

Much of the subject matter of the resolutions is repeated in succeeding congresses and former resolutions reaffirmed. The assembling of the resolutions that the Congresses have passed would require a large volume alone to print them all. These resolutions are not only published in the SAR Magazine but copies are generally sent to Members of Congress and prominent national leaders. Here are some of the important resolutions adopted by the Congresses of the National Society of the Sons of the American Revolution at various times:

1953—Commended Congressional investigation Committees; advocated limitation of the treaty making powers of the President; opposed Federal aid to education and socialized medicine.

1954—Denounced secret diplomatic deals, especially those at Teheran, Yalta and Potsdam; opposed many foreign aid grants; endorsed the Bricker Amendment; protested UNESCO publications; endorsed the McCarran-Walter (immigration) Act; opposed the recognition of Red China.

1955—Demanded that Congress investigate tax exempt foundations; opposed the retention of the so-called Genocide Pact of the United Nations.

1956—Opposed the so-called "Alaska Mental Health Act;" endorsed the Herbert Hoover report advocating the elimination of governmental waste.

1957—Advocated the right of trial by jury in injunction cases; maintained the rights of Senators to free debate in the Senate.

1960—Advocated the local control of public schools and opposed any form of Federal aid, support or grant; opposed the entrance of the United States into any World Government Plan; advocated withdrawal from the United Nations; opposed the Federal control of Urban Renewal.

1961—Deplored the threatened attack of freedom of speech under the guise of security requirements; opposed the political, economical and socialistic One-World activities of the National Council of the Church of Christ in the United States of America; commended the House Committee of Un-American Activities; advocated the restoration of powers not delegated to the United States to the States; advocated the retention of the Connally Amendment; commended General Walker in his fight against communism; inveighed against the United States Supreme Court for its many violations of the Constitution of the United States, particularly with reference to its decisions involving communism.

1962—Reaffirmed the many resolutions adopted in the past.

To summarize, the numerous resolutions relate to loyalty, immigration, education, treason, foreign aid, treaty power, status of forces, investigative committees, Red China, World Government, withdrawal from United Nations, former Senator Jenner's Bill in Relation to the United States Supreme Court, National Council of Churches, States Rights, Federal Bureau of Investigation, Federal Control of Urban Renewal, Metro, Right to Work, and Cultural Exchange Program with Iron Curtain Countries, the "Connally Amendment," attempt to have the United State relinquish control of the Panama Canal, favoring balancing of the Federal Budget, restoring the Gold Standard, reducing corporate and individual taxes, relative to the Air Force Manual, the protection of the contents of textbooks, demanding uncensored reporting of all United Nations news, condemning actions taken by Church denominations presuming to direct governmental policies not related to freedom of the religious or religious matters, opposing participation in any Summit meeting in which the Soviets are represented, and curbing the traffic in pornographic material.

BIOGRAPHIES

PAST PRESIDENTS GENERAL

*Lucius P. Deming, Connecticut, 1889
*Dr. William Seward Webb, Vermont, 1890
*Gen. Horace Porter, New York, 1892
*Edwin Shepard Barrett, Massachusetts, 1897
*Franklin Murphy, New Jersey, 1899
*Gen. J. C. Breckinridge, District of Columbia, 1900
*Walter Seth Logan, New York, 1901
*Gen. Edwin Warfield, Maryland, 1902
*Gen. Edwin S. Greeley, Connecticut, 1903
*James D. Hancock, Pennsylvania, 1904
*Gen. Francis H. Appleton, Massachusetts, 1905
*Cornelius A. Pugsley, New York, 1906
*Nelson A. McClary, Illinois, 1907
*Henry Stockbridge, Maryland, 1908
*Morris B. Beardsley, Connecticut 1909
*William A. Marble, New York, 1910
*Dr. Moses Greeley Parker, Massachusetts, 1911
*James M. Richardson, Ohio, 1912
*R. C. Ballard Thruston, Kentucky, 1913
*Newell B. Woodworth, New York, 1915
*Elmer M. Wentworth, Iowa, 1916
*Louis Annin Ames, New York, 1918
*Chancellor L. Jenks, Illinois, 1919
*James Harry Preston, Maryland, 1920
*Wallace McCamant, Oregon, 1921
*W. I. L. Adams, New Jersey, 1922
*Arthur P. Sumner, Rhode Island, 1923
*Marvin H. Lewis, Kentucky, 1924
*Harvey F. Remington, New York, 1925
*Wilbert H. Barrett, Michigan, 1926
*Ernest E. Rogers, Connecticut, 1927
*Ganson Depew, New York, 1928
*Howard C. Rowley, California, 1929
*Josiah A. Van Orsdel, District of Columbia, 1930
*Benjamin N. Johnson, Massachusetts, 1931
*Frederick W. Millspaugh, Tennessee, 1932
*Arthur M. McCrillis, Rhode Island, 1933-34
*Henry F. Baker, Maryland, 1935
*Messmore Kendall, New York, 1936-39
*Loren E. Souers, Ohio, 1940
*G. Ridgely Sappington, Maryland, 1941
Sterling F. Mutz, Nebraska, 1942
  1304 Sharpe Bldg., Lincoln
*Smith L. Multer, New Jersey, 1943-45
Allen L. Oliver, Missouri, 1946
  506 H-H Bldg., Cape Girardeau
*A. Herbert Foreman, Virginia, 1947
*Charles B. Shaler, Pennsylvania, 1948
*Ben H. Powell, III, Texas, 1948
John W. Finger, New York, 1949
  960 Park Avenue, N. Y. 28

— 172 —

Wallace C. Hall,
 Michigan, 1950-51
 16210 James Couzens Hwy.,
 Detroit 21

*Ray O. Edwards, Florida, 1952

Arthur A. de la Houssaye,
 Louisiana, 1953
 1424 Richards Bldg., N. O.

Milton M. Lory, Iowa, 1954
 3809 Third Ave., Sioux City

Edgar Williamson, Jr.,
 New Jersey, 1955
 972 Broad St., Newark 2, N.J.

Eugene P. Carver, Jr.,
 Massachusetts, 1956
 84 State St., Boston

George E. Tarbox, Jr.,
 Colorado, 1957
 1863 Wazee St., Denver

Walter A. Wentworth,
 New York, 1958
 203 West Campbell St.,
 Frankfort, Ky.

Charles A. Jones, Ohio, 1959
 139 Tibet Road, Columbus

Herschel S. Murphy, M.D.,
 New Jersey, 1960
 320 Chestnut St., Roselle

Horace Y. Kitchell,
 Mississippi, 1961
 Greenwood, Miss.

*Deceased

WASHINGTON IRVING L. ADAMS

Compatriot Adams was born on February 22, Washington's birthday, at Montclair, N. J.

Compatriot Adams was active in patriotic and public organizations. A Major in World War I., he was a banker, a printer, and a 32nd. degree Mason. He was a Presidential elector in 1916 and a Delegate to the National Republican Convention.

Compatriot Adams had two sons; one was killed in action. He was elected President General on May 16, 1922.

LOUIS ANNIN AMES

Louis Annin Ames was born Sept. 5, 1856 on the Island of St. Helena, South Carolina. He moved to New Jersey and then to New York.

Compatriot Ames was President of Annin & Co., flag manufacturers. He was a director of the American Institute of Civics, and Vice-President of the Hudson-Fulton New York Tercentenary Celebration. A civic leader, he belonged to various religious organizations, social clubs, and was a member of numerous patriotic societies and historical associations.

He married Abby Whitney on Jan. 20, 1909 and had two daughters. Compatriot Ames was elected President General on May 21, 1918. He died Nov. 24, 1952.

CHARLES ARNER ANDERSON, M.D.

President General Charles Arner Anderson was born on June 13, 1907, at Cortland, Ohio, a son of James Cossatt Anderson and Halle Clark Anderson.

Compatriot Anderson received his pre-medical education at Ohio Wesleyan University, and his medical degree from the Faculty of Medicine, University of Edinburgh, Scotland. After graduation he became a Fellow of the Royal Medical Society of Edinburgh, and received a Post-Graduate degree from the Royal College of Physicians, Edinburgh.

During World War II, he was Chief of the Urological Service of the 29th Evacuation Hospital, serving in the Southwest Pacific Area, the Philippines, and Japan, for thirty months. He was released from active duty in January 1946, having received several Military Service Awards and Decorations, including the Bronze Arrowhead and four Battle Stars.

Compatriot Anderson's interests in public service have been extensive. He has served as Medical Consultant for the Red Cross Family Service, and is now Medical Consultant for the County Draft Board.

He is a Trustee of the Trumbull County Historical Society; Member, Old Erie Lodge, No. 3, F. & A. M. of Ohio; York and Scottish Rite Mason; and Shrine, Al Koran Temple.

Compatriot Anderson has served as President of the Nathan Hale Chapter, 1952-55; President, The Ohio Society, 1955; Member, The Ohio Society, Board of Managers, 1953-1961; National Trustee from Ohio, 1956; Chairman, The Ohio Society Membership Committee 1959-60-61; Vice President General, Central District, 1958-59; Member, National Society Executive Committee, 1959; Member, American Sovereignty and Americanism Committee, National Society, 1960; Member, National Society Flag Day Committee, 1961-62; and was responsible for the re-chartering of the Ethan Allan Chapter in 1957, and has served as its Secretary-Registrar since that time.

Dr. Anderson received the Minute Man Award at the 72nd Annual Congress, and holds eight certificates from the National Society for distinguished service and appreciation.

Compatriot Anderson is married to Mary Pond Hughes Anderson, a member of D.A.R. They have four (4) children, Charles Arner Anderson, Jr., David James Anderson, Grayson Carroll Anderson, and Warren Rice Anderson. Mrs. Anderson has two children by a previous marriage, Jennifer (Mrs. Ronald) Anderson McGarry, and Thomas Howard Anderson.

Dr. and Mrs. Anderson live at 125 Golf Drive in Warren, Ohio. They are affiliated with the Central Christian Church.

Among the Doctor's hobbies are golf, hunting, and fishing.

FRANCIS HENRY APPLETON

Compatriot Appleton was born June 17, 1847, at Boston. He received his Master Degree from Harvard in 1869. He was noted for his work in agricultural, horticultural and forestry associations. He was President of the Peabody Museum, the Massachusetts Institution for the Blind, a bank director and prominent socially.

He was elected President General on May 3, 1905.

HENRY FENIMORE BAKER

Compatriot Baker was born in Somerset County, New Jersey on March 28, 1859. He later was a resident of Baltimore, Maryland.

He was president of chemical companies and a director of various business organizations. He was a trustee of Goucher College and Chairman of the Manufacturers' Committee of Liberty Loans in World War I.

Compatriot Baker was a member of the Episcopalian Church. He was married to Cora Warman of Trenton, N. J. and had six children and eighteen grand-children.

He was elected President General on May 22, 1935.

EDWARD SHEPARD BARRETT

Compatriot Barrett was born in Concord, Mass. in 1833. He was a volunteer staff officer in the Civil War. He was later Secretary of the Massachusetts State Board of Trade.

For six years he was President of the Massachusetts Sons of the American Revolution Society. He was elected President General on April 30, 1897.

He died Dec. 21, 1898.

WILBERT HAMILTON BARRETT

Compatriot Barrett was born in New Jersey and moved to Adrian, Michigan. He was a manufacturer, banker and active in business and social affairs, and a 32nd. degree Mason.

He organized and was President of the Lenawee Chapter, at Adrian and served the Michigan Society on its Board of Management and as National Trustee and Vice President and on April 15, 1926, was elected as its President for the third term. Previous to his election as President General he served the National Society on the Executive Committee.

Compatriot Barrett was elected President General on June 9, 1926 at the Philadelphia Congress.

He died August 11, 1947.

JUDGE MORRIS B. BEARDSLEY

Compatriot Beardsley was born on August 13, 1849 at Trumbull, Conn. He was a graduate of Yale and subsequently attended the Columbia Law School. He was City Clerk of Bridgeport, Conn. and was later elected Judge of the Probate Court of that city.

Compatriot Beardsley served on various boards and held positions of trust in Bridgeport. He was a scholarly man, a club member and prominent in Masonic and Church affairs. He belonged to several patriotic societies and was active in the Sons of the American Revolution.

On June 5th, 1873 he married Lucy J. Fayersweather, the niece of Samuel J. Fayersweather, a municifent benefactor of Yale University.

He was elected President General on May 1, 1909.

JOSEPH C. BRECKINRIDGE

Compatriot Breckinridge was born in 1855 in Washington D. C. He was elected President General on May 1st, 1900.

EUGENE PENDLETON CARVER, JR.

Eugene Pendleton Carver, Jr., was born at Arlington, Massachusetts, on November 9th, 1891 of the marriage of Eugene Pendleton Carver and Clara Thurston Porter.

He was graduated from Harvard in 1913 and from the Harvard Law School in 1916 and attended the University of London for one year. He was admitted to the Massachusetts Bar in 1916, to practice at the Federal District Bar in 1917 and the Bar of the Federal Circuit Court of Appeals about 1925.

He is a member of the Unitarian Church, and has served it in various capacities for many years. He gave long service as a member of and as Chairman of the Board of Selectmen of the Town of Brookline.

Compatriot Carver served in the Massachusetts National Guard as private, corporal, sergeant and 1st Lieutenant 1910-1919, including Mexican Border Service, and 1st Lt. 8th Mass. Infantry, 1st Lt. 5th Pioneer Infantry, 1st Lt. 56th Pioneer Infantry, U.S. Army, overseas 1918-1919.

He has served as Senior Vice-State Commander, State Commander, National Senior Vice Commander and National Commander of the Veterans of Foreign Wars. He is a member of the American Legion and Disabled American Veterans. He was President of the Massachusetts State Society of the Sons of the American Revolution. He was State President, Deputy President General and President General of the Society of the War of 1812.

He is a member of the Colonial Wars and Sons of the Revolution and has been Massachusetts Governor of the Society of Mayflower Descendants. He has been Exalted Ruler of the Brookline Lodge of Elks and District Deputy of Metropolitan District Elks. A 32nd° Mason he has held many offices in the Masonic Order.

He is a Director of the following Corporations: Metropolitan Coal and Oil Company, Petroleum Heat and Power Company, Frost Coal Company, Boston Insurance Company, Boston Indemnity Insurance Company, and Old Colony Insurance Company.

Compatriot Carver married Dorothy Lee Bell at Brookline, Massachusetts, on September 10th, 1917. They have no children.

ARTHUR A. DE LA HOUSSAYE

Rear Admiral Arthur A. de la Houssaye is a native son of Louisiana, having been born in Franklin, Louisiana, in 1900. His great-great-great grandfather was an officer under General Galvez at the capture of Baton Rouge in September, 1779.

He was graduated from the Franklin High School and later received his L.L.B. from Tulane University and is practicing his profession.

He is a member of Phi Alpha Delta (Legal Fraternity); Beta Theta Pi (Academic) national officer; the Boston Club and the Stratford Club of New Orleans; and the Newcomen Society of England of which he is the secretary for Louisiana.

Admiral de la Houssaye has been a member of the U. S. Naval Reserve since 1929, and entered active duty January 3, 1941 and served 5½ years, with the rank of Captain from 1944. In 1958 he was selected by a Selection Board and on recommendation of the President and Congress was confirmed as a Rear Admiral. Received the Secretary of the Navy Commendation Award, with right to wear ribbon; First Commanding Officer, Volunteer Law Unit 8-2, New Orleans; Judge Advocate for 1949-50 for Louisiana Reserve Officer's Association of U. S.; Member, Naval Reserve Advisory Council of New Orleans.

He has served the Society of the Sons of the American Revolution as Secretary, President and member of the Board of Managers of the Louisiana Society; and as Vice President General, Chancellor General, Member of several Executive Committees, Chairman of Resolutions Committees of the National Congress, and Member of the Constitution and By-Laws Committee of the National Society. He won the Golden Gate Marathon Contest in 1951 and received the Minute Man Award in 1952. Is also a winner of the Florence H. Kendall Award.

He is married to the former Phoebe Dykers and they are the proud parents of a daughter and a son, and reside at 1582 Henry Clay Avenue, New Orleans.

LUCIUS PARMENIAS DEMING

Lucius Parmenias Deming was born in West Stockbridge, Massachusetts, March 10, 1836, the son of John Carlton and Mary (Slauter) Deming.

Compatriot Deming attended school in Westfield and Springfield, Massachusetts, until he was 14 years old.

In 1857 he moved to New Haven, Connecticut, where his parents were then living, and entered General Russell's Military Academy on Wooster Square, where he remained one year. He began the study of law, but because of poor health, upon upon advice of his doctor, adopted a seafaring life and for the following seven years, covering the period of the Civil War, he was master of a schooner running along the Atlantic coast and traveling to many foreign ports.

Returning to New Haven about 1867, he conducted a dry goods business until 1874 when he entered the Yale Law School at the age of thirty-eight years. He was graduated in 1877, 13th in his class. At his graduation exercises he won the Townsend prize for pronouncing the best oration. He was admitted to the bar the same year, and practiced law in New Haven for nearly thirty years. He held office as assistant city attorney, assistant judge and judge of the New Haven City Court, and judge of the Court of Common Pleas of New Haven County. He served as judge advocate of the Second Company Governor's Horse Guards, New Haven, during the administration of Mayor Horace Strong.

Judge Deming was appointed by Governor Andrews, chairman of a committee to investigate complaints in regard to convict labor and its interference with free labor. With committees from other states, they visited nearly every state prison in the United States to learn of the problems involved. A report was made to Governor Andrews, recommending a law limiting contract labor in prisons and other reforms, which were adopted as law and placed on the statute books of Connecticut.

On November 11, 1857, Mr. Deming affiliated with Wooster Lodge No. 79, A. F. & A. M., in New Haven. He was intalled as Master of the Lodge December 31, 1872.

He was an ardent member of the Independence Order of Odd Fellows, becoming a charter member of Relief Lodge, No. 86, June 28, 1864. He was Grand Master of the Grand Lodge in 1883; Grand Representative in 1884. He was a corporator of Odd Fellows Home which was established in Gorton, Connecticut, in 1893.

He was a member of the Congregational Church for 50 years. In politics he was a Republican. Judge Deming traveled extensively through Central and South America. Accounts of his travels appeared in New York and Connecticut newspapers.

Judge Deming married twice. In 1858 he married Laura E. Russell of New Haven. From this marriage there were two daughters and one son. After her death in 1873 Mr. Deming married Eleanor M. Parmelee, December 26, 1874, by whom he had a daughter.

In 1900, Judge Deming was a corporator of The Alessandro Copper Mining Company with principal offices in New Haven and with mines in New Mexico. He moved to Red Rock, New Mexico, in January, 1904, as general manager of the firm's business at Pinos Alto. In 1914 he returned east and located in Auburn, New York. While in Auburn his health began to fail and he was obliged to enter a hospital where his son, Dr. Lucius Deming, Jr., devoted himself to the care of his father during his illness. Compatriot Deming died in Auburn November 28, 1920, at the age of eighty-four. He was buried in the Grand Avenue Congregational Church Cemetery, New Haven, Connecticut.

A "Commemorative Biographical Record of New Haven County," published in 1902, said of Judge Deming: "He is recognized as one of New Haven's ablest and most highly respected sons; a man of place, parts and power."

GANSON DEPEW

Ganson Depew, a nephew of Chauncey M. Depew, was born in Buffalo, N. Y., on March 6, 1866. He was a lawyer and President of the Goodyear Lumber Company, the Buffalo Coal and Coke Company, and a director of the Buffalo & Susquehanna Railroad. He was a philanthropist and contributed to many causes. For years he was a leading figure in the City of Buffalo. Compatriot Depew was a member of many clubs, a 32nd Degree Mason and an Episcopalian.

Ganson Depew married on November 16, 1894, Grace Goodyear and they had two children. He was married the second time on September 30, 1915, to Mrs. Carrie Eviton Ransom.

Compatriot Depew was elected President General on May 23, 1928.

RAY OMER EDWARDS

Ray Omer Edwards was born in Harvel, Illinois, the son of Thomas Stoneham and Sarah Alice (Stevey) Edwards.

His personal military service consisted of eighteen months in Europe with the Second Division in all its major engagements during World War I and of sixteen months in various hospitals recovering from wounds. He previously had been one of the first twenty-four American officers in Anti-Aircraft Artillery and one of the three to write the first textbook in that newly-created branch of the U. S. Heart, French Croix de Guerre and French Fourragere, as an individual decoration. During World War II, he served as Deputy Chief of Public Works and District Chairman of Housing.

Compatriot Edwards attended DePauw University and George Washington University, of Washington, D. C., and received the degree of Bachelor of Science in Civil Engineering from Purdue University in 1922. He was a member of Beta Theta Pi (social fraternity), Contour (Honorary civil engineering) and Tau Beta Pi (honorary engineering scholastic).

He was owner and operator of farms on the Eastern Shore of Virginia as well as rental and resort property in Florida and North Carolina.

He was a member of Rotary, A. F. and A. M., 32nd Degree Mason, member of the York Rite Bodies and of the Shrine, B. P. O. Elks, American Legion, Disabled American Veterans, American Society of Civil Engineers, Boy Scouts of America and a Ruling Elder of the Presbyterian Church.

He had been state, Regional and National President of the National Association of Housing Officials and a former director of the National Housing Conference. He was a Colonel on the Governor's Staff, State of Florida, and held a similar appointment in the State of Georgia in 1940.

In the Sons of the American Revolution, Compatriot Edward had been Treasurer, Genealogist, 1st and 2nd Vice President of the Jacksonville Chapter. For the Florida Society, of which he was a Life Member, he served as Secretary-Treasurer and President and was elected Honorary State President. For the National Society, he served as National Trustee from Florida, as Vice President General, as a member of the Executive Committee, and as a member and chairman of various National Committees.

Compatriot Edwards was married to Lucy Mears Ames of Pungoteague, Virginia, November 28, 1923. They had two sons, both members of the Sons of the American Revolution, Lieut. Ray O. Edwards, Jr., Medical Corps, U. S. Navy, and Captain Thomas S. Edwards, II, Medical Corps, U. S. Army.

He died Sept. 21, 1957.

JOHN W. FINGER

John Whelchel Finger was born August 5, 1907, at Gainesville, Georgia. He was the son of John F. Finger and Lottie Whelchel.

He received the degree of LLB from the University of Georgia in 1928.

He is Chairman of the Executive Committee of the Inter-County Title Guaranty and Mortgage Company.

Compatriot Finger is a member of the Episcopal Church, and holds membership in the Union League Club, New York, Lawyers Club, Schnorer Club, and the Long Island Country Club. He belongs to the Society of Colonial Wars, the General Society of the War of 1812 and the Veterans Corps of Artillery.

On October 28, 1939, he married Carol Smith Allen in the City of New York. They have two children, Allen W. Finger, born September 17, 1942, and John M. Finger, born January 20, 1946.

He resides at 960 Park Avenue in City of New York.

John W. Finger and his wife were the only husband and wife to have simultaneously headed two national societies commemorating the American Revolution. He was the President of the Sons of the American Revolution, and Mrs. Finger was Senior National President of the Children of the American Revolution. He and his wife are known, in some quarters, as "Mr. & Mrs. Broad Ribbon."

ALVAN HERBERT FOREMAN

Compatriot Foreman was born March 1, 1878, at Great Bridge, Va., and was admitted to the Bar of Virginia in 1907. He had taught schools before that and was Superintendent of Schools of Norfolk County, Va. For years Compatriot Foreman was a leader in civic affairs. He was a Rector of the Board of Visitors of William and Mary College and Chairman of the Board of Trustees of Norfolk Polytechnic College. A member of Phi Beta Kappa, he had the degree of LLB from the University of Virginia.

Compatriot Foreman was a Methodist and a Mason. He was elected First Citizen of Norfolk in 1935.

He was President of the Virginia Society of the Sons of the American Revolution; Vice-President of South Atlantic District S.A.R.; member of the National Executive Committee, and recipient of the Florence Kendall Award. He was elected President General of the National Society Sons of the American Revolution on May 15, 1947. Past President General Allan Oliver says of him: "Mr. Foreman was an organizer and very aggressive. For several years after his presidency, he was a leader in the affairs of the Society."

He was married first to Alma Large in 1912, who died in 1937; he then married Grace Carrington in 1940. He had one daughter, Mrs. Margarette Aurelia Hargroves.

Past President General Foreman died March 23, 1958. The Executive Committee of the National Society then passed a resolution which reads in part:

> That the Executive Committee of the National Society of the Sons of the American Revolution expresses its grief and sense of loss in the death of our late Compatriot and Past-President General Alvan Herbert Foreman; and that we particularly acknowledge the contributions he made during his lifetime to patriotic societies and good citizenship and his loyal services to

The National Society of the Sons of the American Revolution while serving as a member of the Executive Committee as President General.

GENERAL EDWIN S. GREELEY

General Greeley was born at Nashua, New Hampshire, on May 20, 1832, later moving to New Haven, Conn. At the beginning of the Civil War he served as First Lieutenant advancing through all grades to Col. of the 10th Connecticut Volunteers. He was brevetted Brigadier General for gallantry and meritorious services.

Compatriot Greeley was the head of a large firm dealing in electric railway supplies. He was Vice President of the Yale National Bank of New Haven, a member of various clubs and service organizations.

On February 20, 1856, he married Elizabeth, daughter of Daniel and Elizabeth Corey of Taunton, Mass.

He was elected President General May 1, 1903.

WALLACE CLARE HALL

Wallace Clare Hall was born on April 12th, 1894. His parents were Charles L. and Ellen Sophia (Greeley) Hall. He received his education at Michigan State Normal College and the University of Michigan.

An educator in his early life, he was admitted to the Bar in 1920, and has since practiced in Detroit, and is a member of the Michigan Bar Association.

He was formerly President of Patriotic Education, Inc., and Chairman of Board of Denton Sleeping Garment Mills.

Compatriot Hall served in World War I with the meteorological division of the Signal Corp, and is Past Commander of the American Legion.

He is a member of Delta Theta Phi Fraternity, the Republican Party, the Presbyterian Church and the Masonic Order. He is the author of "Course Outline and Reference Quiz on the U. S. Constitution."

He married Hazel Harmon Forte on June 17th, 1920. They have a son, Wallace Greeley, and their daughter Ellen Lee is deceased. His home is at 102 Rhode Island Avenue, Highland Park, Michigan.

JAMES DENTON HANCOCK

Compatriot Hancock was born June 9, 1837, at Wilkes Barre, Pa. He was a graduate of Kenyon College in Ohio. He taught mathematics at Western University of Pennsylvania, and later became a lawyer. He was nominated to Congress but declined in 1896 in order to support Palmer and Buckner.

Compatriot Hancock was a writer and an economist. He was elected President General on June 16, 1904.

COLONEL A. S. HUBBARD

Colonel A. S. Hubbard, of San Francisco, because he organized the San Francisco Society on July 4, 1876, was by resolution of the Congress held at Louisville on May 14, 1901, declared to be a past President General of the Sons of the American Revolution.

CHANCELLOR L. JENKS

President General Jenks was born in Chicago on May 11, 1863. He was graduated from Dartmouth College in 1886, studied law at the Union Law College. He was president of the High School Board at Evanston, Ill., president of the Union Club of Chicago and member of civic and social bodies.

He was elected President General on March 20, 1919.

BENJAMIN NEWHALL JOHNSON

Compatriot Johnson was born in Lynn, Mass. He was graduated from Harvard in the class of 1878, *cum laude*, and was a member of Phi Beta Kappa. He studied later at Boston University and became a prominent attorney of Boston. He was a student of history and a member of historical societies. He studied Grecian archeology and crossed the ocean many times in connection with this research.

Compatriot Johnson was a member of numerous clubs and a director of banks and other business organizations. In June 1929, Tufts College conferred upon him the degree of Master of Arts.

He died on February 19, 1932, less than a year after his election as President General on May 18, 1931.

CHARLES A. JONES

Charles A. Jones was born at Deer Park, Maryland, February 25, 1885. The son of Wilbur Clark Jones and Olive Forman Jones.

He was educated in public schools. He later was graduated from West Virginia Conference Seminary (now West Virginia Wesleyan College), in 1904, and received his A.B. from the Ohio Wesleyan University, 1907. In 1949 West Virginia Wesleyan College conferred upon him honorary LL.D.

After graduation from college, Compatriot Jones was engaged in newspaper work for several years. Successively Secretary, Tax Commission of Ohio; manager of campaigns; travelled in China, Japan and Korea for Methodist Centenary Movement; Secretary, United States Senator Frank B. Willis; Federal Bank Receiver; Secretary, Governor Myers Y. Cooper of Ohio; Executive Secretary, Community Fund of Columbus and Franklin County, Ohio; Officer American Education Press, Inc.; Finance Director and Assistant Director, Columbus Hospital Federation, during campaigns for $40,000,000 expansion program.

Member of Methodist General Conferences, 1936, '40, '44 and '48, and of Uniting Conference of 1939; Trustee, Ohio Wesleyan University; Trustee, Treasurer, White Cross Hospital Association, Columbus; Trustee and Treasurer, Godman Guild Settlement House, Columbus.

President, three years, Central Ohio Area, Boy Scouts of America. Received "Silver Beaver" and "Silver Antelope," two of the three highest awards in Boy Scout Movement.

First President, Franklin County Historical Society, and Director for many years. Received Society's "Certificate of High Achievement."

Owns largest Lincolniana collection in private hands in Ohio. Frequent speaker on Lincoln and Civil War subjects. Secretary, Ohio Commission for Celebration of the Sesquicentennial of Lincoln's Birth.

MESSMORE KENDALL

Messmore Kendall was born on December 9, 1872, at Grand Rapids, Michigan. His parents were members of an old New England family. He was graduated from Columbia University Law School (now George Washington) and practiced law in Michigan, Montana and New York.

Compatriot Kendall was connected with many industrial enterprises, Motion Picture corporations such as the Capitol Theater in New York, the Chemical Bank of New York and numerous companies in Canada and South America as well as the United States.

During World War I he was Captain in the Signal Corp. Compatriot Kendall was a member of the leading bar associations and a member of many social clubs. He lived at Dobbs Ferry, which was Washington's headquarters at one time during the Revolution. Compatriot Kendall had a fine library including the entire collection of Harry Houdini and a large part of the libraries of William Winter, Augustin Daly and David Belasco.

Compatriot Kendall married, first, Maude E. Thomason of Memphis on June 21, 1924. They had two children. Second, on June 19, 1925, Catherine G. Flynn of Brooklyn. They had three children.

He was first elected President General on May 20, 1936, and served four terms: 1936, 1937, 1938, 1939.

He died May 1, 1959.

HORACE YEARGIN KITCHELL

Horace Yeargin Kitchell was born at Greenwood, Mississippi, April 7, 1902, the son of Horace Graham and Vesta Georgia (Yeargin) Kitchell.

He is a graduate of Greenwood High School; of Southwestern Presbyterian University, Clarksville, Tennessee, now known as Southwestern University at Memphis; and a member of Sigma Alpha Epsilon Fraternity.

He is a member of the First Presbyterian Church, Greenwood, Mississippi, of which he has been an Elder and Trustee for many years.

His local, state and national record with the Society of the Sons of the American Revolution is as follows: President, Greenwood Chapter S.A.R., which he helped organize; President, Mississippi Society S.A.R.; National Trustee from Mississippi, 1948 through 1954; Chairman of the Bill of Rights Commemorative Committee, five terms;

Vice-President General, Southern District, two terms; Member of the National Executive Committee under Charles A. Jones; Genealogist General; and member of the Membership Committee.

He is a member of the Founders and Patriots of America (Louisiana Society) and a charter member and Organizing Governor of the Society of Colonial Wars in the State of Mississippi.

Compatriot Kitchell is the owner and operator of the Delta Machine Works established by his father in 1891 which is now the oldest organized business in Greenwood, Mississippi.

He is a member of the Greenwood Chamber of Commerce, Kiwanis International, Elks, 100F, Mississippi Manufacturers Association, Delta Council, Leflore County Farm Bureau, and the American Ordnance Association. He is a former President of the Board of Trustees of the Greenwood Separate School District, and of the Leflore County Historical Society; and a member of the Mississippi Historical Society.

He is married to Lillian Blanchard, Greenwood, Mississippi. They have four children, Lillian, Horace, Catherine and Joseph. All are members of either the Sons of the American Revolution or the Daughters of the American Revolution. There are seven grand-children.

He resides at 1008 South Boulevard, Greenwood, Mississippi.

COLONEL MARVIN HARRISON LEWIS

Compatriot Lewis was born on June 16, 1873. He was a stock-broker, prominent in business and social life in Louisville, Ky., and an editorial writer for the Louisville Courier-Journal.

Compatriot Lewis was President of the Kentucky Society S.A.R. for two terms.

He married Isabel A. Rodgers and had one son, Marvin Arthur Lewis.

Compatriot Lewis was elected President General on July 23, 1924.

WALTER SETH LOGAN

Compatriot Logan was born April 15, 1847, at Washington, Conn. He was graduated from Yale and later from both Harvard and Columbia Law Schools. He was President of the New York Bar Association and as an attorney helped win the famous Jumel case in which the title to the Jumel Mansion, at one time Washington's Headquarters, was involved. Through the efforts of the Empire State Society, of which compatriot Logan was President, this property is now a State Park.

Mr. Logan was elected President General on May 1, 1901. During his term the first General Registrar of the Society was published.

He was a writer and speaker on patriotic, historical and scientific subjects as well as economics.

He married Elica Preston Kenyon on April 13, 1875.

MILTON M. LORY

Milton M. Lory in 1919 was a young newspaper reporter in Sioux City, Iowa, fresh from World War I.

The Industrial Workers of the World (I.W.W.) held a Convention at Sioux City, and the editor of the Sioux City Tribune asked for volunteers to cover this Convention, a hazardous reportorial task. In order to gain admission to the Convention, Lory had to join the organization. He had to assume the unkempt and unshaven appearance of a laborer. The press had been refused admittance to the Convention.

The Convention was faithfully covered in the news front-page of the Sioux City Tribune, and 2,000 words a day sent out by the Associated Press wires.

This glaring exposure infuriated the I.W.W. At one time the proceedings were suddenly halted by a "wobbly" saying "there is a reporter in the room." Tough-looking characters went up the aisles scrutinizing every person present looking for the reporter; he was not discovered. This experience of the young man made him dedicate his life to combatting radicalism.

In 1937 at the outbreak of the Japanese-China War, Lory made his way across Korea and Manchuria, and from there he went across the entire Siberia to Moscow. He was one of the last Americans to make this trip before the iron curtain went down.

His sojourn in Russia convinced him of the danger of world conquest by communism. The United States was the number one target. In the Museum of the Revolution he saw a map, much as it appears today, with communist conquests realized. He saw the horrors of the anti-Religious Museum. Upon Lory's return to the United States, he tried to arouse various groups. His lecture entitled "I Saw the Iron Curtain Go Down" was very popular.

Compatriot Lory, when he became a past-president general, was asked to become head of the American Coalition of Patriotic Societies founded in 1929 by Compatriot John B. Trevor. Mr. Lory has experienced the steady growth of this organization to where it now has 117 co-operating patriotic societies with a combined membership of over three million. In the six years he has been president of this organization offices have had to be moved three times because growth has necessitated larger space. The Coalition's principal activities are in the field of immigration. The McCarran-Walter Immigration Act was sponsored and written by the Coalition, its passage in Congress obtained and its preservation maintained.

WALLACE McCAMMANT

Compatriot McCammant was born in Hollidaysburg, Pa., on September 22, 1867. He attended the public schools in Harrisburg, Pa., and later graduated from Lafayette College.

Compatriot McCammant moved to Portland, Oregon, where he was an attorney and afterwards Associate Justice of the Supreme Court of Oregon. He was a delegate to several Republican National Conventions. In 1920 he was on the platform committee and placed in nomination Calvin Coolidge for President of the United States.

Compatriot McCammant was President of the Oregon Bar Association, a 33rd degree Mason, a Presbyterian and a member of various clubs. He was President of the Oregon Society of the S.A.R., and was elected President General on May 17, 1921.

He was married to Katherine S. Davis, of Phillipsburg, N. J., and they had two sons.

ARTHUR M. McCRILLIS

Compatriot McCrillis was born in Providence, R. I., on October 16, 1874. He was graduated from Brown University in 1897. He was active in patriotic work and in the Society of the Sons of the American Revolution. He was interested in history and belonged to several historical societies. He was a member of the Baptist Church.

Compatriot McCrillis was elected President General on May 17, 1933, and again in 1934.

He died September 2, 1957.

NELSON A. McCLARY

Compatriot McClary was born on August 17, 1856, at Albany, Vermont. He was graduated at Dartmouth in 1884. He was first a book publisher and then become interested in gas companies in and around Chicago where he was President of several. A club member, he was a civic leader of Oak Park, Ill.

He was elected President General on June 4, 1907.

WILLIAM ALLEN MARBLE

Compatriot Marble was born on March 4, 1849, at Woonsocket, R. I. For years he was Vice-President and General Manager of the R. & G. Corset Company, one of the largest manufacturers of its kind in the country. He was one of the founders of the Merchants Association of New York, and a Trustee of the Moses Brown School, of Providence, R. I.

Compatriot Marble was elected President General on May 3, 1910.

FREDERICK W. MILLSPAUGH

Compatriot Millspaugh was born in Buffalo, New York, and was a graduate of Syracuse University. He moved to Nashville, Tenn., in 1915, where he was in charge of the Pullman Agency.

Compatriot Millspaugh was a Presbyterian and a Mason. He was active in the Sons of the American Revolution. He married Clyde Burke of Danville, Ky.

SMITH LEWIS MULTER

Compatriot Smith Lewis Multer was born on July 18, 1874, at Worcester, Mass. He graduated from Brown University in 1898 when he was class orator. He received his LL.B. from the New York Law School. He was a prominent attorney of New York City, a Mason and Presbyterian. He belonged to many clubs.

Compatriot Multer was married to Mary Van Huzon and they had a daughter. He lived in Orange, New Jersey.

He was elected President General on May 19, 1943, and was elected again in 1944 and 1945.

He died July 16, 1952.

GOV. FRANKLIN MURPHY

Franklin Murphy was born in Jersey City, N. J., January 3, 1846. He enlisted as a private in the Civil War when he was sixteen years old. He fought at Antietam, Chancellorsville, Gettysburg, and "marched to the sea" with Sherman. He was a first lieutenant at the end of the war.

Compatriot Murphy was prominent politically in New Jersey. He was a Republican, a delegate to five national Republican conventions. He was a candidate for Vice-President of the United States in 1908. Compatriot Murphy was a member of the Newark Common Council and the New Jersey Legislature. He was later Governor of New Jersey.

Compatriot Murphy established The Murphy Company, one of the country's largest manufacturers of varnishes. He was interested in historical and patriotic societies. He was a member of the Union League Club of New York City and other clubs and organizations.

On June 24, 1868, he married Janet Colwel of Newark. They had two children.

Compatriot Murphy succeeded as President General when Edwin S. Barrett died on December 31, 1898. He was elected again on May 2, 1899.

He died February 24, 1920.

HERSCHEL S. MURPHY, M.D.

Herschel S. Murphy, M.D., F.A.C.S., was born February 7th, 1902, at Cleburne, Texas, the son of George L. and Mary C. Brown (Murphy).

Dr. Murphy graduated from Cleburne, Texas, High School, attended the University of Texas and received his M.D. degree from Jefferson Medical College in Philadelphia in 1928. He is a member of Nu Sigma Nu Medical Fraternity.

He is an Associate Attending Gynecological Surgeon at the Presbyterian Hospital in Newark, New Jersey, a Fellow of the American College of Surgeons, a Life Fellow of the International College of Surgeons and a member of the Academy of Medicine of Northern New Jersey, also a Fellow of the American Medical Association. He is the Co-Founder of the New Jersey Obstetrical and Gynecological Society and a Founding Fellow of the American College of Obstetricians and Gynecologists.

Dr. Murphy is a Past President of the Roselle-Roselle Park Rotary Club, the Union County Medical Society, the New Jersey Obstetrical and Gynecological Society, Abraham Clark Chapter of the New Jersey Society, S.A.R. He is a Past President of the New Jersey State Society, S.A.R., a former National Trustee, a former Vice-President General of the North Atlantic District and a member of the National Executive Committee. He is a former Treasurer General, a former Surgeon General and he is the holder since 1954 of the Minute Man award from the National Society, S.A.R.

He is a member of the New Jersey Genealogical Society, the Newcomen Society of North America and is a Knight of Malta—the Soverign Order of St. John of Jerusalem.

Dr. Murphy is a Thirty-Second Degree Scottish Rite Mason, a Knight Templar and a Shriner. He is a member of the First Presbyterian Church of Roselle.

Dr. Murphy married Helen Moore of Roselle, N. J. in St. Luke's Episcopal Church of Roselle on June 30, 1934. Mrs. Murphy is a graduate of Skidmore College, Saratoga Springs, New York.

They have three children: Kenneth, age twenty-six, was married on August 26, 1961, to Miss Kristin Coleman of Beaver, Pa.; Robert F. Murphy, age twenty-two, graduated from the University of North Carolina; Marilyn, age eighteen, is at Wellesley College, Wellesley, Mass. All three of the children have been members of the Children of the American Revolution.

STERLING F. MUTZ

Sterling F. Mutz was born at Burton, Nebraska on March 31, 1888. He was a son of Otto Mutz who has been born in the State of Iowa and Ella Porter Russel Mutz, born in Wisconsin.

He was educated at the University of Nebraska securing the degree of L.L.B. on June 22, 1911. He also attended Peru (Nebraska) State Teachers' College. Admitted to the Bar, Compatriot Mutz has practiced law since 1911 in Lincoln, Nebraska.

He served as Special Assistant to the Attorney General of the United States during World War I, and, again beginning on September 20, 1948, for 10 years; and also as United States Commissioner for Nebraska, 4 years, from 1957 to 1961, inclusive. He served as President of the Lincoln Bar Association for one year.

He was Alternate Delegate to the Democratic National Convention, Baltimore and he was Chairman for Nebraska of the "Woodrow Wilson for President" clubs. He was Nebraska State Chairman of the Roosevelt Business and Professional League from 1952 to 1956.

He has been a member of the Episcopalian Church for 30 years; serving as Delegate from the Diocese of Nebraska he attended eight general conventions as a Lay Deputy beginning with Atlantic City, New Jersey, in 1934. From 1952 to 1961, inclusive, he was a member of the Program and Budget Committee of the General Convention of the Protestant Episcopal Church in the United States of America.

He was married the first time to Jessie Contley Clarke on August 8, 1917 at Auburn, Nebraska. She died in 1943 and he was married the second time on October 11, 1944 to Virginia Lee Mutz. He has two children, Jessica Fahn Mutz, daughter, born in Lincoln, Nebraska, who attended the University of Nebraska, and Mt. Holyoke College, Massachusetts and received her A.B. in 1940; and Sterling Fahn Mutz, Jr., son, born in Lincoln, Nebraska; he attended the University of Nebraska, and is a graduate of Parks Air College, East St. Louis, Illinois, with a degree of B.Sc.

ALLEN LAWS OLIVER

Allen Laws Oliver of Cape Girardeau, Missouri, was born at Jackson, Missouri, January 19, 1886; graduated from Southeast Missouri Teachers College 1905 summa cum laude, and from University of Missouri A. B. 1908 and LL.B. 1909.

He married Olivia Leachman of Prince William County, Virginia, October 28, 1913. They have two sons, Allen L. Oliver, Jr. and John Leachman Oliver.

Mr. Oliver became a member of the law firm of Oliver & Oliver at Cape Girardeau, Missouri, 1910. He is a member of the American Bar Association and Vice-President of the Missouri Bar Association.

Mr. Oliver is an officer in the Presbyterian Church, a Mason and a Rotarian—at one time Governor of the 14th District of Rotary International. He has been active in Boy Scout work. He is Trustee of the Law Foundation of the University of Missouri and Vice-President of the General Alumni Association of the University of Missouri.

After Oliver's administration terminated, at a meeting of the Board of Trustees in Washington, a motion was made to appoint a committee to act on a matter that required diplomacy. One trustee got up and said, "If this committee be formed, Oliver must be put on it; he is the fairest man who ever held high office in this Society." Oliver was elected to the committee.

At a later Trustees' meeting, a member suggested that the Society create the office of Orator-General, so that Oliver could be elected to that office. Oliver objected, saying that such an office would add another to the already numerous national offices and would serve no useful purpose.

MOSES GREELEY PARKER, M.D.

Compatriot Parker was born on October 12, 1842 at Dracut, Mass. He attended the Phillips Academy and later was a graduate of the Harvard Medical School. In the Civil

War he was assistant surgeon and had charge of the First Division Base Hospital, where he received President Lincoln, General Grant, and others. He later studied medicine in London, Paris and Vienna.

Dr. Parker, a scientist and interested in electricity, was in the audience when Bell exhibited his telephone in Lowell, Mass. Dr. Parker later became a Director of the New England Telephone Company.

Compatriot Parker held many positions of trust and honor in the medical, philanthropic and historical associations.

Doctor Parker was elected President General of the Sons of the American Revolution on May 3, 1911.

GENERAL HORACE PORTER

General Horace Porter was born at Huntington, Penn. on April 15, 1837. He was graduated from West Point in 1860, the third rank. During the Civil War he served with the Union Forces for four years and took part in many engagements including the Battle of the Wilderness. He was brevetted on six occasions, his final brevet being that of Brigadier General. General Porter was later on Grant's staff and became his private secretary when Grant was President. On occasions he would represent the President as a speaker when addressing assemblies, and became a distinguished orator. He was a brilliant raconteur and ranked with Chauncey Depew as a speaker. He raised a fund of $600,000 for the erection of Grant's mausoleum on Riverside Drive, New York City, in 1892.

General Porter was President of the Society of the Army of the Potomac; President of the Union League Club of New York; Vice President of the New York Chamber of Commerce; Vice President of the Pullman Company, and a Director of the Equitable Life Insurance Company. He was a member of numerous historical, literary and patriotic organizations. General Porter was appointed Ambassador to France in 1897 and while there was instrumental in locating the body of John Paul Jones and bringing it back to the United States. On this project he spent large sums of his own money over a period of six years.

Congress appropriated the funds to recompense him but he turned the money over to the memorial fund.

Congress voted him the privilege of the floor for life. He was a delegate to the Hague Conference in 1907 and President of the Navy League in 1909.

JUDGE BEN H. POWELL

Judge Ben H. Powell was a native Texan; his parents at an early age came to Texas from States in the deep South. He received his Academic and Law Degrees from the University of Texas in Austin on June 10, 1903.

He was District Judge of a district composed of five counties. For seven years he was a member of the Commission of Appeals of the Supreme Court of Texas; appointed to this last named post by three different Governors. He was presiding Judge of Section B of the Commission of Appeals for about four years. During his seven years of service he wrote some 240 opinions for the Supreme Court, several of which involved very important questions. In one of the later cases he wrote the opinion which held that oil royalties from University of Texas Lands were a part of the Permanent Fund of that institution. He resigned and subsequently headed a successful law firm in Austin.

He was very active in Bar Association work of County, State and Nation. He was president of Texas Bar Association in 1938. He was also very active in the American Bar Association, and served on several of the important standing committees.

He was a Methodist, a Rotarian and a Mason—York rite, Scottish rite and Shriner.

He died Dec. 3, 1960.

CORNELIUS AMORY PUGSLEY

Cornelius Amory Pugsley was born July 17, 1850 at Peeksville, New York. He was a banker and financier, and president of the New York Bankers Association. In 1900 he was elected to the 57th Congress of the United States and in his service was considered one of the best financial minds in Congress. A Republican speaker of the House said of

Cornelius Pugsley, who was a Democrat, that he was "a vigorous talker and thinker, perhaps the ablest Democrat in the House."

Compatriot Pugsley was civic minded. He was ten years a member of the Westchester County Park Commission. He was a philanthrophist who contributed to various charities. He was a club member, a member of the Fifth Avenue Presbyterian Church in New York and a member of various political and civic organizations. He was also widely known as an orator.

On April 7, 1886 he married Emma C. Gregory of New York City. They had one son, Chester DeWitt Pugsley who became a prominent lawyer of New York City.

Compatriot Pugsley was elected President General on May 1, 1906. He died on September 10, 1936 at his home in Peeksville.

In the Encyclopedia of American Biography we find this appraisal:

"Eloquent, sincere, independent, public spirited,
warmhearted and broad-visioned, Cornelius Amory
Pugsley stood high in the applause of the older generation and his influence through his benefactions
and his work will continue for a long time."

HARVEY FOOTE REMINGTON

Compatriot Harvey Foote Remnington was born in Henrietta, N. Y., June 28, 1863, son of William T. and Sarah A. (Foote) Remington.

Mr. Remington practiced law in Rochester, N. Y. and was a director in well known corporations of Rochester and other New York companies.

Compatriot Remington held the office of supervisor, member of the Rochester School Board, assistant corporation counsel, and Judge of the Municipal Court of Rochester, N. Y. He was a 32d degree Mason, member of the Shrine, and other fraternal organizations. He was a life deacon of the First Baptist Church of Rochester, trustee and member of the Executive Committee of the New York Baptist Missionary Convention, a member of the Finance Committee of the Northern Baptist Convention, and sat with the Commission as its Secretary on the affairs of the American Baptist Foreign Mission Society.

He was president of the Rochester Historical Society for three years, president of the Rochester Bar Association in 1923; and member of the New York State and American Bar Associations. He was a member of the New York State Historical Society, the Chairman of the Board of Trustees of Keuka College, and a member of the Board of Trustees of the American Scenic and Historic Preservation Society, and as such trustee a member of the Letchworth Park Commission. He also served as the President of the William Pryor Letchworth Memorial Association.

Judge Remington served several years as President of Rochester Chapter, Sons of the American Revolution, was President of the Empire State Society, 1919-22, Chancellor General of the National Society in 1920, and was elected as President General at Swampscott, Mass., May 20, 1925; he is also a member of the Society of Colonial Wars.

Mr. Remington was active in civic affairs in his home city. He was a member of the Rochester Chamber of Commerce, the Rochester Club, Momal Golf, and other clubs.

He married Agnes Brodie, daughter of Thomas and Martha (Hannah) Brodie, May 28, 1889, and they had seven children. Four of his sons were commissioned officers in World War I, and his daughters served in the Ordnance Department and the American Red Cross.

JAMES M. RICHARDSON

Compatriot Richardson was born June 28, 1849 at Walcott, N. Y. He was a lawyer and a business man. Later he moved to Ohio where he became a civic leader and President of the Presbyterian Union of Cleveland. He was long prominent in S.A.R. affairs and was elected President General on May 21, 1912.

ERNEST E. ROGERS

Compatriot Rogers was born December 6, 1866 in Waterford, Connecticut. He moved to New London, Conn.

Compatriot Rogers was the War Mayor of New London. He served in the Connecticut Legislature and was State

Treasurer for two terms. He was a banker and President of the Connecticut Chamber of Commerce. He was engaged in historical work and belonged to many organizations of this type. He was a member of the First Baptist Church.

Compatriot Rogers was married to Fanny Gaston and had one son. He was elected President General on May 18, 1927.

HOWARD C. ROWLEY

Compatriot Rowley was born in Cortland, N. Y., on March 28, 1876. His family moved to California and he became publisher of the "California Fruit News."

Compatriot Rowley was a member of social and civic clubs in San Francisco. He was a Unitarian. Active in S.A.R. work, he was President of the California Society.

Compatriot Rowley was elected President General on May 23, 1929.

He died August 12, 1958.

G. RIDGELY SAPPINGTON

Compatriot Sappington was born in Maryland on February 4, 1883. He received his LL.B. from the University of Maryland where he later lectured at that law school.

Compatriot Sappington was President of the Maryland Society of the Sons of the American Revolution, and was prominent socially.

He was elected President General on May 21, 1941.

CHARLES BUNN SHALER

Charles Bunn Shaler was born in New Washington, Pennsylvania, January 28, 1884, the son of Lewis J. and Margaret S. Bunn Shaler. He married Hannah Elizabeth Aten and they had a son, named James B. Shaler.

He was a member of Waverly Presbyterian Church of Pittsburgh. He was a prominent Mason, a member of the Council, the Knights Templar, the Consistory, the Shrine and the Royal Jesters.

He was President of the Pittsburgh Guild of Prescription Opticians and was a Director of the National Guild.

As a Captain of the Civil Air Patrol Headquarters Staff, he rendered especially important service to his Country from 1941 to 1945.

LOREN EDMUNDS SOUERS

Loren Edmunds Souers was born December 4, 1882, at Mineral City, Ohio, the son of Judge E. S. and Celestia May Black Souers. Educated in public schools of Philadelphia, Ohio, he was graduated from the Law School of Western Reserve University, Cleveland, in 1905.

He was a distinguished attorney of Canton, Ohio, who had a wide range of civic, fraternal and business interests.

He had been a member of the Canton Board of Education, Canton, Ohio, since 1930, and President of the Board for three years. Compatriot Souers was a Member of his county and state bar assocations, and the American Bar Association.

He was 32nd. Degree Mason; Grand Master of Ohio I.O.O.F. in 1922-23; a Shriner and Kiwanian.

He taught a Bible class for 45 years. Of his life, his pastor said:

"You have loved righteousness; you have delighted in integrity and uprightness in purpose; you have hated lawlessness. Therefore God, even your God, has annointed you with the oil of exultant joy."

Few men who have been President General have been more highly regarded for their wisdom and devotion to patriotic service.

In 1910, Mr. Souers married Ilka R. Gaskell of Canton, Past Regent of Canton Chapter, D. A. R. They had two sons, Loren Eaton and Millard Ball.

JUDGE HENRY STOCKBRIDGE

Judge Henry Stockbridge was born in Baltimore, Md. on September 18, 1856. He received his A.B. degree from Amherst College and his degree in Law from the University of Maryland. He was at one time editor of the *Baltimore American*. He was elected to Congress in 1888 and served one term. In 1891 he was appointed Commissioner of Immigration in Baltimore. In 1896 he was associate judge of the Supreme Bench of Baltimore. He was later appointed to the Maryland Court of Appeals. He lectured on Law at the University of Maryland for 15 years.

Compatriot Stockbridge was Regent of the University of Maryland and President of the Board of Trustees from 1905 to 1924. He was Treasurer of the Enoch Pratt Library.

Compatriot Stockbridge was active in historical association work and was a member of patriotic societies.

On January 5, 1882 he married Helen M. Smith of Hadley, Mass. They had two sons.

He was elected President General of the Sons of the American Revolution on May 1, 1908.

He died March 22, 1924.

ARTHUR PRESTON SUMNER

Compatriot Arthur Preston Sumner, was born in Providence, Rhode Island, on the 8th day of April, 1862. He was the son of Dr. Ossian Sumner and Kate A. (Sayles) Sumner. He was educated in the public schools of Providence, and was graduated from Brown University in 1885 with the degree of A. B. He was admitted to the Rhode Island bar in July, 1888, and practiced before the State and Federal courts till February, 1920, when he was elected a Justice of the Superior Court. He served in the Rhode Island House of Representatives from 1912 to 1920, the last two years as Speaker of the House. He joined the Sons of the American Revolution, May 6, 1893, and attended eight Congresses. He was Treasurer of the Rhode Island Society from 1898 to 1918; was elected Vice President in 1918 and President in 1919. He served as a Vice-President General of the National Society from 1920 to 1923, and was elected President General, May 22, 1923.

Judge Sumner married Sarah E. Potter in 1918. In politics he was a Republican, and a member of the Congregational Church.

GEORGE EDWARD TARBOX, JR.

George Edward Tarbox, Jr., was born on February 11, 1903 in Hartford, Connecticut. The names of twelve of his direct ancestors appear on the Founder's Monument in Hartford. He is the lineal descendant of John Alden, William Mullins, Edward Fuller and Degory Priest, all signers of the Mayflower Compact.

Compatriot Tarbox graduated from the United States Naval Academy at Annapolis, Maryland, in the Class of 1925.

From 1942 to 1944 he was with the War Production Board, in charge of regional priorities for military installations in the Rocky Mountain Area.

Compatriot Tarbox was married, first, on September 26, 1927 to Dorothy Blayney of Denver, Colorado. Their children: Anne (deceased) and John E. Tarbox, III, who is a member of the Colorado Society, S.A.R. and a geophysicist by profession. Dorothy Blayney Tarbox died in 1934 and Compatriot Tarbox married, second, on February 14, 1942, Helen Askling of Denver, Colorado.

Compatriot Tarbox was President of the Colorado Society for two terms, 1945-1947. He was elected a member of the Board of Trustees of the National Society in 1948, 1954, 1955, 1956.

He has served on many National Committees, and was elected to the office of the National Society, for the Rocky Mountain District, at the Jacksonville Congress in 1949, and the following year he was re-elected for a second term. During his tenure of office he made official visits to every State Society in his District, travelling many thousands of miles, in this, the largest District in the National Society. He served the National Society as a Member of its Executive Committee, 1952-1953. He was the recipient of both the Minute Man Award and the Gold Good Citizenship Medal.

ROGERS CLARK BALLARD THRUSTON

Compatriot Thruston was born on November 6, 1858 at Louisville, Kentucky. In 1880 he was graduated from the Sheffield Scientific School of Yale. In later years he was awarded honorary degrees by other universities. He was a specialist in metallurgy, geology and mine engineering, and was a historian and antiquarian. He was a member of scientific and historial societies and socially prominent.

About the turn of the century, he began to devote himself almost exclusively to patriotic and historic endeavors.

He was a devoted member of the Sons of the American Revolution and contributed generously of his time and substance to the State, as well as the National Society. He had held every office in the Kentucky Society and was its only Honorary Life Member.

In 1913 Mr. Thruston organized and headed a pilgrimage which commemorated the journey of George Washington from Philadelphia to Cambridge to take command of the American Army.

In 1923, Compatriot Thruston became President of the Filson Club in Louisville, Kentucky, and continued as such until his death. He had been a member of this organization since 1892. Through this institution he devoted an untold amount of time, effort, and money, to the research and preservation of historical data having to do with Kentucky. He was a member of many State Historical Societies.

His great labors on compilation of "The Signers of the Declaration of Independence," was a monumental work for the Sons of the American Revolution, and in June, 1928, Mr. Thruston made his final report presenting one set of eight volumes, which constituted the results to that date of his vast research, to the National Society.

Compatriot Thruston was elected President General on May 20, 1913 and re-elected in 1914.

He died December 30, 1946.

JUDGE JOSIAH A. VAN ORSDEL

A native of Pennsylvania and a graduate of Westminster College, Compatriot Van Orsdel practiced law in Wyoming and was a member of the Wyoming House of Representatives. As Chairman of the Committee to revise and codify the Laws of Wyoming he did an outstanding job. He later was Attorney General of Wyoming and Associate Justice of the State Supreme Court. President Theodore Roosevelt appointed him in 1906 to be Assistant Attorney General of the United States. In December of 1907, he was appointed as a Federal Judge and Associate Justice of the Court of Appeals of District of Columbia.

Compatriot Van Orsdel was a member of the American Bar Associaiton and of numerous clubs.

He was a Presbyterian. He took a great interest in the S.A.R., and was President of the District of Columbia Society.

He was elected President General on June 4, 1930.

GOVERNOR EDWIN WARFIELD

Compatriot Edwin Warfield was born in Howard County, Maryland, on May 7, 1848. He was an attorney and state Senator. He was Surveyor of the Port of Baltimore in 1886. In 1890 he organized the Fidelity Deposit Company of Maryland, at one time the largest insurance company in the world. He later was elected governor of Maryland.

Compatriot Warfield was a member of many clubs and patriotic societies. He was elected President General on May 1, 1902.

DR. WILLIAM SEWARD WEBB

Dr. William Seward Webb was born in New York on January 31, 1851. He attended Columbia University. He studied medicine in Vienna, Paris and Berlin. He graduated from the College of Physicians and Surgeons in New York in 1875. Dr. Webb was President of the Wagner Sleeping Car Corporation, President of the W. S. Webb & Company, stockbrokers, from which he retired in 1883. He was the President of the Edmondson & St. Lawrence Railway Co. and was a director of many corporations.

He married the daughter of W. H. Vanderbilt.

He was the second President General of the Sons of the American Revolution, having been elected for the first term at Louisville on April 30, 1890 and re-elected in 1891 at the Congress held at Hartford, Connecticut.

ELMER MARSTON WENTWORTH

President General Wentworth, a railroad executive, was born at Newfield, Maine, May 8, 1861, son of John Norris and Nancy Titcomb (Wentworth) Wentworth and a descendant of William Wentworth, who came from Yorkshire, England, about 1627 and settled successively at Hampton and Exeter, Wells, Maine and Dover, New Hampshire.

Mr. Wentworth was married at Peabody, Massachusetts, November 5, 1884, to Sarah Elizabeth Tilton, daughter of Edward Porter Towne, of that place, and they had eight children.

Active in S.A.R. work, he was elected President General on May 16, 1916.

His death occurred at Mount Dora, Florida, April 12, 1936, and he is buried in Pine Hill Cemetery, Dover, New Hampshire.

WALTER ALLERTON WENTWORTH

Walter Allerton Wentworth was born at Dover, New Hampshire on September 6, 1888, the son of Elmer Marston and Elizabeth (Towne) Wentworth. His father was President General of the National Society, Sons of the American Revolution for two terms in 1916 and 1917. This is the only instance in the Society's history where father and son were both President General.

He was graduated from State Center (Iowa) High School and from Iowa State College.

He is the President of the International Dairy Show and formerly the Chairman of the Board of the National Dairy Council; Chairman of the Dairy Industry Committee; President of the Dairy Products Improvement Institute; and President of the Dairy Shrine Club.

He was formerly the Chairman of the Council, First Congregational Church of Columbus, Ohio; and was a Member of the Official Board and Executive Committee of Christ Church Methodist of New York City.

He joined the Iowa Society, S.A.R. in June 1911, transferred to the Ohio Society in 1926 and to the Empire State Society in 1936, thus having been a member for over 50 years. At the 65th Congress he received the Minute Man Award.

Compatriot Wentworth has held the following offices in the National Society of the Sons of the American Revolution:

Member of the Executive Committee, 1956 and 1957; Secretary-General 1954 and 1955; Vice President General,

1951. In his State Society, the Empire State Society, he was President, 1950; First Vice President, 1949; and Member of the Board of Managers, 1944 to date.

He was married the first time to Flora Beatrice Cochrane on August 1, 1912 who died on May 30, 1939, to whom one daughter and two sons were born.

He was married the second time to Aubyn (Chinn) Watson on August 31, 1940. She is a Former Regent of Mary Washington Colonial Chapter (New York) N.S.-D.A.R. and Past President of Oliver Burdick, Jr. Chapter (New York) C.A.R.

He now resides at 203 West Campbell Street, Frankfort, Kentucky, having moved there from New York City on June 1, 1956 upon his retirement, after 27 years with the Borden Company as Director of Industry Relations.

The Empire State Society in presenting Walter Allerton Wentworth for election as President General said in part:

> He combines modesty with a fine personality, and high integrity with executive capacity and a peculiarly effective gift of leadership. We have all loved to work with Al and under Al. We also honor him because he never slights a job or favors himself. Al has a long record of distinguished service to the National Society as well as to Empire State and to his local New York City chapter. We are proud to present him for your consideration.

EDGAR WILLIAMSON, JR.

Edgar Williamson, Jr., was born at Orange, New Jersey on November 24, 1903. He was the son of Edgar and Grace Elizabeth (Van Nalts) Williamson.

He is a graduate of the East Orange, New Jersey, Grammar and High Schools, the LeMaster Preparatory School and the Columbia University Graduate School, 1934-35. He is also a graduate of the Stevens Institute of Technology Graduate School, 1951-52.

Compatriot Williamson is a realtor by profession, heading a real estate, insurance and mortgage firm in Newark, New Jersey.

He is a former member of the New Jersey Legislature, House of Assembly, four terms; and a former Commissioner of the City of East Orange, New Jersey for five terms.

He holds membership in the Calvary Methodist Church, East Orange, New Jersey; the Real Estate Board of Newark, New Jersey; the Board of Governors New Jersey Association of Real Estate Boards; the National Association of Real Estate Boards, the National Institute of Real Estate Brokers; the Down Town Club of Newark, New Jersey; the Chamber of Commerce of Newark, New Jersey; the Advertising Club of New Jersey; the Civic Clubs Council of Newark, New Jersey, and is a director of Mohawk Savings and Loan Association, Newark, New Jersey.

He joined the Society of the Sons of the American Revolution by right of descent from William Williamson of North Carolina, in July, 1929 and is the recipient of the 25 year membership gold bar from the New Jersey Society, October 1954.

Compatriot Williamson's S.A.R. activities include holding all offices (except Chancellor) in the Orange Chapter, President two terms; Member Orange, Newark and Montclair Chapters; New Jersey Society Secretary for two terms; New Jersey Society 2nd Vice President for two terms; New Jersey Society 1st Vice President for two terms; Life member Board of Managers; Trustee of the National Society one term; Vice President General, North Atlantic District, one term; Secretary General of the National Society for three terms; Executive Committee, National Society, two terms; Chairman National Society Membership Committee, two terms; General Chairman of two Congresses (1) Trenton, New Jersey, 1946 (2) Atlantic City, New Jersey, 1960; Recipient of Minute Man Award at the 62nd Congress, Houston, in 1952. He has attended 10 Congresses.

He married Katharine Louis Sibley, daughter of Elmer Parker and Sarah (Tighe) Silbey of Malden, Massachusetts.

He resides at 375 Mt. Prospect Avenue, Newark, New Jersey.

GENERAL ALBERT M. WINN

Past President General elected post-humously at the Third National Congress on April 30, 1892. He was the first President of the California Society.

General Winn died at Sonoma, California, on August 26, 1883.

NEWELL B. WOODWORTH

Compatriot Woodworth was born at Rome, New York, on July 20, 1860. He later moved to Syracuse. He was a graduate of Columbia University—B.A. in 1882, at Law in 1885. He was a member of various patriotic societies, the University Club of New York and other civic clubs.

Compatriot Woodworth was an officer of various public and charitable organizations. He was elected President General on July 20, 1915.

A. HOWARD CLARK

(Secretary General and Registrar General, 1894 - 1918)

A. Howard Clark was born in Boston, on April 13, 1850. He belonged to the class of 1881 at Wesleyan University, Middleton, Connecticut. In 1906 that University conferred upon him the honorary degree of Master of Arts.

Mr. Clark was in the mercantile business in New York from 1867 to 1875. He was an assistant on the staff of the U.S. Fish Commission in 1879. Later he was an expert on the 10th. Census. Since 1881 Compatriot A. Howard Clark was connected with the Smithsonian Institution as Curator of the Division of History and editor of the publications of the Institution. He was a member of the International Geographical Congress held in Paris in 1889 and the same year President Cleveland appointed him as an expert to the Commission at the Paris Exposition of 1889.

Mr. Clark was the Society's first Registrar General and then Secretary-General and held these offices some fifteen years.

Mr. Clark was a member of various patriotic and historical associations. He died December 31, 1918.

FRANK BARTLETT STEELE

(Secretary General and Registrar General of the National Society of the American Revolution)

Frank Bartlett Steele was born in Buffalo, New York.

Frank Steele graduated from Buffalo State Normal School, now State Teachers College; he studied law with George Clinton, grandson of De Witt Clinton, N.Y. Governor, and was admitted to the N.Y. State bar in 1890. He served as Deputy County Clerk of the Supreme Court of New York and Deputy County Clerk of Erie County, and as Clerk of the Board of Supervisors. He was a Republican Committeeman for ten years before leaving Buffalo.

In 1897 Compatriot Steele was admitted to membership in the Sons of the American Revolution. He became Secretary of the Buffalo Chapter, S.A.R. shortly after joining and retained this office until leaving the city.

In 1906 he was a delegate for the first time to the Congress of the National Society S.A.R. which met in Boston.

In April 1908 when the Congress met in Buffalo, Mr. Steele made all the arrangements for both business and social features, the latter including a trip to Niagara Falls.

Mr. Steele attended every succeeding Congress from this time until 1915, when the meeting was held in Portland, Ore. In 1921 the Congress met again in Buffalo, and it was at this meeting that he was elected to the office of Secretary General. Three years prior, the Society had suffered a severe loss in the death of its long-time Secretary General, Mr. A. Howard Clark, who had served since the beginning. He had been temporarily succeeded by Mr. William S. Parks for one year, and Mr. Phillip S. Larner, two years.

At the same Congress at which Compatriot Steele was elected Secretary General, the Trustees decided to merge its two publications—the Annual Year Book and the Quarterly magazine to be sent to every member of the Society. Secretary General Steele was the editor of the magazine until 1949.

One project which Compatriot Steele originated was that of the Good Citizenship Medal Award. This began in

Buffalo and hundreds of these medals were presented each year to boys and girls of the Buffalo schools.

In 1934, at the Congress held in Cincinnati, Compatriot Frank Steele was elected both as Registrar General and Secretary General.

In 1949 Secretary General Steele became ill and the next year, following the Congress at Atlantic City, he retired after some thirty odd years of devoted service. When he retired on March 30, 1950 the District of Columbia Society presented him with a silver coffee tray, and the Board of Managers made him a member emeritus without further dues.

Frank Steele died February 28, 1952. At that time he may have been the only living compatriot of the S.A.R. who actually knew the personalities and leaders of the Society in its early years.

A resolution by Board of Trustees of The National Society of The Sons of The American Revolution on the death of Secretary-Registrar-General Emeritus, Frank B. Steele, reads in part:

> WHEREAS, Frank B. Steele's passing has caused the loss to the Society of a very fine citizen, patriot and compatriot, and
>
> WHEREAS, it is believed that he made a substantial contribution during his lifetime to patriotic societies and good citizenship, and particularly to The National Society of the Sons of the American Revolution while serving for many years as Secretary-Registrar-General;
>
> NOW THEREFORE BE IT RESOLVED, that the Board of Trustees in meeting assembled at Washington, D. C. this second day of March 1950, go on record as expressing its deepest sympathy over the death of our late compatriot and Secretary-Registrar-General, Frank B. Steele; and that we particularly acknowledge the contribution that he made during his lifetime to patriotic societies and good citizenship, and particularly to The National Society while serving as its Secretary-Registrar-General.

HAROLD L. PUTNAM

(Executive Secretary of the National Society of the Sons of the American Revolution)

Harold L. Putnam was born at El Dorado, Kansas, October, 1896, the son of Herbert Lord Putman and Harriett Louise Betts. His parents moved to Los Angeles, California, 1909, in search of a healthful climate for their son. Young Putnam attended public schools in Los Angeles, graduating from Hollywood High School in 1915. He attended Hollywood Junior College until called into service as member of First Fire Command, Coast Artillery, NGC., on April 7, 1917, where he served until honorably discharged December 21, 1918, as gunnery instructor, gas instructor, bayonet instructor and signal instructor.

Compatriot Putnam began his business career in advertising and sales promotion work. He held the position of Assistant Secretary and Treasurer of the California Cooperative Canneries 1922-24. He was a partner in Investment Auditors of California 1924-1926. Then, sales manager of the Johnson-Webb Advertising Agency, 1926-29. Joining the advertising staff of Hearst Newspapers Inc., 1929, he was assigned to the San Francisco Call-Bulletin. He resigned his position as Assistant Advertising Manager of the *Call-Bulletin* in 1950 to become Executive Secretary of the National Society of the Sons of the American Revolution.

Compatriot Putnam has held many offices in the Society of the Sons of the American Revolution, including that of Secretary of the San Francisco Chapter; President of the California Society; Vice President General for the Pacific Coast District, four terms; National Trustee, four terms; and Chairman of the Americanization Committee, five terms.

He is a former Secretary and Director of the Fraternity Club San Francisco; presently a member of the University Club Washington, D. C., and a member of the Academy of Political Science. He has served in his present capacity as Executive Secretary of the National Society, and as Editor of the S.A.R. Magazine, since 1950.

APPENDIX

LIST OF OFFICIALS
and
SOME PROMINENT MEMBERS

PRESIDENTS GENERAL AND DATES OF ELECTION

Date of Congress	Place of Congress	President General Elected	From State of
1889	New York (Fraunces' Tavern)	Lucius P. Deming	Connecticut
1890	Louisville	Dr. William S. Webb	New York & Vermont
1891	Hartford, Conn.	Dr. William S. Webb	New York & Vermont
1892	New York	General Horace Porter	New York
1893	Chicago	General Horace Porter	New York
1894	Washington	General Horace Porter	New York
1895	Boston	General Horace Porter	New York
1896	Richmond	General Horace Porter	New York
1897	Cleveland	Edward S. Barrett	Massachusetts
1898	Morristown, N. J.	Edward S. Barrett	Massachusetts
1899	Detroit	Franklin Murphy	New Jersey
1900	New York	Joseph C. Breckinridge	Kentucky & D. C.
1901	Pittsburgh	Walter S. Logan	New York
1902	Washington	Gov. Edwin Warfield	Maryland
1903	New Haven	Gen. Edwin S. Greeley	Connecticut
1904	St. Louis	James D. Hancock	Pennsylvania
1905	Philadelphia	Francis H. Appleton	Massachusetts
1906	Boston	Cornelius C. Pugsley	New York
1907	Denver	Nelson A. McClary	Illinois
1908	Buffalo	Henry Stockbridge	Maryland
1909	Baltimore	Morris B. Beardsley	Connecticut
1910	Toledo	William A. Marble	New York
1911	Louisville	Dr. Moses G. Parker	Massachusetts
1912	Boston	James M. Richardson	Ohio
1913	Chicago	Rogers Clark Ballard Thruston	Kentucky
1914	Syracuse	Rogers Clark Ballard Thruston	Kentucky
1915	Portland, Oregon San Francisco	Newell B. Woodworth	New York

1916	Newark	Elmer M. Wentworth	Iowa
1917	Nashville	Elmer M. Wentworth	Iowa
1918	Rochester	Louis Annin Ames	New York
1919	Detroit	Chancellor L. Jenks	Illinois
1920	Hartford	J. Henry Preston	Maryland
1921	Buffalo	Wallace McCamant	Oregon
1922	Springfield, Mass.	Major Washington Irving Lincoln Adams	New Jersey
1923	Nashville	Arthur Preston Sumner	Rhode Island
1924	Salt Lake City	Marvin Harrison Lewis	Kentucky
1925	Swampscott, Mass.	Judge Harvey Foote Remington	New York
1926	Philadelphia	Wilbert H. Barrett	Michigan
1927	Richmond	Ernest E. Rogers	Connecticut
1928	Washington	Ganson Depew	New York
1929	Springfield, Ill.	Howard Rowley	California
1930	Asbury Park, N. J.	Judge Josiah A. Van Orsdel	D. C.
1931	Charlotte, N. C.	Benjamin Newhall Johnson (D in office)	Massachusetts
	Ex. Comm. chose	Judge Josiah A. Van Orsdel—to complete term.	
1932	Washington	Frederick W. Millspaugh	Tennessee
1933	Cincinnati	Arthur M. McGrillis	Rhode Island
1934	Baltimore	Arthur M. McGrillis	Rhode Island
1935	Louisville	Henry F. Baker	Maryland
1936	Portland, Maine	Messmore Kendall	New York
1937	Buffalo	Messmore Kendall	New York
1938	Dallas	Messmore Kendall	New York
1939	New London	Messmore Kendall	New York
1940	Washington	Loren E. Souers	Ohio
1941	Columbus	G. Ridgely Sappington	Maryland
1942	Williamsburg	Sterling Fahn Mutz	Nebraska
1943	New York	Smith Lewis Multer	New Jersey
1944	Harrisburg, Pa.	Smith Lewis Multer	New Jersey
1945	No Meeting on Account of War	Smith Lewis Multer	New Jersey
1946	Trenton, N. J.	Allen L. Oliver	Missouri
1947	Huntington, W. Va.	A. Herbert Foreman	Virginia
1948	Minneapolis	Charles B. Shaler (D)	Pennsylvania
	Executive Comm.	(Ben H. Powell)	Texas
1949	Jacksonville, Fla.	John Whelchel Finger	New York
1950	Atlantic City	Wallace C. Hall	Michigan
1951	San Francisco	Wallace C. Hall	Michigan
1952	Houston	Ray O. Edwards	Florida
1953	Cincinnati	Arthur A. de la Houssaye	Louisiana
1954	Williamsburg, Va.	Milton M. Lory	Iowa
1955	Chicago	Edgar Williamson, Jr.	New Jersey
1956	Lake George, N. Y.	Eugene P. Carver, Jr.	Massachusetts

1957	Salt Lake City	George E. Tarbox, Jr.	Colorado
1958	Biloxi	Walter A. Wentworth	New York
1959	Pittsburgh	Charles A. Jones	Ohio
1960	Memphis	Dr. Herschel S. Murphy	New Jersey
1961	Clearwater, Fla.	Horace Y. Kitchell	Mississippi
1962	Philadelphia	Charles A. Anderson, M.D.	Ohio

GENERAL OFFICERS ELECTED AT NEW YORK, APRIL 30th, 1889

President General Hon. Wm. Seward Webb
Vice-President General for Alabama Major G. B. West
Vice-President General for Arkansas Col. S. W. Williams
Vice-President General for California Col. A. S. Hubbard
Vice-President General for Connecticut Maj. J. C. Kinney
Vice-President General for Delaware A. J. Woodman
Vice-President General for Illinois Bishop C. E. Cheney
Vice-President General for Indiana Hon. Wm. E. English
Vice-President General for Kentucky Hon. S. B. Buckner
Vice-President General for Maine Hon. C. H. Denison
Vice-President General for Maryland Rev. John G. Morris, D.D.
Vice-President General for Massachusetts Hon. E. S. Barrett
Vice-President General for Michigan Wm. H. Brearley
Vice-President General for Minnesota Hon. John B. Sanborn
Vice-President General for Missouri Hon. D. R. Francis
Vice-President General for New Hampshire Hon. H. K. Slayton
Vice-President General for New Jersey Hon. Robt. S. Green
Vice-President General for New York Hon. Wm. H. Arnoux
Vice-President General for Ohio Hon. R. B. Hayes
Vice-President General for Rhode Island Hon. E. B. Andrews
Vice-President General for South Carolina Hon. Wade Hampton
Vice-President General for Tennessee Dr. D. C. Kelly
Vice-President General for Vermont Hon. W. P. Dillingham
Vice-President General for Virginia Hon. Fitzhugh Lee
Vice-President General for West Virginia Hon. John J. Jacob
Vice-President General for Wisconsin Hon. Wm. D. Hoard
Vice-President General for District of Columbia Admiral D. D. Porter
Vice-President General for France Edmond de Lafayette
Secretary General Lieut. J. C. Cresap
Assistant Secretary General Chas. J. King
Assistant Secretary General Wilson J. Gill
Assistant Secretary General Wm. F. Cregar
Treasurer General James Otis
Registrar General L. L. Tarbell
Chaplain General Rev. Timothy Dwight

VICE PRESIDENTS GENERAL

1891
Judge Lucius P. Deming, Connecticut
Gov. Simon B. Buckner, Kentucky
Judge William H. Arnoux, New York
Josiah C. Pumpelly, New Jersey
Dr. George Brown Goode, D. C.

1892
Gen. Horace Porter, New York
Jonathan Trumbull, Conn.
Gen. Bradley T. Johnson, Maryland
Judge Albert Edgerton, Minnesota
Col. Champion C. Chase, Nebraska

1893
Jonathan Trumbull
Gen. J. C. Breckinridge
Henry M. Shepard
Gen. T. S. Peck
Paul Revere

1894
Gen. J. C. Breckinridge, D. C.
Col. Thomas M. Anderson, Washington
Wm. Ridgely Griffith, Maryland
Edwin S. Barrett, Massachusetts
John Whitehead, New Jersey

1895
Gen. J. C. Breckinridge, D. C.
Col. Thomas M. Anderson, Washington
Cushman K. Davis, Minnesota
Edwin S. Barrett, Massachusetts
John Whitehead, New Jersey

1896
Col. Thomas M. Anderson, U.S.A., Washington
Edwin S. Barrett, Massachusetts
John Whitehead, New Jersey
Wm. Ridgely Griffith, Maryland
Wm. Wirt Henry, Virginia

1897
Col. T. Anderson, Washington
John Whitehead, New Jersey
James M. Richardson, Ohio
Capt. Samuel E. Gross, Illinois
Gen. J. C. Breckinridge, D. C.

1898
Col. T. Anderson, Washington
John Whitehead, New Jersey
James M. Richardson, Ohio
Franklin Murphy, New York
Gen. J. C. Breckinridge, D. C.

1899
Gen. J. C. Breckinridge, D. C.
John Whitehead, New Jersey
Thos. W. Palmer, Mich.
Jonathan Trumbull, Ct.
James H. Anderson, Ohio

1900
Gen. Thomas M. Anderson, U.S.A., Washington
James Harris Gilbert, Ill.
Gen. Francis H. Appleton, Mass.
Gen. Edwin S. Greely, Ct.
Howard De Haven Ross, Del.

1901
James Denton Hancock, Penn.
Thomas Pitts
Horace Davis
John Whitehead, N. J.
George A. Peane

1902

Cornelius Amory Pugsley,
  New York
Capt. Samuel E. Gross, Illinois

Noble D. Larner, D. C.
Howard De Haven Ross, Del.
Col. Albert J. Logan, Pa.

1903

Maj. Ira H. Evans, Texas
Dr. John W. Bayne, D. C.
Daniel M. Lore, Illinois

John J. Hubbell, New Jersey
Arthur W. Daunis, Rhode Island

1904

George H. Shields, Missouri
John Paul Earnest, D. C.
Col. A. D. Cutter, California

Edward Peyson Cove, New York
Charles Kingsbury Miller,
  Illinois

1905

Morris B. Beardsly, Ct.
Col. John C. Lewis

Henry Stockbridge, Maryland
Nelson A. McClary, Ill.

1906

Dr. Moses G. Parker,
  Massachusetts
Henry Stockbridge, Maryland

Edward Anson Butler, Maine
Lunsford L. Lewis, Virginia
Andrew W. Bray, New Jersey

1907

Trueman G. Avery, New York
William Hamilton Bayly, D. C.
Pelham W. Ames, California

Gen. J. W. Whiting, Alabama
Dr. Clarkson N. Guyer, Colo.

1908

George Wm. Bates, Michigan
William James Van Patten, Vt.
John R. Webster, Nebraska

Dr. Clarkson N. Guyer, Colorado
George Rowland Howe,
  New Jersey

1909

Dr. Clarkson N. Guyer, Colorado
Col. Peter F. Pescud, Louisiana
Willard Secor, Iowa

George C. Sargent, Calif.
Maj. Moses Veale, Pa.

1910

R. C. Ballard Thruston,
  Kentucky
William T. Dewey, Vermont

Com. John H. Moore, U.S.N.,
  D. C.
Col. Samuel E. Bliss, Illinois
R. M. Sims, California

1911

Joseph S. Butler, Jr., Ohio
George Irwin Hale, Colorado
R. C. Ballard Thruston,
  Kentucky

George O. Dix, Ind.
Com. John R. Moore, U.S.N.,
  D. C.

1912

Amedee B. Cole, Missouri
Col. O. D. Baldwin, California
Henry V. A. Joslin, Rhode Island

Newell B. Woodworth, New York
Edwin S. Crandon,
  Massachusetts

1913

La Verne Noyes, Illinois
Wilson Whipple Kirby, Colorado
James Phinney Baxter, Missouri

Wallace McCamant, Oregon
Rear Ad. George W. Baird,
  U.S.N., D. C.

1914

Com. John H. Moore, D. C.
Alvin M. Woolson, Ohio
Herman W. Fernburger, Pa.

Wm. K. Boardman, Tenn.
Lt. Col. M. W. Wood, U.S.A., Idaho

1915

Henry F. Punderson, Massachusetts
Lt. Col. M. W. Wood, U.S.A., Idaho

Samuel Judd Holmes, Washington
William K. Boardman, Tennessee
Samuel Culven Park, Utah

1916 and 1917

Orison J. C. Dutton, Washington
Frederick E. Emerson, Virginia
Thomas W. Williams, New Jersey

Philip F. Tuna, Missouri
William K. Boardman, Tennessee

1918

Charles French Read, Massachusetts
Thomas W. Williams, New Jersey

Albert M. Henry, Washington
Frank W. Rawls,* Arkansas
Thomas A. Perkins, California

1919

George F. Burgess, Ct.
Thomas W. Williams, New Jersey

Moulton Houk, Ohio
Linn Paine, Missouri
Overton Ellis, Washington

1920

George Hale Nutting, Massachusetts
Thos. W. Williams, New Jersey

Moulton Houk, Ohio
Linn Paine, Missouri
Jno. W. Bell, Jr., Washington

1921

George Hale Nutting, Massachusetts
Philip F. Larner, Washington

Marvin N. Lewis, Kentucky
Jno. W. Bell, Jr., Washington

1922

Harry T. Lord, Connecticut
Philip F. Larner, Washington
Louis A. Bowman, Illinois

Henry B. Hawley, Iowa
George Albert Smith, Utah

1923

Dr. Charles H. Bangs, Massachusetts
Carl M. Vail, New Jersey

Louis A. Bowman, Illinois
J. Reid Green, Nebraska
George Albert Smith, Utah

---

* Elected by ex-Com. in place of C. Robert Churchill (La.) who declined the office.

1924

Dr. Charles H. Bangs,
  Massachusetts
Carl M. Vail, New Jersey
Louis A. Bowman, Illinois
J. Reid Green, Nebraska

George Albert Smith, Utah
Frederick W. Millspaugh,
  Tennessee
Jas. M. Breckinridge, Missouri

1925

Benton H. Wiggin,
  Massachusetts
Josiah A. Van Orsdell, D. C.
Frederick W. Millspaugh,
  Tennessee

Louis A. Bowman, Illinois
Charles P. Schouten, Minn.
Jas. M. Breckinridge, Missouri
George Albert Smith, Utah

1926

Benton H. Wiggin,
  Massachusetts
Frederic de Gama Hahn,
  New Jersey
Josiah A. Van Orsdel, D. C.
John F. Jones, South Carolina
C. Robert Churchill, Louisiana

Winford L. Mattoon, Ohio
Harry G. Colson, Illinois
Charles P. Schouten, Minn.
Sam P. Cochran, Texas
Percy B. Hunting, Washington
Howard C. Rowley, California

1927

Albert M. Spear, Maine
Frederic de Gama Hahn,
  New Jersey
Ernest J. Clark, Md.
Jno. F. Jones, South Carolina
George D. Caldwell, Kentucky
Winford L. Mattoon, Ohio

Harry G. Colson, Illinois
Charles P. Schouten, Minn.
Sam P. Cochran, Texas
Parcy B. Hunting, Washington
Howard C. Rowley, California
Marquis de Chambrun, France

1928

George Seymour Godard,
  Connecticut
Ernest J. Clark, Md.
Oliver Benedict Bridgman,
  New York
Cornelius Christianson, Illinois
Norman Milner Couty, Kentucky

David Edwin French, Viriginia
Dr. Frank Ward Hold, Michigan
Harry Benton Moon, Washington
Maj. Charles P. Schouten, Minn.
Howard C. Rowley, California
Marquis de Chambrun, France

1929

George Seymour Godard,
  Connecticut
Oliver Benedict Bridgman,
  New York
Kenneth Sanford Wales, D. C.
Harrison Gray Otis,
  W. Virginia
Ezra C. Potter, Iowa
Robert Stone, Kansas

J. Wilfred Corr, Colorado
Herbert Marston Lee,
  California
Frederick W. Millspaugh,
  Tennessee
David E. French, W. Virginia
Dr. Frank Ward Holt, Michigan
Maj. Charles P. Schouten, Minn.
Marquis de Chambrun, France

1930

Arthur Milton McCrillis, Rhode Island
Miles S. Kuhns, Ohio
Cooper S. Yost, Missouri
Park Mathewson, S. Carolina
Ezra C. Potter, Iowa
Herbert Marston Lee, California
Willard Ives Kimm, New Jersey
Col. Lewis K. Torbet, Illinois
Kenneth S. Wales, D. C.
Frederick W. Millspaugh, Tennessee
J. Wilfred Corr, Colorado
Marquis de Chambrun, France

1931

Arthur M. McCrillis, Rhode Island
Cornelius Doremus, New Jersey
Leslie Sulgrove, Montana
Leland Hume, Tenn.
Col. Lewis E. Torbet, Illinois
Cooper S. Yost, Missouri

Samuel F. Punderson, Massachusetts
Mark F. Finley, D. C.
Ransom H. Bassett, Kentucky
Norman B. Conger, Michigan
H. D. Colquitt, Texas
Judge Walter B. Beals, Washington

Dr. Daniel T. Smithwick, N. Carolina
Mark F. Finley, D. C.
Walter B. Beals, Washington
Miles S. Kuhns, Ohio
Ezra C. Potter, Iowa
Marquis de Chambrun, France

1932

Col. Messmore Kendall, New York
Col. E. L. Baxter Davidson, N. Carolina
Charles A. Breese, Indiana
L. B. Hanna, N. Dakota
Leslie Sulgrove, Montana
Mraquis de Chambrun, France

1933

Samuel F. Punderson, Massachusetts
Col. Jno. L. Walker, Pa.
Ransom H. Bassett, Kentucky
Norman B. Conger, Michigan
H. O. Colquitt, Texas
Judge Walter B. Beals, Washington

Col. Messmore Kendall, New York
Walter B. Livezey, Virginia
Charles Breese, Indiana
L. B. Hanna, N. Dakota
Ben L. Rich, Utah
Marquis de Rochambeau, Foreign Dist.

1934

Willis C. Hall, Maine
Jno. L. Walker, Pa.
Archie M. Smith, Louisiana
Norman B. Conger, Michigan
William H. Arnold, Arkansas
Robert Tucker, Oregon

H. Prescott Beach, New Jersey
Walter B. Livezey, Virginia
Ansel M. Beckwith, Ohio
L. B. Hanna, N. Dakota
Ben L. Rich, Utah
Marquis de Rochambeau, Paris

1935

Willis B. Hall, Maine
Laurence Leonard, D. C.
Archie M. Smith, Louisiana
Charles B. Elder, Illinois
William H. Arnold, Arkansas
Robert Tucker, Oregon

H. Prescott Beach, New Jersey
William A. Graham, N. Carolina
Ansel M. Beckwith, Ohio
Elmour D. Lum, N. Dakota
Ben. L. Rich, Utah
Marquis de Rochambeau, France

1936

Davis G. Maraspin, Massachusetts
Lawrence Leonard, D. C.
Arthur Crouner, Jr., Tennessee
Charles B. Elder, Illinois
Ambrose Deatrich, Kansas
Orville Vaughn, California

H. Prescott Beach, New Jersey
William A. Graham, N. Carolina
Franklin J. Burdette, W. Virginia
Elmour D. Lum, N. Dakota
G. Montagne Butler, Arizona
Marquis de Rochambeau, France

1937

Davis G. Maraspin, Massachusetts
Tom Moore, Virginia
Alex H. Lord, Delaware
Franklin J. Burdette, W. Virginia
Sterling F. Mutz, Nebraska

G. Montagne Butler, Arizona
Harry F. Brewer, New Jersey
Wallace C. Hall, Mich.
Ambrose Deatrich, Kansas
Carl G. Brown, California
Marquis de Rochambeau, France

1938

Howard E. Coe, Connecticut
Alex H. Lord, Delaware
Arthur de la Houssaye, Louisiana
Wallace C. Hall, Michigan
Paul P. Pinkerton, Oklahoma
Carl G. Brown, California

Harry F. Brewer, New Jersey
Tom Moore, Virginia
Clarence A. Cook, Indiana
Sterling F. Mutz, Nebraska
Paul P. Newlon, Colorado
Marquis de Rochambeau, France

1939

Howard E. Coe, Connecticut
Robert C. Trecy, D. C.
Arthur de la Houssaye, Louisiana
Alonzo H. Wilkinson, Wisconsin
Paul P. Pinkerton, Oklahoma
Frank J. Gaunett, Oregon

George Winters, New Jersey
Jas. D. Watson, Georgia
Clarence A. Cook, Indiana
Leavitt R. Barker, Minn.
Frederick H. Ward, N. Mexico
Marquis de Rochambeau, France

1940

Henry D. C. DuBois, Rhode Island
Robert C. Trecy, D. C.
A. Lee Read, Tennessee
Alonzo H. Wilkinson, Wisconsin
Allen H. Oliver, Missouri
Frank J. Gaunett, Oregon

George Winters, New Jersey
Burton Barrs, Florida
Robert Boggis, Ohio
Leavitt R. Barker, Minn.
Frederick H. Ward, N. Mexico
Marquis de Rochambeau, France

1941

Henry D. C. DuBois, Rhode Island
William J. Aiken, Pa.
A. Lee Read, Tennessee
Wm. C. Krickbaum, Michigan
Ben H. Powell, Texas

Harold L. Putnam, California
Richard V. Goodwin, New York
Burton Barrs, Florida
Downey M. Gray, Kentucky
Charles D. Reed, Iowa
Frank M. Keezer, Colorado

1942

Arthur C. Dow, Jr., Massachusetts
William J. Aiken, Pa.
Frank W. Zeigler, Tennessee
Roy V. Barnes, Michigan
Ben H. Powell, Texas

Harold L. Putnam, California
Richard V. Goodwin, New York
A. Herbert Foreman, Virginia
Jno. B. Campbell, Indiana
Charles D. Reed, Iowa
Frank M. Keezer, Colorado

1943

Arthur C. Dow, Jr., Massachusetts
Frederic M. Supplee, Maryland
Frank W. Zeigler, Tennessee
James G. Skinner, Illinois
I. Garfield Buell, Oklahoma

Harold L. Putnam, California
Richard V. Goodwin, New York
William T. Old, Virginia
Jno. B. Campbell, Indiana
Elmour D. Lum, N. Dakota
George A. Smith, Utah

1944

Elmer H. Spaulding, Connecticut
Frederic M. Supplee, Maryland
Percy L. Clifton, Massachusetts
James G. Skinner, Illinois

J. Garfield Buell, Oklahoma
Murray Hulbert, New York
William T. Old, Virginia
Henry J. Smith, W. Virginia
Jno. G. Ballard, Minn.
George A. Smith, Utah

1945

No Congress

1946

Chester R. Martin, Rhode Island
Dr. Clifton P. Clark, Virginia
Furman B. Pearce, Louisiana
Lloyd D. Smith, Michigan
Mason E. Mitchell, Arkansas
G. Ward Kemp, Washington

Harold M. Blanchard, New Jersey
J. Edward Allen, N. Carolina
William M. Pettit, Ohio
Dr. J. A. Goodrich, Iowa
George A. Smith, Utah

1947

Chester R. Martin, Rhode Island
Dr. John A. Fritchey II, Penn.
Furman B. Pearce, Louisiana
Lloyd D. Smith, Michigan
Mason E. Mitchell, Arkansas
Brig. Gen. H. G. Mathewson, California

Harold M. Blanchard, New Jersey
J. Edward Allen, N. Carolina
William M. Pettit, Ohio
Dr. J. A. Goodrich, Iowa
Col. Franklin Riter, Utah

1948

Douglas Sloane, New Hampshire
Dr. John A. Fritchey II, Penn.
Furman B. Pearce, Louisiana
Alonzo Newton Rerm, Illinois
Jno. W. Giesecke, Missouri
Brig. Gen. H. G. Mathewson, California

Jno. W. Finger, New York
Benj. I. Powell, Florida
Hansom H. Bassett, Kentucky
Col. Harold D. LeMar, Nebraska
Brig. Gen. Franklin Riter, Utah

1949

Douglas Sloane,
  New England District
Edgar Williamson, Jr.,
  North Atlantic District
Edward D. Shriner, Jr.,
  Middle Atlantic District
Ray O. Edwards,
  South Atlantic District
Col. Wm. T. Carpenter,
  Southern District
Fred I. Willis,
  Central District

John H. Babb,
  Great Lakes District
Col. Harold D. LeMar,
  North Mississippi District
John W. Giesecke,
  South Mississippi District
George E. Tarbox,
  Rocky Mountain District
Walter S. Bear,
  Pacific Coast District

1950

John Fisher Robinson,
  New England District
Gardner Osborn,
  North Atlantic District
Edward D. Shriner, Jr.,
  Mid Atlantic District
Reuben A. Garland,
  South Atlantic District
Col. Wm. T. Carpenter,
  Southern District
Buford C. Tynes,
  Central District

Ralph D. Johnson,
  Great Lakes District
Albert H. P. Houser,
  North Mississippi District
Dr. Valin R. Woodward,
  South Mississippi District
George E. Tarbox,
  Rocky Mountain District
Walter S. Bear,
  Pacific Coast District

1951

John Fisher Robinson,
  New England District
Walter A. Wentworth,
  North Atlantic District
Theodore Marvin,
  Mid Atlantic District
Carson D. Baucom,
  South Atlantic District
Cyril E. Cain,
  Southern District
Clarence E. Shriner,
  Central District

John E. Dickinson,
  Great Lakes District
Albert H. P. Houser,
  North Mississippi District
Charles E. Gilbert, Jr.,
  South Mississippi District
Robert G. Norfleet,
  Rocky Mountain District
Lewis Addington Smith,
  Pacific Coast District

1952

Harry K. Torrey,
  New England District
Dr. Herschel S. Murphy,
  North Atlantic District
Theodore Marvin,
  Mid Atlantic District

Col. Samuel R. Todd,
  Great Lakes District
Milton M. Lory,
  North Mississippi District
Charles E. Gilbert, Jr.,
  South Mississippi District

Carson D. Baucom,
  South Atlantic District
Cyril E. Cain,
  Southern District
George L. Clark,
  Central District

Robert G. Norfleet,
  Rocky Mountain District
Lewis Addington Smith,
  Pacific Coast District

1953

Harry K. Torrey,
  New England District
Dr. Herschel S. Murphy,
  North Atlantic District
Maj. Gen. Karl Truesdell,
  Mid Atlantic District
Crawford S. Rogers,
  South Atlantic District
Hugh W. Stallworth,
  Southern District
Harry I. Hadsell,
  Central District

Barry T. Whipple,
  Great Lakes District
Howard A. Chapin, Jr.,
  North Mississippi District
Charles E. Gilbert, Jr.,
  South Mississippi District
John R. Gobble,
  Rocky Mountain District
Brig. Gen. Charles D. Y. Ostrom,
  Pacific Coast District

1954

Calvin C. Bolles,
  New England District
Clement D. Asbury,
  North Atlantic District
Maj. Gen. Karl Truesdell,
  Mid Atlantic District
Crawford S. Rogers,
  South Atlantic District
Frederick C. Grabner,
  Southern District
Dr. V. E. Holcombe,
  Central District

Henry C. Fuller,
  Great Lakes District
Howard A. Chapin, Jr.,
  North Mississippi District
Charles E. Gilbert, Jr.,
  South Mississippi District
John R. Gobble,
  Rocky Mountain District
Brig. Gen. Charles D. Y. Ostrom,
  Pacific Coast District

1955

Calvin C. Bolles,
  New England District
Clement D. Asbury,
  North Atlantic District
Louis J. Heizmann,
  Mid Atlantic District
Folks Huxford,
  South Atlantic District
Frederick C. Grabner,
  Southern District
James G. Cecil,
  Central District

Col. Edward N. Wentworth,
  Great Lakes District
Carl A. Herrick,
  North Mississippi District
Col. Frederick W. Huntington,
  South Mississippi District
W. E. Springer,
  Rocky Mountain District
Dr. Burt Brown Barker,
  Pacific Coast District

1956

Stuart H. Tucker,
  New England District
Stanton T. Lawrence,
  North Atlantic District
Louis J. Heizmann,
  Mid Atlantic District
Folks Huxford,
  South Atlantic District
Robert P. Gordon,
  Southern District
Warren M. Taylor,
  Central District

Charles S. Prescott,
  Great Lakes District
Carl A. Herrick,
  North Mississippi District
Col. Frederick W. Huntington,
  South Mississippi District
W. E. Springer,
  Rocky Mountain District
Dr. Burt Brown Barker,
  Pacific Coast District

1957

Stuart H. Tucker,
  New England District
Stanton T. Lawrence,
  North Atlantic District
George Morris Whiteside,
  Mid Atlantic District
Frank W. Hannum,
  South Atlantic District
Robert P. Gordon,
  Southern District
Dr. V. E. Holcombe, Central District

Dr. George A. Parkinson,
  Great Lakes District
James T. Mulhall,
  North Mississippi District
William F. Turrentine, Jr.,
  South Mississippi District
Wood Wormald,
  Rocky Mountain District
Jean A. Hibbard,
  Pacific Coast District

1958

John C. Wroe,
  New England District
Hon. Abram Zoller,
  North Atlantic District
George Morris Whiteside,
  Mid Atlantic District
Carson D. Baucom,
  South Atlantic District
Horace Y. Kitchell,
  Southern District
Dr. Charles A. Anderson, Central District

John E. King,
  Great Lakes District
James Terry Mulhall,
  North Mississippi District
William F. Turrentine, Jr.,
  South Mississippi District
Dr. T. Earl Pardoe,
  Rocky Mountain District
Jean A. Hibbard,
  Pacific Coast District

1959

John C. Wroe,
  New England District
Hon. Abram Zoller,
  North Atlantic District
W. Giles Parker,
  Mid Atlantic District
Dr. Boyce McL. Grier,
  South Atlantic District
Horace Y. Kitchell,
  Southern District
James G. Cecil, Central District

Marion Crawmer,
  Great Lakes District
Lowell R. King,
  North Mississippi District
Col. Ross H. Routh,
  South Mississippi District
Dr. T. Earl Pardoe,
  Rocky Mountain District
Dr. Luther Clagett Beck,
  Pacific Coast District

1960

Stephen C. Luce, Jr.,
  New England District
Ross K. Cook,
  North Atlantic District
Clyde R. Flory, M.D.,
  Mid Atlantic District
Laurens Hamilton,
  South Atlantic District
H. Martin Nunnelley,
  Southern District
James Francis Miller,
  Central District
Read E. Widrig,
  Great Lakes District

Lowell R. King,
  North Mississippi District
Col. Ross H. Routh,
  South Mississippi District
Edwin A. Williams,
  Rocky Mountain District
Jed F. Woolley,
  Inter Mountain District
H. Lewis Mathewson,
  Pacific Coast District
Count Rene de Chambrun,
  Foreign District (France)

1961

Brig. Gen. George A. Davis,
  New England District
William Y. Pryor,
  North Atlantic District
Col. Thurston H. Baxter,
  Mid Atlantic District
Hon. Folks Huxford,
  South Atlantic District
H. Martin Nunnelley,
  Southern District
Chester A. Walworth,
  Central District
Ch. A. Goodwin-Perkins,
  Great Lakes District

Stanley S. Gillam,
  North Mississippi District
Walter G. Sterling,
  South Mississippi District
Clinton M. Roth,
  Rocky Mountain District
E. C. Phoenix,
  Inter Mountain District
H. Lewis Mathewson,
  Pacific Coast District
Count Rene de Chambrun,
  Foreign District (France)

1962

Brig. Gen. George A. Davis,
  New England District
E. Fred Dougherty,
  North Atlantic District
Col. Thruston H. Baxter,
  Mid Atlantic District
Austin R. Drew,
  South Altantic District
Hugh M. Wilkinson,
  Southern District
Samuel K. Houston,
  Central District
Frank L. Lowmaster,
  Great Lakes District

Stanley S. Gillam,
  North Mississippi District
Walter G. Sterling,
  South Mississippi District
John H. Eversole,
  Rocky Mountain District
E. C. Phoenix,
  Inter Mountain District
Olin C. Moulton, M.D.,
  Western District
Joseph C. Long,
  Pacific District
Laurens M. Hamilton,
  Foreign District

EXECUTIVE COMMITTEES

1949-1950

Hon. Sherman Adams
John G. Ballord
Alonzo N. Benn
Harold M. Blanchard
Wheaton H. Brewer

Dr. John R. Fritchey, II
Furman B. Pearce
Ben H. Powell, III
John W. Finger,
    Pres.-Gen., Chr. Ex-Officio

1950-1951

John H. Babb
Wheaton H. Brewer
Ray O. Edwards
John W. Finger
A. Herbert Foreman

Ben H. Powell, III
Clarence E. Shriner
Harry K. Torrey
Wallace C. Hall,
    Pres.-Gen., Chr. Ex-Officio

1951-1952

John H. Babb
Wheaton H. Brewer
Ray O. Edwards
A. Herbert Foreman
Milton M. Lory

Ben H. Powell, III
Clarence E. Shriner
Harry K. Torrey
Wallace C. Hall,
    Pres.-Gen., Chr. Ex-Officio

1952-1953

Arthur A. de la Houssaye
A. Herbert Foreman
Hon. Albert W. Hawkes
Ben H. Powell, III
George S. Robertson

Clarence E. Shriner
Robert H. Smith
George E. Tarbox
Ray O. Edwards,
    Pres.-Gen., Chr. Ex-Officio

1953-1954

Wheaton H. Brewer
A. Herbert Foreman
Rear Adm. William Rea Furlong,
    USA, Ret.
Stanley S. Gillam
Wallace C. Hall

Charles A. Jones
Allen L. Oliver
Edgar Williamson, Jr.
Arthur A. de la Houssaye,
    Pres.-Gen., Chr. Ex-Officio

1954-1955

John H. Babb
Wheaton H. Brewer
Eugene P. Carver, Jr.
Arthur de la Houssaye
A. Herbert Foreman

Rear Adm. William Rea Furlong,
    USA, Ret.
Wallace C. Hall
Edgar Williamson, Jr.
Milton M. Lory,
    Pres.-Gen., Chr. Ex-Officio

1955-1956

John H. Babb
Wheaton H. Brewer
Arthur de la Houssaye
A. Herbert Foreman
Edwin B. Graham

Charles A. Jones
Milton M. Lory
Dr. Herschel S. Murphy
Edgar Williamson, Jr.,
    Pres.-Gen., Chr. Ex-Officio

John H. Babb
Wheaton H. Brewer
Arthur de la Houssaye
A. Herbert Foreman
Edwin B. Graham

Robert C. Garrison
Louis J. Heizmann
Hallan Huffman
S. Denmead Kolb
Frank L. Lowmaster

Calvin C. Bolles
Redmond S. Cole
Ernest S. Crosby
Stanley S. Gillam
Charles A. Jones

Dr. Charles A. Anderson
Horace Y. Kitchell
Stephen C. Luce, Jr.
Charles A. Jones,
    President-General
Robert P. Gordon,
    Secretary General

Harry T. Burn
Charles A. Jones
Donald C. Little

Herschel S. Murphy, M.D.,
    President General
John E. King,
    Secretary General

Charles A. Anderson, M.D.
RAdm. Arthur A. de la
    Houssaye, USNR (Ret.)
Herschel S. Murphy, M.D.
Aaron M. Sargent
Robert L. Sonfield

RAdm. Arthur A. de la
    Houssaye, USNR (Ret.)
Horace Y. Kitchell
Milton M. Lory
Horace R. McDowell
W. Giles Parker

1956-1957
    Walter A. Wentworth
    Edgar Williamson, Jr.
    Eugene P. Carver, Jr.
        Pres.-Gen., Chr. Ex-Officio

1957-1958
    Gen. Charles D. Y. **Ostrom**
    Robert H. Overstreet
    Walter A. Wentworth
    George E. Tarbox, Jr.,
        Pres.-Gen., Chr. Ex-Officio

1958-1959
    Dr. Herschel S. Murphy
    John St. Paul, Jr.
    Ralph J. Stayner
    Walter A. Wentworth,
        President-General

1959-1960
    Walter G. Sterling
    Walter A. Wentworth

    Calvin C. Bolles,
        Treasurer General
    Folks Huxford,
        Chancellor General

1960-1961
    William Y. Pryor
    Col. Robert P. Waters

    Calvin C. Bolles,
        Treasurer General
    Stuart H. Tucker,
        Chancellor General

1961 - 1962
    Horace Y. Kitchell, Pres. Gen.
    John E. King, Sec. Gen.
    Stephen C. Luce, Jr., Treas. Gen.
    Stuart H. Tucker,
        Chancellor Gen.

1962 - 1963
    Charles A. Anderson, M.D.,
        Pres. Gen.
    Howard E. Coe,
        Secretary Gen.
    Harry T. Burn, Treasurer Gen.
    Robert L. Sonfield,
        Chancellor Gen.

SECRETARIES GENERAL

1891-1892—Lt. James C. Cresaps, U.S.N., Maryland
1893   —A. Howard Clark, District of Columbia
1894-1896—Franklin Murphy, New Jersey
1897   —Henry Hall (Acting), New York
1898-1901—Capt. Samuel E. Gross, Illinois
1902   —Charles Waldo Haskins, New York
1903   —Edward Payson Cove, New York
1904-1918—A. Howard Clark, District of Columbia
    (In 1904 Combined with Registrar-General)
1919-1920—Philip F. Larner, District of Columbia
1921-1933—Frank B. Steele, Buffalo, N. Y.
    (In 1933 Combined with Registrar-General)
1933-1949—Frank B. Steele, Buffalo, N. Y.
1950-1952—Edgar Williamson, Jr., New Jersey
1953   —Milton M. Lory, Iowa
1954-1955—Walter A. Wentworth, Kentucky
1956-1957—Charles A. Jones, Ohio
1958-1959—Robert P. Gordon, Alabama
1960-1961—John E. King, Illinois
1962   —Howard E. Coe, Connecticut

SECRETARY-REGISTRAR GENERAL EMERITUS

1949—Frank B. Steele

TREASURERS GENERAL

1891-1892—James Otis, New York
1893-1899—Charles W. Haskins, New York
1900-1901—Cornelius Amory Puglsey, New York
1902-1903—Nathan Warren, Massachusetts
1904-1906—Isaac W. Birdseye, Connecticut
1907-1908—Willard Secor, Iowa
1909-1921—John H. Burroughs New York
1922-1925—George McK. Roberts, New York
1926-1927—Louis A. Bowman, Chicago, Ill.
1928-1950—George S. Robertson, Maryland
1951-1955—Robert H. McNeill, District of Columbia
1956-1957—Dr. Herschel S. Murphy, New Jersey
1958   —Arthur G. Trimble, Pennsylvania
1959-1960—Calvin C. Bolles, Connecticut
1961   —Stephen C. Luce, Jr., Massachusetts
1962   —Harry T. Burn, Tennessee

REGISTRARS GENERAL

1891   —Luther L. Tarbell, Massachusetts
1892   —Dr. Browne Goode, Ph.D., National Museum, Washington, D.C.
1893-1904—A. Howard Clark, Smithsonian Institution, Washington, D.C.

In 1904 the office of Registrar-General was combined with that of Secretary-General. A. Howard Clark was Secretary-General and Registrar-General until 1918 followed by Philip F. Larner in 1920 and 1921.

In 1921 the offices of Secretary-General and Registrar-General were separated and the following held the office of Registrar-General:
1921 —William S. Parke, District of Columbia
1922-1933—Francis B. Culver, Maryland

In 1933 the office of Registrar-General was again affixed to that of the Secretary-General then held by Frank B. Steele and he continued to hold the combined offices.
1933-1949—Frank B. Steele, Buffalo, N. Y.

In 1950 the offices were again separated and Frank B. Steele continued as Registrar-General emeritus. Edgar Williamson, Jr., became Secretary-General and Dr. John A. Fritchey, II, the Registrar-General.
1950-1952—Dr. John A. Fritchey, II, Pennsylvania
1953-1954—Louis F. Ridgway, Ohio
1955 —Edward M. Hall, Ohio
1956-1957—Arthur G. Trimble, Pennsylvania
1958 —Robert G. Norfleet, II, New Mexico
1959-1960—Stanley S. Gillam, Minnesota
1961-1962—Donald C. Little, Kansas

EXECUTIVE SECRETARY

In 1950 Harold L. Putnam was made Executive Secretary to manage and direct the headquarters operations of the Society. He has been the only Executive Secretary so far and has served from 1950 to date (1962).

CHANCELLORS GENERAL

1921-1922—Eugene C. Bonniwell, Pennsylvania
1923-1924—James Edgar Brown, Illinois
1925-1926—George C. H. de Kernion, Louisiana
1927-1928—William J. Askin, Jr., Pennsylvania
1929-1931—Richard Hartshome, New Jersey
1932-1933—Brig. General Lewis W. Stotesbury, New York City
1934-1936—G. R. Sappington, Maryland
1937-1938—Loren E. Souers, Ohio
1939-1940—Smith L. Multer, New Jersey
1941-1942—Henry R. Dutcher, New York
1943-1945—Benjamin H. Powell, Texas
1946-1947—William S. Bennet, New York
1948-1949—Wallace C. Hall, Michigan
1950-1951—Arthur A. de la Houssaye, Louisiana
1952-1953—John H. Babb, Illinois
1954-1955—Lew C. Church, Minnesota
1956-1958—Aaron M. Sargent, California
1959 —Folks Huxford, Georgia
1960-1961—Stuart H. Tucker, Rhode Island
1962 —Robert L. Sonfield, Texas

GENEALOGISTS GENERAL

1920-1923—Walter K. Watkins, Massachusetts
1924-1925—John F. Jones, South Carolina
1926-1930—W. Mac F. Jones, Virginia
1931-1933—John Hobart Cross,
1934-1935—Dr. Clifton P. Clark, District of Columbia
1936-1937—George McK. Roberts, New York
1938-1940—C. Wesley Patten, Massachusetts
1941-1942—Ross K. Cook, New Jersey
1943-1945—Franklyn Hogeboom, New York
1946-1947—Charles W. Tucker, Massachusetts
1948-1949—W. Guy Tetrick, West Virginia
1950 —Dr. Arthur Adams, Connecticut
1951-1953—W. Guy Tetrick,
1954 —Redmond S. Cole, Oklahoma
1955 —Dr. Harold I. Meyer, Illinois
1956 —Col. William T. Carpenter, Alabama
1957-1958—Col. Frederick W. Huntington, Texas
1959 —Clarence H. Gordon
1960 —Horace Y. Kitchell, Mississippi
1961 —Marion H. Crawmer, Michigan
1962 —Same as 1961

HISTORIANS GENERAL

1890 —William Francis Cregar
1891-1897—Henry Hall, New York City
1898-1899—Edward M. Gallaudet, LL.D., District of Columbia
1900 —Gen. Theodore S. Peck
1901-1904—George Williams Bates, Michigan
1905-1906—Prof. William K. Wickes, New York City
1907 —William Frederick Slocum, LL.D., Massachusetts
1908-1909—Walter Kandall Watkins, Massachusetts
1910-1917—David L. Pierson, New Jersey
1918-1921—George Carpenter Arnold, Rhode Island
1922-1923—Joseph B. Doyle, Ohio
1924 —Moulton Houk, Ohio
1925-1927—Henry A. Williams, Ohio
1928 —Roswell Page, Virginia
1929-1930—Monroe M. Hopwood, Pennsylvania
1931-1932—Dr. Henry I. McIlwaine, Virginia
1933-1934—Ben W. Palmer, Minnesota
1935-1936—J. Walter Allen, District of Columbia
1937 —Norman B. Conger, Michigan
1938 —Albert C. McDavid, Texas
1939-1940—William H. T. Squires, Virginia
1941-1942—W. McF. Jones, Virginia
1943-1945—Donald F. Lybarger, Ohio
1946-1947—Louis W. Kemp, Texas
1948-1949—David W. Rial, Pennsylvania
1950-1951—Mason E. Mitchell, Arkansas

1952-1953—Redmond S. Cole, Oklahoma
1954 —Dr. Harold I. Meyer, Illinois
1955 —Clarence A. Cook, Indiana
1956-1957—John E. King, Illinois
1958 —Judge Folks Huxford, Georgia
1959 —John E. Dickinson, Wisconsin
1960-1962—John St. Paul, Jr., Louisiana

CHAPLAINS GENERAL

1890 —Rev. Timothy Dwight
1891-1897—Right Rev. Charles Edward Cheney, D.D., Illinois
1898-1899—Rev. Rufus W. Clark, D.D., Michigan
1900-1901—Rev. Ethelbert A. Warfield, D.D., Pennsylvania
1902-1903—Rev. Rufus W. Clark, D.D., Michigan
1904-1906—Rev. Julius W. Atwood, Ohio
1907 —Rev. J. Harman Randall, New York
1908-1909—Rev. Frank Oliver Hall, D.D., Connecticut
1910-1912—Rev. John Timothy Stone, Illinois
1913-1914—Rev. Wm. Force Whitaker, New Jersey
1915 —Rev. Richard Lightburn McGready, Kentucky
1916-1917—Rev. John Onesimus Foster, Washington
1918-1920—Rev. Lee S. McCollister, Massachusetts
1921 —Rev. Lyman W. Allen, New Jersey
1922-1923—Rev. Frederick W. Perkins, D.D., Massachusetts
1924-1926—Rev. Frank Austin Smith, New Jersey
1927-1928—Right Rev. Philip Cook, Delaware
1929 —Rev. Thornton Whaling, D.D., Kentucky
1930-1931—Rev. J. Romeyn Danforth, Connecticut
1932-1933—Rev. George P. Eastman, New Jersey
1934-1935—Frank C. Rideout, U.S.A., Kentucky
1936-1937—Alva J. Brasted, District of Columbia (Chief of Chaplains, U.S.A.)
1938-1939—Rev. Henry L. Darlington, D.D., New York
1940-1941—Rev. Charles W. Maus, D.D., Philadelphia
1942-1943—Rev. Marion T. Plyer, North Carolina
1944-1948—Rev. William F. Buckley, Utah
1949-1953—Dr. Mott R. Sawyers, Minnesota
1954-1955—Rev. Francis Shunk Downs, California
1956-1957—Rev. Grant Ladd Jordan, Michigan
1958 —Rev. Hansen Bergen, Wisconsin
1959 —Rev. Willis Bergen, District of Columbia
1960-1961—Rev. R. Allan Brown, Virginia
1962 —Rev. Paul Rader, Minnesota

SURGEONS GENERAL

1891 —William T. Parker, M.D., Massachusetts
1892 —Charles E. Briggs, M.D., Missouri
1956 —Dr. John A. Fritchey, II, Pennsylvania
1957-1958—Dr. Olin C. Moulton, Nevada
1959 —Dr. Herschel S. Murphy, New Jersey
1960 —H. Ryerson Decker, M.D., Pennsylvania
1961-1962—Clyde R. Flory, M.D., Pennsylvania

LIBRARIANS GENERAL

1934-1940—Louis C. Smith, D. C.
1941-1947—McDonald Miller, D. C.
1948-1949—Dr. W. Harvey Wise, D. C.
1950 —Robert H. McNeill, D. C.
1951-1957—P. Harry Byerly, Virginia
1958-1962—Robert S. W. Walker, Virginia

PRESIDENTS OF THE UNITED STATES—MEMBERS OF THE
NATIONAL SOCIETY OF THE SONS OF THE
AMERICAN REVOLUTION

Rutherford B. Hayes
William McKinley
Theodore Roosevelt

Warren G. Harding
Herbert C. Hoover
Dwight D. Eisenhower

SOME FAMOUS MEMBERS OF THE SOCIETY OF
THE SONS OF THE AMERICAN REVOLUTION

Baruch, Bernard, Financier and Adviser of Presidents
Davis, Richard Harding, Writer and War Correspondent
Dewey, Admiral George, Naval Hero, Spanish American War
Dewey, Thomas E., Governor of New York
Hanna, Marcus A., "Maker of Presidents"
Hughes, Charles E., Chief Justice, U.S. Supreme Court
MacArthur, Douglas, General USA (Ret.)
Miles, General Nelson A., Famous Indian Fighter
Pershing, John J., General USA
Porter, Admiral D. D., of Civil War Fame
Rayburn, Sam., Speaker, House of Representatives
Root, Elihu, Secretary of State
Vanderbilt, William K., Financier and Railroad President
Wainwright, General Jonathan Mayhew, "Bataan March," World War II

MEMBERS OF S.A.R. WHO ARE OR HAVE BEEN GOVERNORS
OF STATES

Adams, Sherman, New Hampshire, (Asst. to Pres. Eisenhower)
Baldwin, Raymond E., Connecticut (Justice, Supreme Court of Conn., Senator)
Cooper, Myers Y., Ohio
Cox, Channing Harris, Masachusetts
Cross, Wilbur L., Connecticut
Dewey, Thomas E., New York
Dickinson, Luren D., Michigan
Dillingham, W. P., Vermont
Driscoll, Alfred E., New Jersey
Duff, James H., Pennsylvania (U.S. Senator)
Dwinell, Lane, New Hampshire
Fisher, John S., Pennsylvania
Foss, Joseph J., South Dakota
Francis, David R., Missouri
Fuller, Alvin T., Massachusetts
Green, Robert H., New Jersey

Griffin, S. Marvin, Georgia
Guild, Curtis, Jr., Massachusetts (Ambassador to Russia)
Hammond, Winfield Scott, Minnesota
Hampton, Wade, South Carolina
Hawkes, Alfred W., New Jersey (Senator)
Long, John Davis, Massachusetts (Sect'y of Navy)
Mabry, Thomas H., New Mexico
Miller, Leslie A., Wyoming (National Resources, First Hoover Commission 1947-49)
McKay, Douglas, Oregon (U.S. Sect'y of Interior)
Murphy, Franklin, New Jersey
Proctor, Redfield, Vermont (Senator)
Proctor, Mortimer R., Vermont
Retner, Payne H., Sr., Kansas
Richardson, J. F., South Carolina

Rollin, Frank W., New Hampshire
Saltonstall, Leverett, Massachusetts (Senator)
Sprague, Charles A., Oregon (Alternate Delegate to U.N.)
Talmadge, Herman, Georgia (Senator)
Thurmond, J. Strom, South Carolina (Senator)
Tuck, William M., Virginia (Representative)
Warfield, Edwin, Maryland
Whitman, Charles S., New York
Williams, G. Mennen, Michigan

MEMBERS OF THE SONS OF THE AMERICAN REVOLUTION WHO ARE SERVING OR HAVE SERVED IN THE UNITED STATES CONGRESS AS SENATORS

Baldwin, Raymond E., Connecticut
Bayard, Thomas P., New Jersey
Boggs, James Caleb, Delaware
Bridges, Styles, New Hampshire
Bricker, John W., Ohio
Burdick, Quentin N., North Dakota
Byrd, Harry F., Virginia
Capehart, Homer E., Indiana
Connally, Thomas T., Texas
Cotton, Norris H., New Hampshire
Copeland, Royal S., New York
Cushman, New Jersey
Daniel, Price, Texas
Daniels, John W., North Carolina
Depew, Chauncey M., New York
Ervin, Samuel J., Jr., North Carolina
Graham, Frank P., North Carolina
Gurney, Chan, South Dakota
Hanna, Marcus A., Ohio
Hayden, Carl, Arizona
Hickenlooper, Bourke B., Iowa
Jordan, B. Everett, North Carolina
Keating, Kenneth B., New York (Also Representative)
Kilgore, Harley M., West Virginia
Knowland, William F., California
Long, Edward V., Missouri
Lodge, Henry Cabot, Massachusetts
Martin, Edward, Pennsylvania
Monroney, A. S. Mike, Oklahoma
Morse, Wayne L., Oregon
Morton, Thruston B., Kentucky
Murphy, Franklin, New Jersey
Overton, John H., Louisiana
Palmer, Thomas W.
Platt, Orville H., New York
Robertson, A. Willis, Virginia
Russell, Richard B., Georgia
Taft, Robert A., Ohio
Vandenberg, Arthur A., Michigan
Wadsworth, James W., New York

SOME MEMBERS OF THE SONS OF THE AMERICAN REVOLUTION WHO ARE SERVING OR HAVE SERVED IN HOUSE OF REPRESENTATIVES

Avery, William, Kansas
Baumhart, Albert D., Jr., Ohio
Bennett, Charles E., Florida
Bentley, Alvin M., Michigan
Boggs, Hale, Louisiana
Bolton, Oliver P., Ohio
Burdick, Usher L., North Dakota
Campbell, Courtney W., Florida
Chamberlain, Charles E., Michigan

Chiperfield, R. B., Illinois
Clavenger, Cliff, Ohio
Curtis, Laurence, Massachusetts
Frelinghuysen, Peter H. B., New Jersey
Haley, James A., Florida
Harrison, Burr P., Virginia
Hinshaw, Carl, California
Hope, Clifford R., Kansas
Judd, Walter H,. Minnesota
Mathias, Charles McC., Jr., Maryland
Mumma, Walter M., Pennsylvania
Patten, Harold A., Arizona
Perkins, Bass, New Hampshire
Rayburn, Sam, Texas
Reed, Chauncey W., Illinois
Rivers, Al Ralph Jr., Alaska
Robison, Howard W., New York
Roosevelt, Jr., Franklin D., New York
Roosevelt, James, California
Saylor, John P., Pennsylvania
Schenck, Paul F., Ohio
Schweiker, Richard S., Pennsylvania
Seldon, Armistead I., Alabama
Slack, John M., Jr., West Virginia
Smith, Frank E., Mississippi
Smith, Lawrence H., Wisconsin
Taber, John, New York
Tuck, William M., Virginia
Van Zandt, James E., Pennsylvania
Walter, Francis E., Pennsylvania
Wilson, Robert C., California

SOME PROMINENT MEMBERS OF THE SOCIETY OF THE SONS OF THE AMERICAN REVOLUTION

Alger, Frederick M. Jr., Ambassador to Russia
Allen, Clinton L., President—Aetna Insurance Co.
Anderson, Gen. Thomas W.
Arnold, Frazer, Brig. Gen., Colorado National Guard World War II
Austin, Warren R., Ambassador to United Nations, Sect'y of State
Baker, Walter S., Major General—Former Chief Chemical Warfare Service
Barber, Rear Adm. Albert S.
Balch, Everett P.
Barker, Dr. Burt Brown, Vice President—Univ. of Oregon
Beals, Walter B., Retired Judge—Washington Supreme Court
Bradford, George H., Associate Justice—Colorado Supreme Court
Brewer, David J., Associate Justice—U.S. Supreme Court
Brosman, Paul, Judge U.S. Court of Military Appeals, Washington D.C.
Burton, Harold H., Associate Justice Supreme Court
Bushnell, George E., Sovereign Grand Commander Northern Masonic Jurisdiction, Ancient Accepted Scottish Rite—Former Supreme Court Justice, Michigan
Buckner, Maj. Gen. Simon B. II USA, Killed at Okinawa
Carmichael, Dr. Leonard, Secretary Smithsonian Institution, Washington, D.C., Former President Tufts College
Code, Maj. Gen. James A.
Creeley, Gen. A. W.
Cullen, Hugh Roy
Delaplaine, Edward S., Chief Judge Court of Appeals, Maryland

Dana, Charles A., New York Sun
Danforth, Charles H., Brig. Gen. USAF (Ret.)
Dalton, John M., Attorney General, Missouri
Dalton, J. P., Chief Justice Supreme Court of Missouri
Dessez, Lester A., Brig. Gen. USMC (Ret.)
Devers, Jacob L., General USA
Dwight, Timothy, President of Yale University
Fenton, Dr. Ralph A., Internationally Known Surgeon
Fake, Guy L., Federal District Court Judge
Fortier, Alcee, Professor, Linguist and Historian
Fortier, Louis, Brig. Gen. (Ret.)
Fries, Amos A., Maj. Gen. USA (Ret.)
Fletcher, William B., Rear Adm. USN (Ret.)
Furbush, Richard I., President State Senate Mass.
Furlong, William R., Rear Adm. USN (Ret.)
Gannett, Frank E., Gannett Publications
Gilmer, Daniel Cort, LL.D., President Johns Hopkins University
Grant, U. S. III, Major Gen. USA (Ret.)
Grant, Gen. Frederick D.
Goren, Charles H., Bridge Expert
Gurley, Fred G., President Atchison, Topeka & Santa Fe RR.
Hartshorne, Richard, Federal District Court Judge
Hearst, William Randolph, Jr., Hearst Publications
Hinds, Sidney R., Brig. Gen. USA (Ret.)
Hopkins, Dr. Ernest Martin, Former President Dartmouth College
Horn, Stanley F., Editor Southern Lumberman
Houghton, Alenson B., Ambassador to Great Britain
Howe, Brig. Gen. Walter
Johnston, Gen. Joseph Eggleston
Kellogg, Frank B., Sec. of State
King, Gen. Charles
Lee, Gen. Fitzhugh, Virginia
Loring, Charles, Former Chief Justice Minnesota Supreme Court
McClung, Lee, Treasurer U.S.
Malthie, William M., Former Chief Justice Supreme Court of Conn.
Matchett, Henry J., Brig. Gen. (Ret.)
Merrill, Maj. Gen. Frank, USA
Miles, Gen. Nelson A., Commanding General of the U. S. Army
Morrison, deLesseps S., former Mayor New Orleans. Ambassador to A. O. S.
Morton, Levi P., Vice President U.S.
Muir, James Irvin, Maj. Gen. (Ret.)
Nickell, Joe, Maj. Gen. Kansas National Guard
None, Rear Adm. John W., USN
Parkinson, Dr. George A., Director Univ. of Wisconsin, Rear Adm. USN
Peale, Rev. Norman Vincent, Noted Clergyman and Author
Perkins, Louis Waite, Rear Adm. USN
Pettengill, Samuel B., Author, Lecturer, Former Member of Congress

Pound, Roscoe, Dean Emeritus Harvard Law School
Reid, Ogden, Publisher New York Herald Tribune
Reincke, Frederick G., Maj. Gen., Adjutant General State of Conn.
Rucker, Colby Guequierre, Rear Adm. USN (Ret.)
Scofield, Rear Adm. USN
Shafter, Gen. William R., Spanish-American War
Shake, Curtis G., Judge Indiana Supreme Court (1938-44)
Shriver, Thomas A., Judge Tennessee Court of Appeals
Smead, Col. Burton A., World War I Commander 89th Div. - DSC
Stahlman, James G., President and Publisher Nashville Banner
Starbird, Alfred A., Brig. Gen. USA (Ret.)
Stillman, W. Paul, Chairman of the Board Mutual Benefit Life Ins. Co.
Sternberg, George W., Surgeon General USA
Sulzberger, Arthur Hays, Publisher New York Times
Summerall, Gen. Charles P.
Swift, George H., Jr., Chairman of the Board Swift and Co.
Thomas, Charles E., Jr., Maj. Gen. USAF (Ret.)
Thomas, Lowell, Lecturer and Commentator
Train, Harold Cecil, Rear Adm. USN (Ret.)
Trousdale, Maj. Gen. G. W.
Truesdell, Major Gen. Karl
Warner, Harold J., Chief Justice Supreme Court Oregon
Wessels, Theodore F., Brig. Gen. (Ret.)
Wheeler, Gen. Joseph, Confederate General
Woodford, Stewart L., Ambassador to Spain
Wilson, Gen. Thomas U.S.A.
Whitney, Otis Minot, Brig. Gen. 26th Div. Commissioner of Public Safety Mass.
Williams, L. Kemper, Brig. Gen. (Ret.)
Wooley, George F., Brig. Gen. USA (Ret.)
Wortendyke, Reynier J., Jr., U.S. District Judge

THE STAMP WHICH CAUSED THE AMERICAN REVOLUTION

(From an article by Compatriot Lothrop Lee Brown, of the Illinois Society, in the November 1950 issue of the S. A. R. Magazine).

Grenville's Stamp Act passed by the British Parliament in 1765 led directly to the Revolution. When the stamps arrived in the colonies they were received with rioting, and mobs burned and destroyed property of government officials. It was difficult to find men to act as distributers.

Although repealed the next year, the repeal was accompanied by a declaratory act that Parliament had sovereign right to tax the colonies and this stirred up the colonists so that they began to think of "taxation without representation," and other injustices foisted upon them by the mother country. The Tax yielded only £4000, less than the expense of putting it into effect.

The documentary tax of 1765 on the Colonies was represented by an adhesive stamp about one and five eighths inches square, stamped, impressed or more correctly, embossed on a separate piece of coarse, heavy, dark-greenish blue paper. The design was somewhat in the shape of a shield with a five-petal flower in a circle with a crown above. Above this was the word "America." On each side was a branch design and the amount of the tax at the bottom. Around the center circle was the inscription "Honi-Soit-Qvi-Mal-Y-Pense."

The stamp was glued or pasted on the document.

The above picture of the 2 Shilling 6 Pence stamp is of one of the genuine stamps issued by Great Britain in 1765. This stamp has been handed down through the Brown family from an ancestor who lived in Boston at the time of the American Revolution. It is probably the only stamp (1765) of this denomination in existence.

PATRONS

In the following pages are the names of the Patrons of the publication of "The History of the National Society of the Sons of the American Revolution" who supported the project by a pre-publication subscription. The names are arranged by states. Because some Patrons live in one state and belong to the society of another state, it was sometimes not possible to list them under the name of the state society of which they are members since few subscribers mentioned the society to which they belong. Patrons are, therefore, listed in accordance with the addresses given.

PATRONS

ALABAMA

Alves, Walter Johnston (M.D.)
Armistead, William R.
Bragg, James W., Jr.
Brasfield, Charles T., Jr.
Browning, G. F., Jr.
Camp, Ehney A., Jr.
Carpenter, William T. (Col.)
Clarke, John T.
Cleere, George L.
Coburn, Robert E. III.
Coleman, Wade Hampton, Jr. (Pres. Ala. Soc.)
Coleman, Wade Hampton III
Crigler, Arthur D.
Daves, Alfred C.
Douglass, Hiram Kennedy (Rev.)
Garrison, Robert C.
Glover, Charles Williamson, Jr. (1st Lt.)
Gregory, William F.
Guttery, John McQueen
Hewes, E. Thompson
Jones, Catesby ap R.
Jones DeVane K.
Koenig, Frederick G., Jr.
Kohn, John P., Jr.
Lawrence, G. Saxton
Lee, George B. (Lt.)
Lukens, John N., (Rev.)
Lyon, Henry L., Jr. (M.D.)
McCrary, George Laurence
McCrary, Henry Zeitler
McKinney, Roy
Marks, David S.
Mason, John J.
Meek, Robert C.
Morgan, Ryall S.
Morris, Enoch Carter
Morris, William Chester, (Col.)
Pearson, Albert Matthews, Jr.
Sizemore, James Middleton
Smith, Frank Chester
Speigner, Donald H.
Stallworth, N. J.
Stoval, J. T.
Strange, Luther Johnson, Jr.
Walker, Alfred
Ward, Charles Bondurant
Whilldin, David O.
Woodson, Lewis Green III

ALASKA

Carroll, Joseph R.
Firmin, Lewis G.
Jensen, Thomas B., Sr.
King, James J.
Rasor, John C.
Rozell, Donald C.
Orton, Louis S.
Wolverton, James N.

ARIZONA

Blaisdell, Lowell S.
Dorland, Frank Norton
Heineman, Frederic W.
Hibbs, D. G.
McGrew, Baird L.
McGrew, James Henry III
McGrew, Samuel J.
McKesson, Theodore G.
Pabst, Ralph M.
Ruffalo, William Taft
Robinson, Wliliam K.
Springer, William E.
Suter, William P.
Tarbell, O. H.
Walker, Duncan Cameron
Wheeler, Harold Parker II
Woolley, G. B.

ARKANSAS

Cabler, Cleveland
Dickens, Marion Thomas
Coleman, George Monroe
Gholston, Thomas M.
Glenn, Harold V., (M.D.)
Greene, John H.
Hain, Veit A., Jr.
Herrington, Pat C.
Johnson, Rodney K., (M.D.)
McCartney, Scott L.
Neuberger, Jean E.
Reynolds, Seth C.
Weaver, William S.

CALIFORNIA

Abbott, Lyle Shepley
Adams, Frank P.
Adams, Frank R.
Allen, Frederick S.
Allphin, Don J.
Anderson, William E.
Arnold, Hubert Andrew
Ash, Lloyd Radcliffe (Capt., U.S.N.R.)
Austin, Calvin T.
Babb, Jerrell
Berger, Sholes
Bemis, Grant Squires
Bentley, Chesley I.
Bishop, Horatio Warren
Blair, Joe W.
Boggis, Robert P.
Bosley, Bradford
Bowman, Guy Grant
Bradford, B. P.
Brooks, Clifton E.
Brownridge, George W. (M.D.)
Burch, Douglas T., Sr.
Byers, Russell Conwell
Carpenter, Mark C. (M.D.)
Carver, C. Ellis (M.D.)
Caseten, Charles R. (Col., Ret.)
Cates, Harold D.
Chetham, Alfred Howard (Son of Organizer)
Chord, J. T.
Clark, Max A. X. (M.D., F.R.G.S.)
Clementson, Merrill Kinsell (Rear Admiral Ret.)
Code, James A., Jr. (Maj. Gen.)
Cofer, L. K.
Corr, J. Wilfred
Cotton, Aylett R. (Judge)
Crawfurd, Hal Lindsay
Criglar, William Louis
Crippen, John H., Jr.
Dana, W. L.
Daniels, Edgar E. (M.D.)
Davies, Phillips S.
Davis, John J.
Doty, James K.
Downey, M. H.
Drake, Arthur B.
Duke, Charles L. (Lt. Col.)
Durnford, James A.
Edwards, Ben E.
Elliott, Roy H.
Engle, Donald R.
Evans, Jack Robert
Faithorn, N. R.
Fin-Kelson, John M., Jr.
Fitch, Joseph P.
Folmar, Cecil John, (M.D.)
Folmar, Cecil Lee (Col.)
Folmar, Raymond Hale
Folmar, Roger Lee
Fravel, Maris T.
Freeman, Harvey Bartlett
Frost, C. M.
Gallison, Harold Bailey
Gary, George L.
Goethe, C. M. (M.D.)

PATRONS

CALIFORNIA—Continued
Gorton, Julius C. (D.O.)
Hall, Glendon Colwell
Hayes, Emmet B.
Hebel, Walter E., Jr.
Heizer, Joseph J. (M.D.)
Hooper, Frederick R.
Hutchinson, Robert H. (M.D.)
Irwin, William B.
Jenkins, Kenneth M. (M.D.)
Jepson, W. R. (M.D.)
Johnson, Willard L.
Jones, Benjamin C. (Judge)
Jones, Enoch R. L., Sr.
Jones, Paul McR.
Kahlert, Charles G. (Prof.)
Kiehl, Ralph A.
Lipscomb, Joseph A.
Livingston, Ivan
Lowery, Doane M.
McCluer, Paul
McKerrihan, R. B.
Manley, Orville
Marsh, Edward Earl
Marsh, Edward E., Jr.
Mathewson, H. Lewis (Vice President General)
Maurice, Rosseter (Capt. U.S.N.R. Ret)
Mauzy, Charles S.
Meyer, Stanton H.
Millard, Theodore B. (Col. U.S.M.C. Ret.)
Miller, Arthur H. (Maj.)
Miller, Marvin, H.
Miller, Robert Warburton (M.D.)
Millholen, John H.
Mitchell, Chester E. (Lt. Col.)
Montgomery, Edwin J., Sr.
Moore, H. F.
Morrison, Robert W.
Northrop, J. H.
Parks, William Frederick
Paulson, Donald H. (M.D.)
Payne, Lawrence R.
Peale Robert R.
Pearmar, Ben F., Jr.
Pharo, John Birdsall
Plaister, Deane M.
Pray, Ralph M. (Capt. U. S. Navy)
Reed, George William
Riley, Thomas E.
Rockwell, John Edward
Roper, Frederic R.
Rose, Gordon W.
Rosenkrans, Dale D.
Rucker, Robert

Rutledge, P. W.
Sadler, C. Boone
Sanders, Wallace, (Dc. Phc.)
Shafer, Warren Wesley
Sigler, Allen Jefferson
Smith Craig Patterson (Comdr. U.S.N.R.)
Smith, Edward F.
Stanford, John H.
Storm, John L. (Rt. Rev.)
Sutton, Francis W.
Taylor, James R.
Teed, John W.
Terry, Carl C.
Thomas, R. L. (M.D.)
Tinkham, Kenneth Otis
Todt, George
Turrell, Franklin M. (M.D.)
Updegraff, James Gill III
Veith, Milton P.
Warn, Carl E.
Webster, Francis X. (Col.)
Wesson, Miley B. (M.D.)
Weydell, Walter T.
Whitehair, Francis Darel
Winchester, Robert Wood
Wood, William F.
Young, W. F.
Zahn, Dene W.

COLORADO

Barnes, G. S. (Rev.)
Brehm, Gill (M.D.)
Carpenter, Claude M.
Collins, Hubert W. (Col.)
Davis, Raymond J.
DeSollar, Tenney C.
Downing, Warwick M.
Dye, Peter L.
Frye, Baldwin Abbott
Godsman, Sidney P.
Ives, Richard
Jarrell, James Floyd
Jarvis, William Bancroft, Jr.
Miller, Victor A.
Morse, Bradbury B.
Murphey, Bradford J. (M.D.)
Shattuck, Robert C. (M.D.)
Tarbox, George E., Jr.
Williams, Edwin A.
Wolbert, Robert Douglas Timberlake

CONNECTICUT

Anderson, James Thorn
Baruch, Hartwig N., Jr.
Bolles, Calvin C.

Boughton, Clark
Brooks, Whitney L.
Brown, William Morris
Bryan, Errol H.
Bulkeley, W. H.
Cavanagh, Alvin E.
Coe, Howard E.
Cook, Howard P.
Dailey, John M.
Darlington, Henry, Jr.
Deardorff, Claire Wilson
Eldred, Roger M.
Farnsworth, Francis P.
Gale, Robert Allan
Goodsell, Lewis E., Sr.
Hathaway, Chester E.
Kaschub, C. A. LeRoy
Leavitt, Charles T.
LeConche, Richard B.
Lindquist, Warren (Lt. Col.)
Livingston, William A.
McMaster, Fitzhugh, (Capt. U.S.N. Ret.)
Merriman, Henry (M.D.)
Moore, James C., Jr.
Morsman, Joseph J., Jr.
Morsman, Joseph J. III
Norcross, Arnold B.
Parsons, Allan F.
Pauley, Robert Reinhold
Pelton, Howard L.
Roberts, Wilson B.
Sanger, Edmund Phipps
Sias, Arthur Cowles
Skeels, Charles R.
Stewart, John E.
Towner, Winthrop Hoadley
Tuttle, Theodore Frederick
Van Etten, Carl C.
Whittemore, Harris, Jr.
Williams, Wayne
Woodward, J. W.

DELAWARE

Baldwin, Norman F.
Beggs, Albert, Jr.
Bird, Samuel B.
Chambers, George E. Sr.
Child, Edgar
du Pont, Nicholas R.
Ellis, Howard
Fulling, Roger W.
Greene, David B.
Logan, Arthur G.
Marshall, Joseph L.
Mires, Maynard H., Jr. (M.D.)
Mullin, Mac Sumner, Jr.
Peirce, Joseph J.
Rheuby, William P.

PATRONS

Ridgely, Henry J.
Sellers, John
Sprankle, Lynn D. (Col.)
  (Pres. Delaware Soc.)
Swezey, Robert J.
Weldin, Walter Joel
Weldin, William C., Jr.
Whiteside G. Morris II
Wright, Evan R.

DISTRICT OF COLUMBIA

Austin, John H.
Baldwin, William Perry, Jr.
Ball, Walter V.
Bennett, Benjamin H.
Biddle, Richard Knight
Billingley, Henry E.
Birely, William C.
Black, Revus R.
Blum, William, Jr.
Bowen, John F.
Britton, Alexander T.
Bryan, H. Eugene
Burr, Samuel Engle, Jr.
  (M.D.)
Cain, William Morris
Calder, Albert R.
Carll, George S., Jr.
Childs, James B.
Clark, Raymond B., Jr.
Dessez, Lester A.
  (B. Gen. U.S.M.C. Ret.)
Devers, J. L. (Gen.)
Dixon, Peter A.
Dorman, John Frederick
Folk, Serge W.
Forkner, Austin H.
Foster, Allen R.
Fryer, Loren Hansbrough
Furlong, William Rea
  (R. Adml. U.S.N.)
Gaylord, William S.
Gibbs, Frederick R.
Glover, Charles C., Jr.
Gravatt, R. H., Jr
Harris, Ray Baker
Henshaw, Newton L.
Hoes, Laurence G.
Ireland, Mark L. (Col.)
Jackson, Edgar B.
Jarrott, Wallace Smith T.
Kephart, Calvin J.
  (Col. U.S.A.R. Ret.)
Kerr, James W. (Lt. Col.)
King, Thomas Cobb
Lansford, Willis R. (Col.)
Lockmiller, David A.
McKeever, Robert L.
Mainey, Louis B.
Manbeck, Jesse B.

Murch, James DeForest
Purvis, R. Scott
  (Lt. U.S.N.)
Putnam, Harold L.
Shaw, James A.
Skeels, Simon C.
Smallwood, Grahame T., Jr.
Smith, Henderson L.
  (Maj. USAF)
Spence, William Thornton
Stecher, Karl
Sweeny, Robert P.
Sweitzer, C. McG.
Sarno, Ronald Scott
Tuggle, Kenneth H.
Walker, Robert S. W.
Turrell, Orban Clyde
Weaver, Rufus M.
Williams, George Livingston
Wirt, Raymond E., Sr.
Withers, Guy (Maj.)
Wooley, George F., Jr.
  (Brig. Gen. U.S.A. Ret.)
Young, W. Harvey

FLORIDA

Abernethy, W. Bruce
Applewhite, Eric Leon
Baskin, H. H., Jr.
Bateman, William
Bittenbender, Horace W.
Blackburn, W. W.
Booth, Eden C.
Bothwell, Cecil L.
Boyd, John Wright
Bransford, L. E., Jr. (M.D.)
Brock, Kenneth Guthrie
Brotherton, Robert T.
Carleton, Walter George
Cartwright, Charles B.
Chandler, Herbert William
Child, F. M.
  (Col. U.S.A. Ret.)
Chinnock, Harry S.
Clute, W. T.
Cole, Robert F.
Colburn, Layton Rogers
Coleman, P. N.
Combs, Willis B.
Cubbedge, Cooper M.
Dame, Flem C.
Day, William A.
Denton, Marion G.
DeVane, Claude L.
DeVane, George Albert
DeVane, Dozier A. (Judge)
Dickinson, J. H., Sr.
Dodenhoff, Harry C.
Drew, Austin R.

Fairman, Harold
Florence, Robert S.
Fyler, W. G.
Garretson, Gerald B. (M.D.)
Gaskins, Thomas
Gerhart, Luther F.
Gee, Herbert C.
Getzen, Robert L.
Getzen, W. L.
Gillmore, Frederick III
Gramling, L. G., Sr.
Graves, Howard B., Jr.
Harding, Gerald M.
Haynes, Preston C.
Hoffman, Carl K.
Holcomb, Lyle Donald, Jr.
Hopkins, Russell N. (M.D.)
Howells, Joseph H.
Jackson, James J.
Langstroth, Francis W.
Lanier, John F.
Lanning, Harley M.
Lewis, Reese Cleaton
Lybass, James H.
McGarry, Mark R.
McKesson, H. D.
McLester, R. L. (Col.)
Marlow, Clyde D. (D.D.S.)
May, John Alden
Meadors, John Allen
Mead, D. Richard
Mease, John A., Jr. (M.D.)
Mumme, Henry T., Jr.
  (Capt. U.S.N.)
Murray, Eric F.
Nevins, Elmer Hibbard
Norris, Garland C.
Norris, Hardgrove S. (M.D.)
O'Hara, V. Winthrop
Osterhout, Charles H.
Parish, Alonzo N.
Park, Arthur H.
Parmelee, Charles J.
Phelps, Harold E.
Pickens, Myron Ashley
Porter, Robert Treat
Potter, James Berry
Reese, William E. (Col.)
Remington, George C. T.
Richards, John A.
Richardson, Henry R.
Ristig, James Paul, Jr.
Rives, Howard P.
Roberts, Herbert C. (Col.)
  (Pres. Florida Soc.)
Rundles, J. Clinton
Sanders, Ola, Jr.
Sawyer, Bickford E.
  (Maj. Gen.)
Schaefer, Harold C.

PATRONS

Scharf, John Regester
Schooley, Bernal L.
Scoville, Samuel S.
Shipman, William F., Jr.
Sias, Azariah B.
Shriner, Clarence E.
Snyder, John W., Jr.
Steele, R. C. (M.D.)
Storm, Walter Everson
Thompson, Vedric III
Trice, C. V. W., Jr.
Turnburke, H. M.
Turrentine, John W.
Upchurch, Frank D.
Van Brunt, Raleigh W.
Van Ness, Harold J., Sr.
Waite, W. Edwin (Judge)
Weidenhamer, Frank E.
Westervelt, Daniel E., Jr.
Westervelt, Derek John
Wilbur, Jerry F.
Williams, Clyde W.
Wilson, L. Elbert (Rev.)
Wilson, E. Meade II
Willcut, William Bacon (Hon.)
Younger, J. R. (Col. U.S.A. Ret.)

GEORGIA

Ansley, David H.
Austin, William H., Jr.
Boardman, W. K., Jr.
Bowden, J. Richard
Brannen, William L.
Brock, W. C. (D.D.S.)
Brogdon, Rembert E.
Brown, Hugh Bennett
Bush, R. Harold
Carter, William J., Sr.
Cordle, Charles G.
Cowart, Troy Allison
Crummey, James B.
Daughtry, William Le Roy
Davenport, Paul Mitchell
Davis, LaFayette
Freret, William A., Jr.
Gibson, Charles E.
Green, Henry H.
Groves, Robert Walker
Halsey, LeRoy
Hammond, Edmund J.
Harper, C. N.
Hilkey, Dean Charles J.
Hooks, Eugene James
Howell, Hugh H., Jr.
Huxford, Folks
Ladson, James B.

Ledbetter, A. W., III
Lester, James Jackson, Jr.
Linthicum, Thomas G.
Long, Robert Dearing
Lovejoy, Hatton
Lunceford, A. Mell, Jr.
McCool, Dennard I.
McLaughlin, L. H.
McLeod, James A.
Mikell, Charles Bazemore
Moore, Harvin C., Jr.
Moseley, L. O.
Mosher, William Edwin
Mygatt, Lucien L. (M.D.)
Owens, Arthur Lee, Jr.
Pentecost, Otis J.
Phillips, John T., Sr.
Pye, Durwood T. (Judge)
Respess, Edwin K.
Rhoden, Vascoc
Sibley, Erwin
Slaton, John M., Jr.
Smith, William M.
Spitler, Raymond A., Sr.
Stevens, Pat M. (Col. Ret.
Thompson, William D.
Tipton, A. Lee
Tyson, W. A., Sr. (Rev.)
Wallace, George J.
Wells, Guy H. (M.D.)
Workman, Charles C., Jr.
Worthington, James Drewry
Wright, Ernest Linwood
Younts, Charles R.

HAWAII

Cloward, Ralph Bingham (M.D.)
Edgecomb, Frederick A.
Kepner, Richard DeMonbrun (M.D.)
Shootman, Thomas W.
Southwell, Gilbert Lee (Lt. Col. USAF. Ret.)
Waipa, Stephen Parker

IDAHO

Brackett, Charles O.
Davison, W. H.
Dunckel, Neil V.
Eldridge, Jay Glover
Gooding, E. G.
Henry, Weston Rush
Phoenix, E. C.
Smith, Courtland B.
Wright, Earl Stanger

ILLINOIS

Abbott, W. L.
Anderson, George L.

Ashenhurst, James G.
Ashenhurst, John Watson
Asmann, Edwin N.
Babcock, David Hinman
Barney, Albert S.
Beal, Charles J.
Benjamin, R. Allen
Bishop, Mars P.
Bogert, Gilbert P.
Bone, Robert G.
Boroughf, Arthur E.
Bowker, Herbert H.
Brainerd, George S.
Brewster, Edward Sumner (M.D.)
Brian, Floid B.
Brisbin, John D.K.
Brockie, John Meikle, Jr. (Col.)
Brown, Cecil David (M.D.)
Brown, Joy Stone
Brown, Warren W.
Brush, Herbert Sherman, Jr. (1st Lt.)
Brush, Herbert Sherman, III
Bryan, H. H.
Bryan, Leslie A. (M.D.)
Burgess, Frank K.
Carr, Robert C.
Case, Charles Center
Chapman, Dave
Chilgren, Arthur D.
Coleman, E. P. (M.D.)
Colvin, A. A.
Combs, Willis B.
Converse, Arlan W.
Cook, Junius F., Jr.
Cooper, W. Roger
Coover, Lloyd
Corrough, Clifford J.
Cowger, Rolla E.
Crakes, C. R.
Creigier, E. B.
Cricks, John Clifton
Crippen, John K.
Crouch, Harold
Cummings, John H.
Cureton, T. K.
Davis, James Casey
Davis, Laurence Ralph
Dawson, John A.
Deffenbaugh, W. I.
Deneen, Charles A.
Dillon, Elmer C.
Downen, **Leigh Crim**
Dunham, Claire Arthur
Edmunds, **Palmer D.**
Eldredge, **Charles H.**

— 246 —

PATRONS

ILLINOIS—Continued
Fairbanks, William Earl, Jr.
Farnsworth, James E.
Flanders, C. Norman
Flinn, Bernard W.
Fowler, Sharron J.
Frazer, Richard S.
Galbreath, Walter E.
Grauman, H. Richard
Gifford, A. Mead
Goodwin-Perkins, Charles A.
Gregg, Clifford C.
Gregg, Philip H.
Griffith, James S.
Gunn, Waylen Leon
Haagen, Paul T., Jr.
Hall, Carrol C.
Hargrave, Homer P.
Harwood, Thomas A.
Harrison, Robert M.
Haynes, John T.
Hayward, Thomas Z.
Hazen, Parker Rowland
Hewett, Douglas
Horn, B. F.
Hurlbut, Willis Alden III
Hutchins, Evert O.
Jenkins, Arthur D.
Jenkins, David M.
Jepeway, Ross M.
Johonnot, Robert I.
Knight, B. Jay
Knight, Winstanley
Lamb, Gilbert C., Sr.
Larsen, Webster Gay
Line, Rial Dunton
Loughnane, John P., Jr.
Lum, Dudley Field
Lynn, John R.
Mace, Clarence E.
Mackin, Robert D. (Comd.)
Maley, Charles David
Maley, W. Forrester (M.D.)
Mason, E. C.
Mehringer, Ernest Putnam
Mershimer, J. D. (M.D.)
Meyer, Harold I. (M.D.)
Moody, William L.
Mooney, Russell E.
Mustell, Frederick Peter
Nehring, Wayne H.
Noone, Donald
Oliver, C. B., Jr.
Orndorff, John R. (M.D.)
Pagles, Claude C.

Parker, David Brewster
Parkhill, Harry Anderson
Patton, Francis F.
Pomeroy, Paul G. (M.D.)
Porter, Hilton T.
Potter, T. W.
Richardson, George M.
Ricketts, Ernest A.
Roberts, Daniel A. (Judge)
Robertson, Hayes
St. Paul, John III
Seaver, Jay J.
Simpson, Burney J.
Simpson, L. M.
Smith, Amos K.
Smith, Earl J.
Smith, Harold Byron
Smith, Len Young
Smith, W. Gorin
Staehle, Jack C.
Stanton, Harlan Mayne
Stern, Tracy R.
Stoll, John E. (M.D.)
Strawn, E. W. (M.D.)
Sullivan, Frank R.
Tarleton, Earl R.
Taylor, Orville
Tenney, Harold M.
Thorpe, James H.
Tobin, James W. (M.D.)
Todd, Samuel R. (Col.)
Topping, Harry L.
Tucker, Robert G. (M.D.)
Turner, Harry A.
Veirs, Willard L. (M.D.)
Voss, Howard Wicklund
Vreeland, H. K.
Walker, Frederick Burgess
Walmsley, James N.
Willis, Thomas H.
Witt, D. Vernon
Weston, George W.
Windsor, Henry A., Jr.
Winship, Fred C.
Wright, Theron

INDIANA
Bailey, Lindon A.
Barry, Maurice Joseph, Sr. (M.D.)
Boyd, Robert Lowell
Boyer, Clyde C.
Breece, Charles A.
Cruger, Frank M.
Dillon, T. O.
Fairbanks, William Earl, Jr.
Gaskins, Charles Eugene

Haberly, H. Paul
Hawkins, Joseph Loughery
Hollingsworth, Irvin C.
McClelland, Stewart W. (M.D.)
Maddox, Harry A.
Mohler, Floyd B.
Patterson, Arthur E. I.
Patterson, William Fletcher, Sr.
Raffensperger, Hiram J.
Rush, Gail Edward
Traver, Perry C. (M.D.)
Warfel, Stanley L.
Wetzel, Miles T.
Woolling, Kenneth K.

IOWA
Anderson, George L.
Atwater, Carleton W. (D.D.)
Denham, Thomas S.
Giese, Henry
Kirkham, Don (Prof.)
Lory, Milton M.
Reeder, James E., Sr. (M.D.)
Walker, Ralph E.

KANSAS
Axton, Charles B.
Carkener, G. Guyton
Deatrick, Ambrose Winston
Helm, Frank
Lash, Earl A.
Nash, Clifford E. (Rev.)
Piper, Ralph H.
Turrentine, W. F., Jr.
Wilbert, Paul L.
Wilkie, Horace T.

KENTUCKY
Bach, Marion T., Jr.
Brandenburgh, Estill C.
Caldwell, George D.
Chenault, William Anderson
Dilley, Morris McDonald
Dumas, Province P.
Duncan, Joseph G.
Evans, Richard Claypool
Featherston, Robert E.
Garred, E. W. (M.D.)
Garrison, C. Erskine
Gilkeson, Frank P.
Hall, Lyman S. (M.D.)
Herrman, Jesse Edward
Jones, John Spenser
King, Harold William
Kitchen, Travis B.
Kovacic, Joseph Howard

PATRONS

McDonough, T. H.
Miller, James Francis
Morris, Benjamin Hume
Moss, Clive A.
Nelson, Howard M. (Col.)
Nisbet, William A.
Norman, John Colgan
Osborne, Adam G. (M.D.)
Paine, Stuart R.
Pipes, Charles Breckenridge
Pipes, William Breckenridge
Shannon, Roy L. (Capt., Ret.)
Smith, Selby E.
Spencer, Henry L.
Spencer, Herbert W.
Stewart, Manning
Tarrant, John E.
Thompson, Edward M. (M. D.)
Watkins, Lowry
Wentworth, Walter A.

LOUISIANA

Adams, Reed McC. B.
Allain, Daniel A., Jr.
Allen, Samuel L., Jr.
Andry, Maurice G., 111
Barnes, Robert M.
Blue, Daniel O., (Capt., U.S.N.R.)
Bolles, Amanuel Joseph
Borman, Joseph I.
Boudousquie, Charles E.
Bozeman, Joseph R.
Brewster, W. Rogers (M.D.)
Brown, James H. (M.D.)
Christy, Alfred S. (Rev.)
Clement, W. E.
Cooper, George William Noel, (M.D.)
Culver, Fred M.
Curry, Robert H.
Dalehite, Bob
Dart, Albert L.
Dart, Henry P., Jr.
de la Houssaye, Arthur A.
de la Houssaye, B. C., Sr.
de la Houssaye, Malcolm L.
deLassus, Louis St. John deHault
de la Vergne, Hugues J., II
de la Vergne, J. Hugues
de la Vergne, Jules
De Verges, Ed J.
Dinkins, H. H., Jr.

Douglas, Hiram Kennedy (Rev.)
Dudding, James Leslie
Dula, Harry L.
du Mont, John S.
Dunaven, Ralph Jackson
Eustis, Clifford H.
Ewing, Donald M.
Farrar, Floyd R.
Favrot, Henry Richmond
Fontenot, Paul Alfred
Forman, William Harper
Gandolfo, J. C., Sr.
Gandolfo, J. C., Jr.
George, J. S. (M.D.)
George, Frank J.
Goodspeed, Lawrence A.
Grabner, Frederick C.
Greenwood, Lyman
Hagaman, Frederick P.
Heckert, J. E.
Hopkins, Orren Battle, Jr.
Howard, David Burton (Lt.)
Howard, W. J.
Hunley, H. Martin, Jr.
Hutchison, J. B.
Jackson, Virgil T., Jr. (M.D.)
Johnson, Ben III
Jones, Robert Randolph (Lt. Col. Afres.)
Jordan, Clarendon
Jordan, E. Clarendon, III
Jordan, Bishop
Jordan, Harry B.
Jordan, Harry B., Jr.
Kernion, Richard J.
LaFargue, Myron Joseph
LaFleur, Edwin G.
LaFleur, Wallace Aaron
Leaming, Christian R.
Leche, Richard W., Jr.
Leigh, Thomas W.
Leigh, W. E.
Lewis, Southerner M. L.
Lyons, George D. (M.D.)
McCaleb, Alfred F. (Col.)
McShane, John W., Sr.
Meador, H. G.
Mehurin, Chester A.
Miller, Ben R.
Mitchell, Lansing L.
Mithoff, H.
Moore, P. Albert
Moyer, R. Kirk
Ogden, Michael M.
O'Kelly, William Abram III
Olivier, André A.
Olivier, Frederick J.

Parker, Herbert C.
Pattison, George P.
Pearson, John R. (Lt. Col.)
Persell, Ralph M.
Pettie, Hawthorne
Pharr, H. N.
Plauche, Hester
Pratt, George K. III
Prowell, Jones T.
Prutzman, William James
Querens, Perey L. (M.D.)
Richardson, Beale Howard IV
Richardson, Frank Byron
St. Paul, Hugh C.
St. Paul, Hugh V.
St. Paul, John, Jr.
Saunders, W. H., Jr.
Sinclair, F. W., Jr.
Snider, Donald Graves
Soniat, Robert Upshur
Strachan, Frank G.
Sutherlin, George H. (Col.)
Suthon, Walter J., Jr.
Thurber, George A.
Trousdale, G. W. (Maj. Gen.)
True, Gratz A.
Turner, Franklin T.
Turner, William S., (Rev.)
Van Denburgh, Archer G.
Veith, Gordon S.
Veith, Milton P.
Verret, C. J.
Walton, John M., Jr.
Weitz, John S. (M.D.)
Whitley, Andrew R. (M.D.)
Wilkinson, Hugh Sr.
Wilkinson, John B.
Williams, L. Kemper (Brig. Gen.)
Wilson, Earl B.
Wilson, Sloan J. (M.D.)
Wood, Charles Spencer (M.D.)
Woodyard, Lawrence D.
Wright, William J.
Zatarain, Charles Clements

MAINE

Baker, Silas K. (Col.)
Clark, Carroll H.
Gren, Axel Henry
Hamilton, Harlan
Jeffries, John
Johnson, John R.
Marquis, W. James (M.D.)
Sloggett, John B. (Capt.)
Wright, Frank Vernon

PATRONS

MARYLAND
Adams, Reed M. B.
Ankeney, F. H.
Baxter, Thurston H. (Col.)
Bennett, Timothy Read
Biddle, Richard Spencer
Blacklock, Aubrey Henry
Bridges, John F.
Brooks, Clifton R. (M.D.)
Cockey, Edward W.
Ferrell, Collier P.
Fillian, George B.
Fisher, Lawrence M.
Herndon, Albert D.
Houston, George Porter
Johnson, Hiram E.
Knickerbocker, Ralph E.
Kelb, S. Denmead
Maddox, H. Randolph
Norris, Abell A., Jr.
Parker, W. Giles
Puryear, Robert M.
Robertson, George Sadtler
Seegar, J. King B. E., Jr. (M.D.)
Stein, Charles Francis
Steiner, Edward E.
Stick, Gordon M. F.
Trieschmann, Herbert E.
Wampler, French, Jr. (Capt. U.S.N.)
Warburton, William Thomas
Watkins, Ira D.
Wilmoth, Harold E.
Wood, William Meredith, Jr

MASSACHUSETTS
Amon, Carl H., Jr.
Archer, Gleason, L.
Baldwin, J. Thomas
Barter, Forest H.
Bessom, Philip E.
Boynton, Gordon D.
Brink, William Raymond
Canedy, Albert W.
Carman, Ernest W.
Carver, Eugene P., Jr.
Chamberlin, John Alvin
Cheever, Frederick E.
Crowell, Howard W.
Currier, Ross H. (Cdr. U.S.N.R., Ret.)
Dana, Edward
Drew, William J.
Farley, Charles Judd
Folsom, Charles Emerson
Foster, Granville J., Jr.
Gardner, George O.
Glodell, Leroy Marcus (Col. A.U.S., Ret.)
Grebenstein, George W.
Grebenstein, Henry D.
Grout, Charles E.
Hall, John Alden
Hanckel, Robert C.
Hatch, Lincoln D.
Heath, Milton Weeks
Heath, Milton Weeks, Jr.
Hemenway, George W.
Hobbes, Alan Buxton
Hotchkiss, Henry
Johnson, Frank W.
Karr, Paul W.
Keddy Albert Willard
Kenerson Horace E.
Kenney, Matthew W.

Luce, Stephen C., Jr.
Lyon, Frederick W.
MacArthur, Arthur Paul
MacArthur, William Arnoux
Miller, Frank E.
Orcutt, Milton Haynes
Phinney, Charles Wills
Plumley, H. Ladd
Powell, Norman L.
Rollins, Edwin Butler (Prof.)
Roscoe, Theodore Swan
Rowe, Frank E. (M.D.)
Salois, Irving R.
Shaul, Edwin Hilton
Shaul, H. Edwin
Smith, Francis E.
Smith, Leroy
Stevens, Harold F.
Ver Planck, Philip
Vogt, Albert A., Jr.
Wagner, Andrew James
Wall, Lester S.
Walter, George R. L.
Warner, Leonard J.
Winslow, Henry D.
Winslow, Henry J.
Woods, George Clayton
Woods, Walter Clayton
Wroe, John C.

MICHIGAN
Angell, James C.
Arnold, Albert
Baker, J. Herbert
Bauer, Richard Maxwell
Bricker, Charles
Cadieux, Eugene Rogers
Camp, Max W.
Cleveland, William F.
Coleman, Thomas W., Sr.
Crawmer, Marion H.
Dougherty, Clifford L. (M.D.)
Ellington, Harold S.
Favorite, William P.
Fisher, Stewart H.
Gibson, Clelland A., Jr.
Goodman, Harold Oton
Goodrich, Francis L. D.
Gordon, Lynn S.
Hall, Wallace C.
Hamilton, Charles Andrew
Harris, Gerry Sutphin
Henry, Burns, Jr.
Jones, Duane A.
Jordan, Grant Ladd (Rev., D.D.)
Kales, Robert G.
Keys, John G.
Kull, John Prescott
Leib, Emmett J.
Livingston, Archie Lyon
Lowmaster, Frank L.
Lyon, Arthur G., Jr.
McCracken, Harold M.
McCurdy, Walter H.
McIntyre, B. D.
Marshall, Gerald R.
Norton, Edwin Perry
Prescott, Charles S.
Rice, Merrill B.
Rowe, Ernest Perry
Salot, R. F. (M.D.)
Semmes, Prewitt
Slade, C. Blount, Jr.
Thomas, John P.

Washburn, J. B., II
Waters, Lewis Dudley
Westcott, Hanson C.
Wiggins, Lawrence W.

MINNESOTA
Barrows, Edward Pickering (Col. JAGC).
Cory, Harry H.
Denison, Ralph Tillinghast
Evans, Joseph T.
Fisher, Sam Kendall
Frank, Harry O.
Gillam, Stanley S.
Gooding, Arthur Faitoute
Hayward, Charles L.
Hooper, William S.
Jameson, Sanford C.
Jones, Lawrence M.
McGregor, Byron C.
Markoe, Francis A.
Patterson, Norman G.
Paul, James Richmond, Jr
Peck, Roderick Daniel
Reed, Frank E. (Judge)
Royce, Franklyn Amherst
Sawyers, Mott R. (Rev.)
Skinner, Harvey O. (M.D.)
Stoner, Paul Abbott
Storer, Harold Sheldon
Wheeler, Walter H.
Young, Lloyd, Jr.

MISSISSIPPI
Ashford, Charles Rabb
Brady, James O.
Brady, Thomas P. (Judge)
Brady, Tullius
Butler, James Barnard (Ph. D.)
Cain, Cyril E.
Carter, Charles N.
Carter, Claude B.
Chandler, H. T.
Cook, Edward L., Jr.
Craig, Louie V., Jr.
Dribben, W. B.
Dodenhoff, Harry C. (Col.)
Flowers, T. F.
Flurry, James Alvin
Flurry, Robert L.
Flurry, Robert Luther, Sr.
Fraser, Donald Rayburne
Fraser, Merle Caswell, Sr.
Frazier, John M.
Harper, M. J.
Harris, William A.
Jordan, Walter G., Sr.
Kelly, Carl M.
Kimball, Hunter Hudson
Kitchell, Horace Y.
McNees, L. L.
Owen, Ben
Pettis, Charles R.
Rhodes, Francis Arlington
Smith, Hobart A. (M.D.)
Smith, Prentiss Edward, Jr. (M.D.)
Spencer, Sidney B., Sr.
Taylor, Lloyd D. (Capt.)
Vaughn, J. Rigg
Welch, David C.
Williamson, Frank Henderson
Wood, Edward Watson

PATRONS

MISSOURI

Cordry, William S.
Crossen, Kay M.
Cusimano, Richard (S.J.)
Doubler, Francis T. H.
Hamilton, Harlan
McClure, T. Rex
Miller, Jo Zach, III (Col.)
Ockerhausen, Bobby Joe
  (Lt. U.S.A.F.)
Oliver, Allen L.
Osborne, Charles D.
Pagenstecher, William
Robinett, Paul M.
  (Brig. Gen. U.S.A., Ret.)
Roney, Robert H.
Rose, Roy Delos
Siegfried, M. H.
Thomas, C. Prentiss
White, R. C.
Williams, Maxwell
Young, Gary Edward

MONTANA

Clutton, Sam William
Higgins, Grove Lawrence, Jr.
Johnson, Howard A.
Marquard, Hugo M.

NEBRASKA

Barnes, Lynn G.
Binder, Frank H.
Blease, Ernest Basil
Bodenbach, Max N.
Borchers, F. Edward
Brown, August H.
Buffett, Howard H.
Colvin, Albert A.
Conover, Earle V. A.
  (Rev. D. D.)
Cresap, Robert D.
Daniel, Herbert S.
Davis, Reed E.
Dorsey, Guy P.
Fislar, Leslie E.
Isreal, Wesley Ambrose
Kent, Royce N.
Leroy, W. Lee (M.D.)
Likes, Fred. R.
McPherren, Wayne
Moseley, Ralph S.
Mutz, Sterling F.
Neely, Robert D.
Quest, Wallace Guhl
Roberts, J. Gordon
Smith, Edson
Sutherland, Charles M.

NEW HAMPSHIRE

Brooks, Albert L.
Chandler, John Parker Hale, Jr.
Fiske, Herbert I.
Furbush, Spencer S.
Hutchins, John Walbo
Johnson, Hiram W.
Lougee, Carl M.
Margeson, Henry B.
Ouellette, Arthur R.
Shepard, John S.

Turner, Gardner C.
Waldo, Henry C.
Webber, Paul Baron, Jr.
Weeks, Harold (Judge)
Wesson, Earle Frederick
Wood, Charles Ernest

NEW JERSEY

Allen, Leon B.
Alesbury, Alfred W.
Angus, William A.
Angus, William A., Jr.
Arrington, J. Neil
Beard, William M.
Bennett, David K.
Borden, A. H.
Brown, Lewis Woodbridge
Buckman, Williamson
Bull, Warren N.
Butterworth, T. H.
Campbell, Herbert R.
Canfield, George R.
Case, M. D. III
Castle, C. Ward
Chamberlin, William Orr
Colburn, Harold L. (M.D.)
Cole, Arthur F.
Colyer, Douglas Sanford
Cook, Richard L.
Cook, Ross Keelye
Cowles, Harry D.
Crowell, Robert S.
Culin, Curtis Grubb
Dennis, G. Vernon
Dodd, Frank N.
Eld, Terry J. H.
Eldred, Richard T.
Fischer, Herman Allen
Frazee, John Henry
Freeman, Walter H.
Gilman C. Malcolm B.
  (Col., M.D.)
Gilman, Charles M. B., Jr.
Graff, Manton L.
Hammond, Cleon E. (Col.)
Hamner, James Garland
Hight, William E., Sr.
Hopper, I. B.
Hough, James Elverson
Hurtado, Edward, Jr.
  (Capt. U.S.A.F.R.)
Johnston, Carey William
Kemble, Joseph F.
Kling, G. Nelson
Knapp, Howard R.
Kuykendall, C. Fremont
Laine, Edmund Randolph
  (Rev., L.H.D.)
Lamb, Richard
Larsen, Lyle F.
Leavens, William Barry, Jr
Lomax, Paul S.
McDowell, E. O.
McLagan, S. J.
McMahon, Ernest E.
MacRae, A. Kenneth
Maben, S. M.
Markle, Arthur Davis
Meinzer, Harry Valentine, Jr.
Merrion, A. Robert
Miller, C. Gifford
Murphy, Herschel S.
  (M.D.)
Naisby, John R., Jr.
Naulty, Charles W., Jr.
  (M.D.)

Newkirk, Earl S.
Newkirk, Stanley C.
Oakes, A. Bliss
Parsons, Robert W., Jr.
Pearce, Owen C.
Pryor, William Y.
Rindell, Donald
Ritter, P. E.
Rook, Harry Beckurth
Rowand, Carlton W.
Rule, George A., Jr.
Ryder, Guy M.
Samson, David P.
Schomp, A. L., Jr.
Seely, Raymond Dunbar
Segoine, H. Richard
Seibert, Franklin J.
Smith, Charles H. (M.D.)
Smith, David R.
Stevens, Elmer O.
Stevens, Wilbur A.
Stokes, Albert L.
Story, Allen Lawrence
Stratton, Lawrence (Maj. U.S.A., Ret.)
Templeton, John M.
Thomas, H. Emerson
Tobey, Albert K.
Vanderhoof, William W., Jr.
Van Inwegen, Vincent
Van Name, Elmer G.
Wesner, Wilton W.
Wismer, Raymond P.
Wickware, L. H.
Williams, Arthur Julius
Williamson, Edgar, Jr.
Williamson, George P.
Wolfe, J. Albert
Woodruff, Leslie R

NEW MEXICO

Frazier, Lake Jr., Jr.
McDowell, Horace R.
Norfleet, Robert G., 2nd

NEW YORK

Abelein, Gilbert R.
Adams, William George
Allis, Leonard G. K.
Avery, Albert G.
Avery, C. Howard
Asbury, Edward Bennett
Babcock, George S.
Baker, R. Lynn
Baker, William C., Jr.
  (Maj. Gen.)
Bance, Edlow S.
Barker, C. Austin
Barnes, Norman
Barton, Ralph M.
  (Pres. Empire State Soc.)
Bassett, Conrad J. B.
Baumann, Walter S., Jr.
Beers, George R.
Bellows, Charles Franklin
Benkhart, George F.
Bennett, Eugene C.
Birch, Everett P.
Birch, Richard J.
Birdsall, John T.
Bishop, E. W.
Bothwell, Cecil L., Jr.
Bowlby, Harry L.
  (Rev., D.D.)

PATRONS

NEW YORK—Continued

Brady, William H.
Bresee, Wilmer G.
Brush, Henry G.
Bryant, Frederick E., Sr. (D.D.S.)
Bryson, Clark
Buck, J. Orton, Jr.
Buchanan, H. J.
Bundy, Clifford H.
Burns, Ward
Byrnes, Horace Marsellus (Col. U.S.A.F.R.)
Caldwell, Ethan LeRoy
Campion, Washington Custis Lee
Chamberlin, William O.
Childress, Clifford C.
Clark, Franklin P.
Clark, George S.
Clark, Chester M.
Clark, Henry C.
Cobean, George G.
Code, Ralph J., Jr.
Coe, Neile H.
Cole, Thomas Harris
Colvin, Harold B.
Comfort, Harold W.
Conklin, John P., Jr.
Conklin, Kenneth W.
Cox, Thomas R.
Crandall, John Cortland
Crispell, Reuben B.
Crosby, Ernest S.
Darlington, Gilbert (M.D.)
DeWitt, Fred. P.
Dohmann, George W.
Dougherty, E. Fred.
Doughtie, V. L.
Dow, Hicks B.
Doxsee, Robert L.
Dresser, Frank E.
Dudley, Ralph W. (Capt.)
DuRant, Henry L.
Dutcher, Henry Redman, Sr
Edison, Charles
Edwards, Charles Nelson
Egbert, Richard F.
Elias, Cloyd L.
Emmons, James E., Jr. (Lt.)
Fallon, Carlos E. (M.D.)
Fay, Allyn C.
DeFere, Paul E., Jr.
Finger, John W.
Fish, Mark H.
Fisher, George Howard
Fitch, Allen Homer
Fleury, Scott Marvin
Fort, William Lapham
Freeman, David A., Jr.
Friedlander, Robert George
Gaines, Furman V.
Gardiner, James B.
Garretson, Douglas
Giffin, Stewart Hamilton
Goepel, Floyd Vansise
Goodding, R. A.
Gordon, William F., Jr.
Gore, Roland F.
Greeley, Horace (M.D.)
Gregar, Willis A.
Gregory, George M.
Gregory, Robert H.
Gregory, William H., Jr.
Griswold, Hovey H.
Gros, Frederick J.
Guggenheim, William III

Gurnee, Richard McKenzie
Hagey, William Anderson
Hall, Clifton Reed, Jr.
Hall, David R.
Hallauer, Carl S.
Hamilton, A.
Hamilton, Leon W.
Harding, Gerald Merritt
Harwood, Charles, Jr.
Harned, John Randolph
Harris, Scott
Harvey, Roger C.
Heath, J. Franklin
Heinen, George W.
Henchey, Curtice Bickford
Hiers, James Lawton
Hinds, William L.
Holden, William C., Jr.
Hollister, George W.
Holman, James M. (M.D.)
Henlahan, Thomas J. (Lt. U.S.M.C.)
Hopkins, Wallace
Howell, Chester E., Jr.
Howes, John E. (Capt.)
Hunt, Frank P.
Huntley, Wesley Y.
Irving, Walter V.
Isaacson, H. Harding
Jenkins, Palmer H. (D.D.S.)
Johnson, George B. (Rev.)
Johnson, Ralph Dodge
Johnson, J. Ray
Joseph, Julius, Jr.
Jones, Robert H. III
Keeler, David Armour
King, Raymond M.
Kirch, James H.
Krais, Frederick V., Jr.
Laird, J. R. Durham (M.D.)
Lancaster, Robert Vaughan
Larned, George L.
Latimer, C. V. (M.D.)
Lee, Alva D.
Lemon, Elmer H.
Livezey, T. Ernest
Livingston, John W.
Lobaugh, Lawrence C. Sr.
Loeb, John L., Jr.
Love, Frank C.
Lovely, Thomas J.
Luther, Gordon C., Sr.
McCormic, Joseph A.
McGarvey, Michael R., Jr.
Martin, Robert Bruce
Marwig, Carl H.
Mattison, Harold
Melvin, Crandall, Jr.
Merritt, Charles E. (Maj., C.E.)
Messner, Charles A.
Messner, Charles A., Jr.
Metcalf, Reginald Herford Sr.
Metcalf, Reginald H., Jr.
Militello, Daniel H.
Miller, Ralph T., Jr.
Monell, Harry Stanbrough (Col. CAC Ret.)
Moore, John H.
Morrell, John Dorrance
Morse, Clarence F.
Mottram, Floyd W.
Mumper, John Everett
Munroe, Sydney P.
Murphey, Douglas J.
Neal, Ray C.

Northern, S. T.
Osborn, Gardner, Jr.
Osborn, Harold H.
Osborne, William H.
Palmer, Bryant S. III
Parker, Thomas W.
Parsons, Gerald J.
Parsons, Robert W.
Payne, James Hamilton III
Peabody, A. Stuart
Peelle, John W. J.
Penny, A. C.
Pharr, Eugene A., Jr.
Phillips, Albert Ira
Pierce, Claude D.
Pierce, Robert
Place, Lyman Tripp
Porter, A. R.
Potter, Harold Taft
Pratt, Roger Sherman
Prine, William J.
Pringle, Edward T.
Proper, Theodore R. (M.D.)
Pugsley, Chester DeWitt
Quinn, David C.
Radke, John A.
Ranney, Everett J.
Robinett, H. Maurice
Root, Howard D.
Rossell, Clare C.
Rowland, R. B. (Lt. Col.)
Ruland, John H.
Russell, William Fiero
Sanders, D. H., Jr.
Sattley, Robert B.
Selleck, Zeno
Shepard, Charles
Shope, Perry Reese
Sitgreaves, Edwin J.
Smith, David H., (Lt. Col.)
Snell, Charles D., Sr.
Souza, Edgar M.
Stevens, Robert C.
Stephens, Willis H.
Sterne, Willard F. (Pres. Empire State Soc.)
Stockwell, L. Albert
Stoddard, Herbert Richmond
Strohl, John L. II
Sullivan, Charles H.
Sunderland, Edwin S. S.
Talbert, Ansel E. M.
Tandy, Russell H., Jr.
Templin, W. W.
Thompson, William Rodney Jr.
Titus, Paul
Tomkins, Sydney E.
Treman, Leonard C.
Trevor, John B., Jr.
Trumpore, George E.
Tudor, Frank G.
Turner, Ralph E.
Turrell, Orban Clyde
Unkefer, Jarrett B.
Utley, George Dexter II
Vale, George W.
Vanderkloot, W. J. (Capt.)
Veith, G. James (D.D.S.)
Vollmer, E. Clinton (M.D.)
Vosburgh, Charles W., Sr.
Warrick, William Henry
Way, Glenn C.
Weed, F. Malcolm
Weed, Joseph J.
Weidlich, Clifton F.
Wells, Charles Joseph (M.D.)

PATRONS

Wilber, Donald J.
Williams, Mackenzie
Wilson, Bruce A.
Wingfield, Morris R.
Winter, Clark B.
Wolfe, A. Royce
Wood, Charles P.
Woodbury, Cyrus H.
Woodruff, Frank B.
Woodward, Warren S.
Woolley, Gordon Byron
Woolsey, Floyd E., Jr.
Worthington, Herbert E.
Wright, Charles E.
Wright, G. Hoyle
Young, Earl E.
Zimmerman, Herbert A.
Zoller, Abram

NORTH CAROLINA

Allison, William L. (Maj.)
Barber, Joseph William
Baum, Edward D.
Breckenridge, Clarence E.
Brown, Junius Calvin
Carter, Bruce Randall
Cherry, George D.
Croom, Mebane F.
Dawson, Wallace H., Jr. (Col.)
Garibaldi, Linn D.
Grady, Henry J.
Hanes, Pleasant Huber
Hardee, David L. (Col.)
Harding, William T.
Highsmith, W. C. (M.D.)
Horne, Josh L.
Idol, Victor H.
Jordan, John Y., Jr.
Lindsey, I. A.
Logan, Howard M.
McKeown, Douglas Oneal
MacLamroc, James
Moore, John H.
Overman, George Reid
Parker, William A.
Pickell, Yawger
Placak, Joseph C., Jr. (M.D.)
Ramsey, William Lee
Reece, R. P.
Robbins, Marvin R.
Ross, Robert A. (M.D.)
Smallwood, Charles
Smith, Edwin C.
Springs, Eli B.
Wall, William S.

NORTH DAKOTA

Davenport, Willard E.
Spare, John C.
Stevens, O. A.
Wright, Dana

OHIO

Abell, J. Richard
Anderson, Charles A. (M.D.)
Andrews, Florian Albert
Assel, Joseph H.
Ayars, David P.
Bahrenburg, J. H. (M.D.)
Baker, A. F.
Baker, Robert A.
Baldwin, Lewis Morse, Sr.

Barba, William M. (M.D.)
Barefoot, Charles R.
Baxter, F. H.
Beatty, Hugh G. (M.D.)
Beebe, David William (Rev.)
Beeks, Frank Cone
Berthold, Paul W.
Blair, George N.
Blair, Tully D.
Blauvelt, Roland George
Blue, H. T. O.
Bobo, Jarrot
Bolton, Kenyon C.
Bordur, Paul W.
Bourne, R. M.
Bouic, Fredric V.
Bowen, William C.
Bracy, Rex F.
Bradley, A. Ilsley
Branson, Don S.
Brehm, G. Wayne
Breininger, Charles H.
Bricker, John W. (U.S. Sen.)
Bright, William Woodson
Brinton, Hugh P.
Brouse, Edwin W.
Brown, C. Donald
Brown, Maltbie S.
Bruner, Clark S.
Bryan, Clarence P.
Bryant, Thomas T.
Burgner, Walter C., Jr.
Burrows, Charles D.
Carry, William L.
Carstarphen, E. T.
Chubbuck, Stephen L.
Coberly, Edward William
Colley, Josiah Van K.
Congleton, Ernest W.
Converse, John H.
Cox, Jesse R.
Crampton, P. S.
Crouch, Howard B.
Davidson, Frederick E. (Lt. Col.)
Davis, B. G.
Davis, J. Boyd
Davis, Eugene W.
De Benedictis, Robert Pogue
Dice, Max G.
Dickey, M. R.
Diefenbach, Allan B.
Dieffenbach, C. Maxwell
Dilley, Mark E.
Durst, Ross Compton
Dye, Theodore C.
Emery, Ira Joseph (Lt. Col., U.S.A., Ret.)
Fackler, Joseph J.
Fawcett, Joseph R.
Fetterman, Harold B.
Ford, James Dudley
Fellers, Forest S.
Fellers, Robert W.
Forney, Howard G.
Foust, Fayette William
Gray, Charles E.
Guthrie, John D. (2nd Lt.)
Hale, Clayton G.
Hamel, Claude C.
Hammond, W. A. (M.D.)
Harbaugh, Donald L.
Harding, Warren G. II (M.D.)
Harroun, Francis E.

Harshman, W. A.
Hartley, Charles A.
Heavilon, Ernest B.
Heckman, Henry T. S.
Heltzel, Carl J.
Henderson, Herbert Long
Herrick, Clay Jr.
Herrick, Meriam Clay
Hills, Frank L.
Hoffman, Lewis D.
Houston, Samuel K.
Hoyer, William B.
Hyatt, Hudson
Ives, William M., Sr.
Jackson, S. D. L., Jr.
Johnson, Phineas C.
Johnston, Homer B.
Johnston, Kenneth B.
Jones, C. A.
Jones, Archbold M., Jr. (M.D.)
Kimball, Carl R.
King, K. R.
Knox, Ewing Pendleton
Kroehle, Vernon
Lamb, John K.
Lamon, Earl W.
Larned, Andrew D.
Lawrence, Keith
Leach, Sagito J.
Lewis, Charles H.
Lewis, Maxwell Pelton
Locke, John F.
Long, Harold J. (M.D.)
Lorenz, Karl E.
McClure, Edward V.
McCoy, Orlando Zeben
McDonnell, Lester R.
McDowell, Robert A.
McGlothin, Harvey C.
McGuire, Eugene C.
McIntyre, Ruluff D.
Manchester, Harry S.
Martin, Andrew P.
Martin, John Cephas
Martin, William G.
May, George S.
Mead, Edward G.
Mellen, William Henshaw (Maj. A. U. S., Ret.)
Middleton, Henry A.
Miller, John I.
Miller, A. Clarke
Mitchell, Osborne
Moore, Leland E.
Moore, James H.
Moore, Philip St. John, Jr.
Munn, Ray E.
Murch, Maynard H.
Nearing, Charles E.
Nesbitt, Keith E.
Nicholls, Malcolm B.
Nims, Joel B.
Packer, William F.
Paterson, John N.
Paterson, Peter C., Jr.
Peck, Carlos E.
Pelton, Frank H.
Phipps, Russell W.
Pieratt, Thomas S.
Pierce, Robert R.
Pleasants, J. G.
Plumb, J. G.
Pool, C. H.
Puterbaugh, John C.
Quine, Kenneth D.
Richards, Gayl Roe
Riegler, Howard E.

— 252 —

PATRONS

Roelle, Franklin J.
Roller, Clyde Calvin (M.D.)
Romaine, Millard
Rosenberg, Karl
Rosensteel, John L.
Ruple, Ferdinand W.
St. Paul, John, III
Sanford, Elroy
Scott, S. Hubbard
Shafer, James C. F.
Shook, John T.
Slutz, W. Hol
Simmons, Percy Q.
Smith, Warren H.
Smith, Wayne G.
Souers, Loren E., Jr.
Sparks, Aubrey L.
Stanley, Welles Kirk
Stewart, William E.
Stone, Ray W.
String, A. C.
Swearingen, J. K.
Taylor, Ralph Ensign
Taylor, Everett E.
Taylor, J. Wallace
Taylor, Warren M.
Thwing, Leman Samuel
Tilton, David E.
Tod, David
Tubman, Charles S.
Umbarger, Harold N.
Unkefer, Jarrett B.
Upton, Charles B.
Van Buren, Donald C. (Judge)
Van Iden, Starr S.
Van Koughnet, L. H.
Van Patten, DeWitt
VonderHaar, Edward P.
Waggoner, Alfred
Waldo, R. E.
Walker, Robert G.
Ward, Lucius A.
Welker, William C.
Wetherbee, Ralph H., Jr.
Wilson, Thomas B.
Wineland, Park
Wineland, Lisle Garber
Wolfe, French Eugene
Wood, David Baker
Wykoff, L. C.
Zimmer, Ralph R.
Zimmerman, Charles B. (Judge)
Zimmerman, Henry A. (M.D.)

OKLAHOMA

Adams, Wiley J. (M.D.)
Campbell, James A.
Darling, Sturgis Williams
Dwen, James G.
Edmund, Angus Bowen, Jr.
Erwin, Harry P.
Gill, Joseph A., Jr.
Golderman, W. E.
Greenfield, Henry F., Jr.
Hamilton, William S.
Hawk, Darall G.
Hefner, R. A.
Howe, Elliott H.
Kimbrough, Felix A.
Logue, William F.
Nisbet, Watkins F.
Ricks, James R. (M.D.)
Stovall, David A.

OREGON

Barfield, John R., Sr. (Maj. Ret.)
Barker, Earl Basil
Garlough, Francis Earl
Griffin, Frank Loxley
Jones, Walter H.
Maddox, Robert I.
Metsker, Charles F.
Morrow, R. W. (M.D.)

PENNSYLVANIA

Aiken, W. James, Jr.
Alcorn, Cyrus Cope
Anderson, Russell S. (M.D.)
Baily, Kenneth G.
Baldwin, Harrison R.
Bashline, O. O.
Baum, Paul James
Beard R. Edward
Bergey, C. R.
Bergey, Norman
Bergey, J. Paul
Bigoney, Thomas W.
Bikle, H. Dwight (M.D.)
Bittner, William J., Jr.
Bohart, P. H.
Borneman, John K. (Gen.)
Bowman, Norwood D.
Boyer, George H. (Lt. Col.)
Braddock, James S.
Brallier, J. Merle
Branthaver, Milton E.
Brown, Oliver W.
Brownley, Richard L.
Butz, George W.
Buzzard, J. F. (M.D.)
Campbell, Charles K.
Campbell, Lucius P.
Canan, William Truscott
Carringer, Marion A.
Carty, William H. (D.D.S.)
Cassady, John C.
Champlin, Carroll D.
Cheuvront, Brooks K.
Christy, Martin B., Jr.
Cleveland, Paul Wood
Cochrane, Walter E.
Cole, Scott
Coleman, Ernest H.
Cope, Ernest E.
Cornwell, Ralph T. K.
Crane, Herbert B.
Crisman, Howard B.
Daugherty, G. Wallace
Daume, Robert E., Jr.
Dengler, Ernest H. (M.D.)
Dixon, Jesse F.
Dorworth, Charles D.
Drake, James F. (Col.)
Dunkelberger, J. A. (M.D.)
Eaker, Arthur T. (Lt. Col.)
Ehrgood, A. H.
Evans, George Webster
Faust, Alvin Girard (Rev., Ph. D.)
Faust, Nile Eugene
Fish, Charles R.
Flory, Clyde R. (M.D.)
Frederick, John B.
Friedly, Roy E.
Fritchey, John A., II (M.D.)
Gare, Marshall S.
Gehman, Paul F.
Geiger, Robert B.
Graham, William Creigh
Grimm, Luther J.
Groves, K. Deane
Hamilton, Harlan
Hartranft, Nelson S.
Harvey, Jay C.
Henry, William E.
Hay, George (M.D.)
Hummel, Clarence D. (M.D.)
Hennessy, J. J., Jr.
Hesser, Vernon Cassel (Maj. A. F. R.)
Hillard, Arch R. (Rev.)
Hillegass, Russell M.
Hodgdon, Maurice E. (M.D.)
Hoenstine, Carl R.
Hoenstine, Floyd G.
Horn, Harold R.
Hubbell, Randolph H.
Hunsberger, Charles L.
Ingham, Robert
Jackson, Samuel McCartney II
Jolly, Thomas D.
Jopling, John M.
Jordan, Murray J.
Keller, Lester A.
Kerstetter, Newton
Kling, Vincent George
Knipe, Norman L., Jr. (Cdr., U.S.N.R.-R.)
Lathrop, Donald E.
Lehr, Earl H.
Leibensperger, Bruce T.
Leis, Edmund Ross
Leitzinger, William A. E., Sr.
Lemmon, John L.
Lenny, Donald Blackburn
Lightbourne, James H.
Limberg, Henry T., Sr.
Linn, Jay G. (M.D.)
Lovell, Harry C. (D.D.S.)
Luhrs, H. E.
Lupfer, James R.
MacFarland, E. G.
McFarland, K. T. H., Jr. (M.D.)
McMillin, H. C. (M.D.)
McNeil, Robert L., Jr.
McVay, Demas L., Jr.
Magenau, J. M., Jr.
Mercer, H. Fred, Jr.
Miles, George Hobart (M.D.)
Millbach, Alph L.
Milnor, Mark T.
Moore, Carl H.
Moyer, Raymond A.
Murray, John Allen (M.D.)
Neece, Harold Augustus
Neish, Lee D.
Nixon, Clarence B. (Judge)
Parke, Francis W. (Col.)
Park, W. L.
Pangburn, Edward W.
Persing, Harry M., Jr. M.D.)
Person, Morgan D. (M.D.)
Phillips, John Howard
Pollock, Lloyd E.
Potts, T. A.
Rahauser, William S.
Randall, J. Landis

PATRONS

Reed, James O.
Rhoades, Charles R.
Richards, Earl M.
Rodgers, Jacob Robert
Rohn, James H.
Rossman, W. F. (M.D.)
Reid, L. Gordon
Reinhold, Paul B.
Robb, W. Graham
Roberts, W. Kendrick
Rockwood, Henry
Russell, John McBride
Sadtler, Edward Hill, Jr.
Schlecht, Ellerslie Wallace, Jr.
Schroeder, Henry J. Jr. (Col.)
Shaffer, Charles I. (M.D.)
Shaner, Philip K.
Sherrard, J.
Smith, William H.
Smith, Kenneth G.
Smith, R. Stanley
Smith, Ward Tolbert
Snyder, John M. (M.D.)
Snyder, Paul A.
Solliday, John C., Jr.
Sorber, G. Stoy
Spanogle, John Paul, Sr. (M.D.)
Stains, Cameron
Stein, John Walter
Stewart, William E.
Stolz, John C. (M.D.)
Strite, Frank S.
Sturgis, Samuel B.
Taylor, George III
Thomas, Lewis J.
Thorne, Thomas R.
Trautman, B. E.
Trimble, A. G.
Vaughan, Paul A., Sr.
Vernon, Thomas H.
Vicary, Arthur C.
Walker, E. F. (Brig. Gen.)
Walmer, C. Richard
Walter, Henry M., Jr.
Ward, N. M.
Waters, Robert S.
Weikel, C. H. H.
Whitaker, Tristram Coffin
Whittaker, William Alexander
Williams, Lowell W.
Wilson, Harold H., Sr.
Wilson, Massey F. (Col.)
Wilson, William E.
Wood, Vernon M.
Woods, A. G.
Woolever, Harry, Jr.
Wright, R. P.
Wyatt, John S.
Yeager, James G.
Zacharias, W. O.
Zepp, Edward G.
Zimmerman, Richard P. (M.D.)

RHODE ISLAND

Adams, Harold E. (Lt. Col.)
Briggs, Frank G.
Cranston, William I.
Davies, Stanley D. (M.D.)
Dresser, Robert B.
Dumas, Warner
Eddy, Robert F.

Jackson, Henry Greene
Lander, Norman
Magruder, Cary Walthall
Martin, Walter R.
Mays, W. Clarke S., Jr.
Peirce, Frederick A., Sr.
Remington, T. Elliot
Smith, Norman B.
Stewart, Donald L.
Stewart, Earle W.
Tefft, Benjamin Franklin (Col., M.D.)
Tucker, Stuart H.
Vories, Lawrence F.

SOUTH CAROLINA

Calhoun, Charles N.
Cork, William Neville (Brig. Gen.)
DuRant, Henry L. (Lt.)
Farlow, E. Allison
Field, John O., Jr.
Hook, Julian Martin
Moore, Austin T. (M.D.)
Smith, James Roy, Jr. (Lt. J.G., U.S.N.)
Tonge, Maner Lawton

SOUTH DAKOTA

Gifford, Lester B.

TENNESSEE

Adams, J. Louis
Barringer, L. T.
Barret, Paul Weisiger
Breckinridge, E. L. D.
Brown, A. Paul
Burn, Harry T.
Brunson, William R., Jr.
Clevenger, Ernest A.
Coombs, Edwin F.
Duff, Charles L., Jr.
Figuers, Sherrell
Fort, Dudley C.
Furman, Henry J. (Lt. Col.)
Gardiner, Laurence B.
Gill, Harrison W. (Col.)
Hagan, George B.
Haagen, Paul T., Jr.
Hart, Alexander Ewing
Hays, Mark H.
Hedges, D. E.
Herring, A. Lynn (M.D.)
Hollingshead, John R.
Jameson, W. Miller
Leffler, William Skilling
Lipscomb, Edward L.
MacDonald, Daniel Harman
Magruder, Lauch
Mays, Harvey J., Jr.
Miles, John Keathley
Mount, Oliver E.
Myers, Thomas S.
Nelson, E. H.
Nunnelley, H. Martin
Peacock, Charles K.
Perry, J. L., Jr.
Rawlings, John H.
Reed, Forrest F.
Reynolds, John Lacey
Rhea, George Hearn
Rodgers, Hillman P.
Rule, Elmer D.
Senter, William R. (Rev.)

Stallworth, Hugh W.
Stephenson, Jay G.
Todd, John Hart
Turnley, Edmund Wright
Turnley, Edmund Wright, Jr.
Valentine, John J.
Warner, Porter, Jr.
Webster, B. H. (M.D.)
White, Weldon B. (Judge)
Whitman, A. L.
Whitman, Finner D.
Whittington, Earle Ligon
Wilson, Oscar M., Jr.
Wirt, Ralph Howard

TEXAS

Allison, Roy H.
Anderson, C. H. C.
Andrews, James Ray, Sr.
Armstrong, James M.
Armstrong, R. Wright
Atwood, Charles Nobel
Baldwin, Raymond W.
Bannister, John Howard
Barbee, Robert L.
Bell, Frank F. (Brig. Gen., AUS. Ret.)
Berryhill, E. J. (Col.)
Boatwright, C. Rene
Boggess, Albert
Boone, James Leroy
Boswell, Lorin A.
Bosworth, Laurence S.
Bosworth, Laurence S., Jr.
Bourke, Clyde Edwin, Jr.
Boyd, Robert Sherrill
Brown, William LaFayette
Buxton, Coburn A.
Caldwell, Walter O., Jr.
Calvin, Elvis Aubrey, Jr.
Campbell, Lionel Lockard, Jr.
Carthew-Yorstoun, Charles Morden
Carthew-Yorstoun, John Maynard Andrew
Casey, Allan M.
Cashion, M. Lyle, Sr.
Chamberlin, Oliver B.
Crutcher, Howard K. (M.D.)
Culver, H. Dillon
Curtis, James R.
Darnall, Joseph R. (Col. U.S.A. M.C., Ret.)
Davidson, J. Whitfield
Dickinson, A. C.
Dingwall, William M., Jr.
Doughtie, Venton Levy, Sr.
Earp, Thomas Jefferson
Eastmond, T. L. (Col. U.S.A.)
Eby, J. Brian
Etzel, William W.
Farrar, Charles S., Jr.
Flores, Vetal
Flowers, H. Fort
Folk, R. G.
Foster, J. Lewis
Frank, Anton J. (Very Rev.)
Goar, Everett L. (M.D.)
Golden, Gabriel Hawkins
Green, John Plath
Guinn, Edwin D.
Haagen, Paul T., Jr.
Hamman, John, Jr.

— 254 —

PATRONS

Harper, Sam Hay, Jr.
Heafer, Henry Wallace
Hazelrigg, Hal
Held, Edward C. (M.D.)
Holden, Henry M.
Holland, T. L. (M.D.)
Hills, J. Huntington (Col.)
Hofer, Harry V.
Hough, Walter C.
Huson, Hobart
Hutchinson, Ben B. (M.D.)
Huntington, F. W.
 (Col. U.S.A. Ret.)
Ingram, T. Robert (Rev.)
Jackson, James C. (Col.)
Jefferies, Clarence B.
Jessup, William J.
Johnston, Floyd Allen
Jones, Wayne V.
Jones, Paul
Kelley, R. H.
Kellogg, W. H.
Kyle, Jack Polk, Jr. (M.D.)
Larkin, Christopher
Lane, James Lavelle, Sr.
Lea, Walker A., Sr.
Lefevre, Arthur, Jr.
Lewis, John L.
Logan, Bard A.
Logan, E. Winter
Lomax, O. Q.
Loughridge, Frank P.
Lowe, Joe Forrest
McCain, Augustus C.
McClure, Charles Boone
McCormick, Zeb Motley
McDavid, Albert Calhoun
McDuff, Louis Clarence
Malone, Edwin Scott III
Masterson, Harris
Mathews, H. W.
Miller, Raymer H.
Miller, Robert V.
Morris, Arving E.
Morrow, Tarlton
Neff, Frank R., Jr. (Rev.)
Neill, Robert T.
Newsome, J. A.
Nichols, Marvin C.
Park, Samuel, Jr'
Perkins, John
Polk, Lucius J.
Prescott, C. B.
Read, Hill Patterson
Red, Samuel Clark
Rembert, William Adair, Jr.
Reynolds, Francois H. K.
 (Col.)
Riley, Solon F.
Robertson, French M.
Robertson, Ralph A.
Robinett. C. H.
Robinson, Verner A.
Rogers, Sam D.
Rooke, Allen Driscoll
Roth, John W.
Royall, Richard R.
Sartwelle, J. W.
Saunders, J. K.
Shelby, Maurice C.
Shepherd, Robert A.
Sherman, Frantz H.
Shirey, Floyd L.
Shivers, Allan
Simmons, W. L.
Sleeth, Joseph C., Sr.
Smith, B. Brown
Smith, Charles L. (M.D.)

Smith, Tevis Clyde, Jr.
Smith, Stanley S.
Soar, Everett L. (M.D.)
Spradley, B. E.
Stalnaker, Paul R. (M.D.)
Sterling, Walter G.
Swigart, Theodore E.
Taylor, Thomas H.
Van Eman, J. H.
Vallette, Charles N.
Walker, Dee Brown
Wallace, George J.
Walsh, Tracy R.
Warner, Addison W.
Warren, Guy I.
Washington, John W.
Werlein, Presley E., Jr.
Weaver, W. T.
Wessels, T. F.
 (Brig. Gen. Ret.)
White, Frank G.
White, Joseph M.
Wilson, Hugh Bascom
Witherspoon, James W.
Williams, Samuel T.
 (Lt. Gen., U.S.A. Ret.)
Woodward, C. S. (M.D.)
Woodward, Valin (M.D.)
Wray, Andrew Jackson
Zuber, Charles B.

UTAH

Anderson, Robert Clair
Brimhall, Mark H.
Fox, George Wallace

VERMONT

Arthur, Harold J.
Brooks, Albert L.
Ditmars, Walter Earl
Phipard, Charles W.
Proctor, Mortimer R.
Putnam, Ralph W.
Rixford, Oscar A.
Swezey, H. Joseph
Tracy, Robert M.
Van Scolk, Roy H.

VIRGINIA

Ackiss. Collis Leon
Adams, Edwin F.
Adams, William Arthur
Adelstein, Thomas E.
Andrews, Mallory Sinclair
Babcock, David Hinman
Bailey, David Leonard, Jr.
Baldwin, Donald Winston
Bartlett, C. L.
Batte, Du Roc Jones
Bellamy, C. Carroll
Bemiss, Samuel Merrill
Betzer, William E.
 (Capt., U.S.N.)
Black, William E., Jr.
Blankenbeckler, George K.
 (Col.)
Blunt, Charles P., Jr.
Boland, John N.
 (Capt., U.S.N. Ret.)
Bonney, Frederick P.
Brandt, A. Frankland
 (Maj.)
Brown, Harold Norwood, Sr.
Brown, Ray Eber

Bryan, Joseph III
Butt, James Hunter
Bywaters, Richard W.
Carneal, Charles W.
Caskie, Marion M.
Chrisman, Thomas L.
Cox, James E.
Crockett, W. Chaffin Jr.
Culpeper, Willoughay B.
Curry, Lucien R., Jr.
Dawson, S. C., Jr.
Dewar, Joseph Ralph
Dixon, Peter A.
diZerega, Thomas W.
Dunbar, Jimmie J.
Easley, Harold T.
Edwards, James W.
Edwards, Thomas Henry
Ervin, Sam R.
Farris, Hansford Lee
Fergusson, E. Bruce
Fifield, Ren A.
Fleming-Parsons, Tarlton II
 (Maj.)
Friend Earl T.
Galt, James Colquhoun
Gibson, John F., Jr. (M.D.)
Gillmore, William B.
Graham, Martin T., Jr.
Grigg, John Edward
Grubert, Reese T.
Gunnell, Bruce Covington
 (Lt. Col.)
Hamilton, Laurens M.
Hamilton, Warren M.
Hamlin, Charles Hughes
Harvie, Malcolm G.
Hawes. Richard P.
Heflin, James L.
Hickson, E. W. (M.D.)
Henley, John R.
Hodgkins, Howard W. (Col.)
Holt, Yuille, Jr.
Ilyus, Edmund Burwell
 (Col.)
Jones, John Kirwan
Jones, Robert Parke
Kellam, Harold B.
Kendall, Paul G. (Col.)
King, John S.
Kingman, John P.
Knott, Charles L.
Leach, Claude L.
Lipscomb, Bryant B.
Lyon, David A. III
Lucas, J. Lynn
MacBryde, M. H., Jr.
McConnel, Murray, Jr.
Marshall, Thomas E., Jr.
Marsteller, D. L.
Marston, William Frank
Massie, Williams E.
Motley, Charles G.
Menken, Harold D.
Minick, Don C.
Millan, John A.
Moffett, C. K.
Murray, Thomas A., Jr.
Osborne, B. Sam
Pannell, Clifton Wyndham
Parker, Frederic T.
 (Col., U.S.A.R. Ret.)
Parramore, William P.
Peake, James R., Sr.
Phillips, E. Turpin
Phillips, E. K.
Powell, Robert C.
Powell, Wm. Ptolemy

PATRONS

Purvis, R. Scott
  (Lt. U.S.N.)
Roche, L. B.
Ragsdale, Homer C., Jr.
Scott, R. Walker
Shank, J. Edward
Shepherd, Lemuel C.
  (Gen.)
Siegfried, J. W., Jr.
Sigourney, Daniel P.
Simmons, Richard F. (M.D.)
Slaydon, F. Donald
Smith, Claude H. (Lt. Col.)
Smith, Roy
St. Paul, Jerome M.
Stewart, William B.(LCDR)
Swope, Ralph R.
Thompson, Allen R.
Tuck, Parham Franklin
Turner, Stephen R.
Walker, Robert S. W.
Wall, H. Ewing
Waller, E. P.
Waters, Robert Powers
Webster-McGarvey, H. H.
Whittle, S. G. III
Whitehead, Paul
Whitescarver, Roy S. (Rev.)
Whitley, W. J.,
  (LCDR, U.S.N.)
Wilkins, James R.
Williams, Hutter
Williams, Richard E.,Jr.
Williams, Winslow
Wroton, James C.
Young, Clinton J. T.

WASHINGTON

Balch, Cyril H.
Cordon, C. H.
Edgerton, E. Ralph
Lee, T. Bailey, Jr.
Louis, Lyman G.

Marshall, Joseph Wöehler
  (Maj.)
Mitchell, W. E.
Phifer. John P.
Raymond, C. B. W.
Shafer, Sydney D.
Smith, Lewis Addington
Stallcup, Jack L.
Voorhees, G. M.
Wilson, John N.
Wright, Roscoe M.

WEST VIRGINIA

Anderson, Jack Sandy
Atkinson, Merrill R.
Batten, J. E., Jr.
Boltz, Howard William, Sr.
Buckles, Frank Woodruff
Clarke, George Sharpe
Counts, Kilby Palmer
Cruikshank, Dwight P. III
Farley, Erman P.
Gebhardt, Walter Leslie
Gorrel, Harland P.
Holt, Robert H.
Holt, Wendell H.
Hornor, Thomas R.
Langfitt, E. Carl
McIntosh, C. Leon
Lowe, Malcolm Jackson
Mansperger, Martin M., Sr.
Mastin, Kenneth C.
Musser, Junius K.
Myers, Karl J., Sr. (M.D.)
Peters, Luke T., Sr.
Silver, Gray, Jr.
Starr, Paul Floyd
Stutler, Martin I.
Trippett, K. H.
Turley, Joseph C.
Umstead, William O.
Van Metre, Thomas E.
Vest, Walter E., Sr. (M.D.)

Walworth, Chester A.
Ward, LeMoyne
Way, Fred E., Jr.
Wood, E. B., Sr.

WISCONSIN

Benton, Roy W. (M.D.)
Gombar, Francis
  Sutherland, Sr.
Kostomlatsky, Mat S.
McNeel, J. H.
Parker, Charles G.
Stone, Thomas S.

WYOMING

Davis, Porter A.
Everett, W. Hume

SUNDRY

Bowles, Mrs. William Carter
  Chevy Chase, Md.
Edwards, Mrs. Ray O.
  Jacksonville, Fla.
Howell, Mrs. John D.
  Knoxville, Tenn.
Milligan, Mrs. H. W.
  Sioux City, Iowa
Plotner, Mrs. Charles H.
  Washington, D.C.
Post, Mrs. Roswell D.
  Birmingham, Ala.
Powell, Mrs. Benjamin H.
  Austin, Tex.
Sappington, Mrs. G. Ridgely
  Baltimore, Md.
Smead, Edward L.
  Mexico City

www.ingramcontent.com/pod-product-compliance
Lightning Source LLC
Chambersburg PA
CBHW022050160426
43198CB00008B/181